Clinical Supervision

Clinical Supervision

Morris L. Cogan
School of Education
University of Pittsburgh

Houghton Mifflin Company · Boston
Atlanta   Dallas   Geneva, Illinois   Hopewell, New Jersey   Palo Alto

Library of Congress Catalog Card Number: 72-85906

ISBN: 0-395-14027-7

For
Mildred, Jeremy, Daniel, and Jessica

Table of Contents

Foreword

This is a book born of hard work, painful honesty, and dearly bought experience. Its roots go all the way back into the middle 1950's when Morris Cogan and his associates, supervising student teachers in Harvard's MAT program, faced the fact that what they were doing was not working.

The significant thing was that they admitted it. For, by all the evidence, the supervision they supplied was at least as good as student teachers— *any* teachers—generally receive. And yet the results were thin, and the "customers" were dissatisfied.

Out of that tension grew a long, groping effort to devise something better. Little by little the supervisory crew hammered out ways of working that yielded greater gains and more satisfaction. The procedures and the results were scrutinized at every step. Soon the scope of the work reached out beyond the little world of student teaching to the huge world of in-service education. At the University of Pittsburgh, under Dr. Cogan's leadership, faculty members kept experimenting, and doctoral candidates put everything under the microscopes of their dissertations.

The result is complete authenticity. Any experienced schoolman reading this volume will hear the ring of reality on every page. The examples come through the way school is. The portrait of the hopes and fears and hesitations of the teacher-supervisor relationship is sensitive and discerning. The advice is solid and specific, with the maturity of experience.

On two points the book is uncompromising. First, the author emphasizes that there is no use talking about instructional innovations unless the teachers are given enough expert help to make the innovations stick; the trail of education is strewn with half-tried improvements, discarded before they had a chance. Second, the book clearly states that the kind of precise help the situation demands will *not* be delivered by scatter-shot supervision amounting to little more than sporadic "visits" followed by some global comments. "Teachers are better left alone," says the author, "than merely tampered with."

Dr. Cogan is playing for keeps. He lays out a system of supervision with enough weight to have impact and with the precision to hit the target. He knows that it will be expensive, that it will call for a sizable corps of supervisors backed up by collateral specialists of a wide variety; he simply insists that it is cheaper than poor teaching and failure to change. He calls his system "clinical supervision" because it operates right in the clinic of the classroom and depends on direct observation of manifest behavior. He fully recognizes that there are other essential elements in "general supervision"—that teachers also grow through cooperative curriculum development, for instance—but this book is about one-to-one, in-class observation and the assistance that can be built on that base alone. It concentrates on that one job and carries it all the way.

In these times, anyone who advocates such supervision—coming into the classroom and studying the performance—must take into account the feelings of teachers, which are often fearful and half-suspicious, if not downright antagonistic. Dr. Cogan faces that set of problems squarely, and provides a realistic set of answers. He describes a careful preparatory sequence, to be worked through at whatever length it takes before the supervisor ever comes to the teacher's classroom to observe. The key to this preparation is that the teacher himself studies the supervisory process. He becomes familiar with its purposes and its methods. He practices it, at least in a simulated way, perhaps with other teachers in the free setting of a summer's workshop. He learns a good bit about *self*-evaluation and diagnosis. The objective is to ripen up a genuine partnership, in which there is no superior-subordinate relationship, no assumption of the supervisor "teaching the teacher."

Once that mutually supportive partnership has taken root, the real work of cooperative planning, detailed analysis, and shared evaluation can get under way. The guides to that ongoing process constitute roughly the last half of the book. They are as explicit as anything can ever be, in an enterprise so dependent upon personal trust and rapport. They are technical, and yet at every point they are informed with a deeply sympathetic feeling for all our human frailties, our best aspirations but also our self-deceptions and our timidities.

I believe that Dr. Cogan and his associates have spaded out a way of working that is consonant with an overwhelming need of our schools, in these times when we are trying to reach so high for educational progress. If we are to succeed there must be expert help, but the modes of supervision must change at least as much as the modes of teaching must.

In the preparation of new supervisors this book will be an invaluable aid. At the same time, for every seasoned practitioner whose work includes the improvement of instruction the book will provide something more—not only new insights and skills, but also a new surge of faith and enthusiasm, in a job that is all too often a continuing drain upon one's inner strength.

Fred T. Wilhelms
*Association for Supervision
and Curriculum Development*

Preface

This book has two principal purposes. The first is to develop and explicate a system of in-class supervision that, in competent hands, will prove powerful enough to give supervisors a reasonable hope of accomplishing significant improvements in the teacher's classroom instruction. The second purpose is to help correct the neglect of in-class or clinical supervision and to establish it as a necessary complement to out-of-class ("general") supervision. The lack of clinical supervision is conceived to be one of the major factors in the failure of many useful instructional innovations to secure a foothold in our schools and universities. One reason for this failure is that the teacher who is trying to develop new classroom competences generally needs the continuing in-class support of specially trained colleagues in order to be successful. Without such specialized help the major and minor failures that a teacher almost always experiences in attempts to change established behavior will ultimately tend to press him back into familiar, and "safer," modes of teaching.

Such regressions have too often transformed the history of attempts to improve instruction into a history of potentially useful educational innovations enfeebled and finally defeated by the failure to provide the teacher with the professional support required for the tasks of innovation.

Although *supervision* is part of the title of this book, it is addressed as much to experienced teachers and future teachers as to supervisors. The reason for this is that clinical supervision is conceptualized as the interaction of peers and colleagues. It is *not* unilateral action taken by the supervisor and aimed at the teacher. On the contrary, the teacher is called on to assume almost all the roles and responsibilities of a supervisor in his interaction with the clinical supervisor. He initiates action, proposes hypotheses, analyzes his own performance, shares responsibilities for devising supervisory strategies, and is equally responsible for the maintenance of morale in the supervisory processes.

Such parity of responsibility between teacher and supervisor in clinical supervision makes it imperative for the future teacher and the experienced teacher to learn new skills and assume new roles in the process of improving their instruction. It follows then that the fullest benefits of clinical supervision cannot be realized unless the teacher has gained adequate mastery of its rationale, ethics, practices, and technology. This volume is therefore designed to serve as a handbook for both teachers and supervisors. It seems probable that a study of the book may offer economies of time and effort for teachers and their supervisors alike.

Clinical Supervision may also be both useful and interesting to school administrators responsible for the organization and administration of supervision.

This book may perhaps be more readily understood if the reader is aware of its central frame of reference. Clinical supervision is conceptualized insofar as possible from within the teacher's viewpoint. That is, it is principally shaped to be congruent with the teacher's universe, with his internal landscape, rather than with that of the supervisor. (We have found this same point of departure to be useful to the teacher in conceptualizing the instruction of students.)

Some distinctive features of the book include: (1) the concept of the cycle of supervision, with its provision for continuities and inputs substantial enough to make a lasting difference in the teacher's behavior, (2) an emphasis on the identification of patterns of teaching behavior, (3) the imperative need of teacher and supervisor to gain useful self-knowledge about their own behavior while they are involved in clinical supervision, and (4) the emphasis on the professional-ethical controls required of both teacher and supervisor.

Acknowledgements

Many people and several institutions have helped to make this book possible. I have been most fortunate in my students. They have my thanks for their critical and substantive contributions.

Colleagues at Harvard University and the University of Pittsburgh have often taken an important and formative role in the development of the rationale and practice of clinical supervision. I am indebted to the following, among others too numerous to list here: G. Bradley Seager, David W. Champagne, David E. Purpel, and Maurice L. Belanger.

Two men made time and resources available to me for the development of clinical supervision and the writing of this book. My sincere thanks go to Francis Keppel, former Dean of the Graduate School of Education, Harvard University, and to Paul H. Masoner, Dean of the School of Education, University of Pittsburgh.

I have drawn important ideas from the work of Ned A. Flanders, Gilles

Dussault, Barak Rosenshine, C. M. Galloway and M. L. J. Abercrombie, which I acknowledge with thanks.

Thanks are due also to Carol Fiumara, who typed innumerable revisions with skill and patience.

I could not have written this book without the sustaining help of my wife, Mildred.

Morris L. Cogan

Clinical Supervision

PART ONE

The First Phase
of Clinical Supervision

CHAPTER 1

Overview of Clinical Supervision

Educational Reforms and Clinical Supervision

The history of the American school could well be written as an account of educational reforms and recurring crises in the schools. The attempted reforms have included efforts to implement a long (and generally un-connected) series of innovations: universal free public education and the relating of schools to the technological revolution, for example. On a smaller scale, campaigns have been mounted to establish "progressive" schools, the core curriculum, the middle school, programed instruction, modern mathematics, and the open classroom.

Such attempts at reform have been punctuated by school crises, rang-ing in recent years from the illiteracy explosion (*Why Johnny Can't Read*) to the dreadful inadequacies of the "educationist bureaucracy" (*Quackery in the Public Schools*), and culminating in the "mutilation" of school children (*Crisis in the Classroom*) and the "spiritual and psychological murder" of black children (*Death at an Early Age*).

Two important facts become evident when we examine the educational history of the past half-century. The first is that almost every reform that attained national scope embodied some valuable innovative educational ideas that deserved to be incorporated into the instruction offered in the schools. The second is that most of the innovations were poorly understood in the schools (the activity school) or were starved for resources to implement them (the core curriculum), and were therefore delayed and deformed in their implementation (team teaching) and often perished, sweeping good ideas into oblivion along with the bad.

The reasons why this wasteful process is permitted to continue are to be found partly in the low priority our society accords to education. But educators themselves must also accept part of this responsibility. They have been unwilling or unable, first of all, to develop the processes by which innovative ideas are critically and exhaustively examined prior to being adopted by the schools. Superintendents and school boards are therefore driven to "buying blind," a practice that results in the phenom-ena of educational fads and styles that have their season and then are allowed to wither. Secondly, an innovation once "bought" is rarely tested; it is promoted. What superintendent of schools is ready to admit that he spent *x* dollars of the taxpayers' money to test an idea that turned out to be a lemon? And if a new departure *is* adopted, it is usually handed to the teachers for implementation, with only subminimal resources and training to support them in their efforts.

As a result, school teaching is one of the professions that in this century has been least effective in raising the level of its average performance. Certainly it trails far behind most other professions in the utilization of new technology and in the testing of innovations in the uses of specialized personnel.

This lack of all but the simplest progress that commonly accrues to a modern vocation through the adoption of improved practices points to the granite insolubility of some problems of teaching-learning and to a general failure to disseminate and implement new practices that *do* show promise for the improvement of the teacher's classroom performance. These last tasks—disseminating and implementing new practices and improving the teacher's performance—constitute precisely the domain of clinical supervision. It follows, then, that the development of a large corps of clinical supervisors might create a powerful force in the schools—a force competent to implement reforms in the classroom.

Such a broad claim demands some explanation. In characteristic American fashion, most educators and the public alike envisage the solution to their educational problems in terms of a need for new technology, new organization of schools, new content and methods of teaching, and new "plant" and physical resources. In a discussion of the lag in applying educational knowledge to the problems of teaching-learning, Thelen has written:

> As judged by what could be done if we were to understand and apply modern knowledge to educational problems, all our schools are obsolescent. . . . But most of this knowledge has so far made almost no dent at all on educational practices, and, with the present tendency to think that educational problems can be solved with money and organizational changes, the likelihood of any significant improvement is discouragingly slight.[1]

Thelen's discouragement is understandable, and the difficulties that stand in the way of improvements in schooling are indeed dispiriting. Yet the delay that Thelen deplores is not simply a lag in the *dissemination* of knowledge about better ways of teaching. Dissemination works best

[1]Herbert A. Thelen, *Education and the Human Quest* (New York: Harper and Bros., 1960), p. 1.

when accompanied by the support necessary to help teachers fulfill the new roles and functions they are to learn and implement. This support must be provided in the schools, in classrooms. It must be supplied by individuals specially trained to work with teachers and to develop *individualized programs* of supervision. In contrast, the supervision that teachers usually receive today may average out to two or three classroom visits per teacher semiannually.

Without systematic, in-class assistance, the teachers are asked, as it were, to *invent* the new methods, the new relationships with students, and the roles the students themselves are to assume in the new instruction. To say this is simply to say that for most teachers, useful knowledge about new forms of instruction is in itself not enough. The teacher needs a sustained, expert program to help him relinquish his existing classroom behavior in favor of new behavior, a program strong enough to help him apply such new competences to the specific conditions that obtain for each child, for each class, and for the teacher himself. Such a program must focus on *in-class supervision,* on what we have been calling "clinical supervision."

Why this emphasis on in-class supervision? It is because the American experience so far indicates that it is in the classroom, at the point of application, that new methods of teaching break down. The risks involved in essaying new teaching behavior and the pain of complete or even partial failure often become too great for many teachers to endure. As a result, teachers revert to familiar patterns, and another potentially effective innovation vanishes quickly, often without leaving a trace.

The response of the schools to innovative programs is often institutionalized. A small corps of teachers receive special training preparatory to the introduction of new ways of teaching. These teachers tend to become partisans rather than testers of projects. They are often encouraged to view themselves as a select team with an important mission. The nonparticipating teachers, on the other hand, often feel excluded—removed from the scene of innovative action—and therefore tend to ignore the novelty or to form an underground resistance to it. In either event, they almost never have the benefit of a sustained program that will prepare them to try out a new departure with the company of supervisor-colleagues specially trained to implement innovation.

When a small group of teachers receive special training and support while the rest are expected to learn by observing or by osmosis, the consequences are generally tragic. The most common outcome is that the non-participating teachers generally attribute any success the innovators may achieve to the special resources funneled into the project. In this manner the teachers in a school or school system become divided into two camps—the minority "ins" and the majority "outs." When the majority group, with too little training and only occasional supervisory help, is required to implement the new practices, the result is too often a shambles. The useful core of innovation is lost or perverted, and a few ritual behaviors are substituted. As for the group of trained "ins," their energies are undermined by institutional resistance and inertia, and their numbers quickly depleted by promotions, transfers, and defections. Replacements are poorly prepared, and the empty, melancholy cycle of innovation winds down to a stop again.

It is our belief that an important part of the delay and failure characteristic of innovation in the American schools is attributable to the lack of trained, continuing in-class support for the teachers. The important words here are *in-class support*. It is true that many promising preliminary techniques are available for helping teachers learn new behavior—microteaching, simulation exercises, and observation, for example. Such minor inputs are, however, insufficient as a basis for permanent change because of the psychological and institutional forces that press new teaching behavior back into old molds. Even new teachers with modern methods almost universally yield to these institutional pressures in about five years and begin to teach more and more like the existing models—unless they have help. As for experienced teachers, change is doubly difficult for them. They must unlearn the safe and comfortable ways of teaching they know so well and undertake the toilsome and risky tasks of replacing them with new, untried patterns of behavior. Very few teachers can achieve this goal without the continuing collaboration of expert supervisors. It is our hope that clinical supervision can provide such help.

We need no economist to tell us that the preparation and employment of enough clinical supervisors to make a real difference in teaching and learning in our schools is bound to be costly. The present corps of clinical supervisors is so minuscule in relation to the number of teachers to be served that most teachers are deprived of in-class help in improving their day-to-day instruction, to say nothing of mastering innovations. Certainly the preparation and employment of a corps of clinical supervisors numerous enough to make a difference in the quality of instruction will cost a great deal. But could anything be as expensive as the wasteful and ineffective teaching so many schools are now paying for?

The educational systems of the United States can afford to prepare adequate numbers of clinical supervisors. If the nation does in fact commit itself to this task, it may be taking a small but important step toward the improvement of schooling, the facilitation of educational reform, and the defusing of at least some of the recurrent crises in education.

Beginnings of Clinical Supervision

Clinical supervision was born out of great travail, and the pain of the process was shared by many supervising teachers, student teachers, and university supervisors. It started more than fifteen years ago with students in the Master of Arts in Teaching program at Harvard. These candidates for teaching merited the best instruction we could develop for them: many were talented, rich in ideas, in enthusiasm, in empathy for their pupils, and in love of the subjects they taught. Most of them anticipated that their first teaching experiences would be carefully planned and competently supervised and that these early experiences would constitute a valuable induction into promising and rewarding careers. For too many of them it turned out to be an induction in which their supervisors failed them.

The students' testimony about this failure was full and convincing: university supervisors did too little or too much; what they did, did not make sense, did not offer much real help to them in becoming teachers. So, too, for their cooperating teachers—many were well meaning but unskilled; others were either indifferent or full of fervor and hell-bent on delivering intact their own personal revelation about how to teach, whether their defenseless student teacher wanted that particular revelation or not.

Each year evaluative feedback was conscientiously collected from these students in an effort to improve the supervision of their teaching. And year after year the feedback left the supervisors shattered by the testimony that many of the students thought their mentors were doing a miserable job. This misery lasted for some years. Then, gradually, we began to put together a few practices that the students found helpful.

Supervisors began to team up with students, working more intensively for longer periods of time in more sustained sequences of planning, observation, and analysis. The post-teaching conferences became a careful study of the observation data—a quest for the meaning of what had happened in the classroom. These emerging practices, to be sure, were not uniformly successful, and failures sometimes came so thick and fast that occasionally the small successes seemed only accidental. Gradually, however, a body of fairly useful practices took shape. Supervisors spent more and more time in the classrooms, observing student teachers and trying at the same time to scribble notes about what was going on, to capture both verbal and nonverbal interaction between teacher and students and among students.

Eventually some of these practices began to take on systematic form, and there appeared to be some hope for a breakthrough. Students and supervisors alike found it rewarding to approach classroom data not as isolated events or brief sequences, but in terms of an analysis of patterns of classroom behavior. *Pattern analysis* quickly became one of the foundations of the supervisory structure. It made sense to the future teachers. It was convincing in that it dealt so unswervingly with what had happened in class. The use of data and the analysis of patterns operated to anchor supervisors and supervisees firmly in rationality and formed a foundation for the inference-play of the post-observation conferences. Working together in such sequences, supervisor and student could begin to ask about the connections between the latter's objectives, his behavior in class, the pupils' behavior, and the likely relations of all these to the pupils' learnings. But above all, a new role for the student teachers began to take shape. They themselves began to form larger planning groups, teaming up with supervisors in observation, analysis, and conferences. In sum, we began to induct our future teachers not only into teaching and the analysis of teaching but also into the practices of supervision. In these new roles and processes, and especially in these new relationships, we found some cause for optimism, and we began to refer to our basic procedures as "the cycle of clinical supervision."

And for the first time our students began to tell us that we were really helping them to become teachers. They didn't go berserk with delight, but they did stop telling us we weren't helping very much.[2]

Very soon thereafter various public school systems became interested in applying clinical supervision to teachers already in service, and by 1958 the author was lecturing fairly widely on the topic. In 1961 he addressed the Rhode Island Association for Supervision and Curriculum Develop-

[2]Morris L. Cogan, "Supervision at the Harvard-Newton Summer School," mimeographed (1961).

ment, and in 1962–63 a group of school and university teacher educators came from Oregon to Harvard, and later to the University of Pittsburgh, to study the subject. By 1963 the state of Oregon had instituted clinical supervision for candidates for the Master of Arts in Teaching at major colleges and universities in the state. In 1964 a paper written by the author, entitled "Clinical Supervision by Groups," appeared in *The College Supervisor.*[3]

Since that time clinical supervision has continued to be adopted and adapted. Men and women in some communities and universities have been able to make contributions to the theory and practice while experimenting with it. So, too, have many of the writer's students and colleagues. This book is an attempt to set out in some usable form the rationale, the practices, and the principal strategies of clinical supervision.

Definitions of General and Clinical Supervision

Some difficulties have been noted above in the account of the "travail" that accompanied the development of clinical supervision. Among the less important but still irksome tribulations was the resistance to the introduction of the term *clinical.* Several colleagues at Harvard objected forcefully to the writer's use of the word in associations clustering around a proposal he had prepared in 1961, entitled "Case Studies and Research in Clinical Supervision." His co-workers pointed out pungently and colorfully the denotations and connotations of the word *clinical,* with many allusions to sickbeds, hospitals, and mortal illnesses.

The author stuck to his guns, perhaps ill-advisedly, and countered by citing *Webster's Third New International Dictionary* to the effect that clinical also means "of, relating to, or conducted in or as if in a clinic . . ." and "involving or depending on direct observation. . . ." The reference to dependence on direct observation seemed to catch exactly one of the distinguishing characteristics of clinical supervision. The dictionary further supported arguments for the appropriateness of *clinical* by referring to "the presentation, analysis, and treatment of actual cases and concrete problems in some special field. . . ."

In all seriousness, the word *clinical* was selected precisely to draw

[3]Association for Student Teaching, *The College Supervisor: Conflict and Challenge* (Dubuque, Iowa: W.C. Brown Co., Inc., 1964), pp. 114–31.

attention to the emphasis placed on classroom observation, analysis of in-class events, and the focus on teachers' and students' in-class behavior. In brief, *clinical* was designed both to denote and connote the salient operational and empirical aspects of supervision in the classroom.

At this point it may be helpful to make a distinction between the use of the terms *general supervision* and *clinical supervision*. As used in this book, *general supervision* subsumes supervisory operations that take place principally outside the classroom. The events occurring inside the classroom are treated by supervisors and teachers mainly as a background of shared professional understandings about schooling. *General supervision*, therefore, denotes activities like the writing and revision of curriculums, the preparation of units and materials of instruction, the development of processes and instruments for reporting to parents, and such broad concerns as the evaluation of the total educational program.

In contrast, *clinical supervision* is focused upon the improvement of the teacher's classroom instruction. The principal data of clinical supervision include records of classroom events: what the teacher and students do in the classroom during the teaching-learning processes. These data are supplemented by information about the teacher's and students' perceptions, beliefs, attitudes, and knowledge relevant to the instruction. Such information may relate to states and events occurring prior to, during, and following any segment of instruction to be analyzed. The clinical domain is the interaction between a specific teacher or team of teachers and specific students, both as a group and as individuals. Clinical supervision may therefore be defined as the rationale and practice designed to improve the teacher's classroom performance. It takes its principal data from the events of the classroom. The analysis of these data and the relationship between teacher and supervisor form the basis of the program, procedures, and strategies designed to improve the students' learning by improving the teacher's classroom behavior.

It is clear that this separation of clinical from general supervision is both arbitrary and artificial. It is made simply to stress the narrower focus of this book and to distinguish clinical supervision from the extremely inclusive, not to say global, definitions of supervision.[4]

A Caution   This book is an attempt to set out in usable form the rationale and procedures for systematic classroom supervision of teachers. The

---

[4]As used in this book, the term *supervision* refers to clinical supervision unless the context makes clear a reference to supervision in general.

word *usable,* however, requires an explanation. The book is not usable in the sense that a person may study it and learn directly how to become a clinical supervisor. The competences needed by the clinical supervisor are generally too complex and too difficult to master in this fashion. For the very large majority of people, the professional competences of the practicing clinical supervisor must be learned in an extended program of preparation that includes a carefully planned and supervised practicum, that is, in a systematic and critically examined induction into practice. During the induction process, which is individualized for every candidate, the future supervisor is helped to examine the rationale and practices of clinical supervision and to relate them to his own behavior in his own style.

In sum, for most people, this book and a "textbook course" on clinical supervision are inadequate as preparation for practice. Supervisors must build their competences through supervised practice related to a carefully examined rationale. In the latter process this book may be useful.

The purpose of the book is to improve supervision, but not to develop a "school" or a cult of supervision. On the contrary, clinical supervision is conceived of essentially as a set of empirically developed practices centering around classroom teaching-learning. Clinical supervision is an attempt to begin systematic practice and to focus on new specializations of roles and functions in supervision. In brief, it is an attempt to move toward better control and greater expertise in a specific educational domain.

Above all, the book will not try to promote clinical supervision in any doctrinaire fashion. Rather, it is offered to the reader as an examined synthesis developed out of long experience, in the hope that the reader will find some ideas to examine, some to assimilate, and others to reject.

The Cycle of Supervision and Its Phases

Much of what is said in the following chapters will be more readily understood if the reader has some knowledge about what is referred to as the *cycle of supervision.* The cycle consists of eight phases, each of which is discussed, with examples, in later chapters. The phases are as follows:

THE CYCLE OF SUPERVISION

Phase 1. Establishing the teacher-supervisor relationship

The first phase of clinical supervision is the period in which the supervisor—

    a. establishes the clinical relationship between himself and the teacher;

    b. helps the teacher to achieve some general understandings about clinical supervision and a perspective on its sequences; and

    c. begins to induct the teacher into his new role and functions in supervision. These first-phase operations are generally well advanced before the supervisor enters the teacher's classroom to observe his teaching.

Phase 2. Planning with the teacher
The teacher and supervisor together plan a lesson, a series of lessons, or a unit. *Lesson* generally is taken to mean an instructional process oriented by objectives of fairly limited scope and designed to be accomplished in a span of time varying from part of a class period to a school day or two. Plans encompassing more complex objectives and more extended periods of time are referred to as *units*. Whatever the scope of the planning, the entire design and each of its constituent lessons are planned in terms of the objectives for the students and the teacher. Plans commonly include specification of outcomes, anticipated problems of instruction, materials and strategies of teaching, processes of learning, and provisions for feedback and evaluation.

Phase 3. Planning the strategy of observation
The supervisor plans the objectives, the processes, and the physical and technical arrangements for the observation and the collection of data. His functions in the observation are clearly specified, as are those of other observers if any are to participate. The teacher joins in the planning of the observation and takes a role in it as he becomes more familiar with the processes of clinical supervision.

Phase 4. Observing instruction
The supervisor observes the instruction in person and/or by way of other observers and other techniques for recording classroom events.

Phase 5. Analyzing the teaching-learning processes
Following the observation, the teacher and the supervisor analyze the events of the class. Initially they usually perform this task separately. Later in the program they may do so together or with other participants. Decisions as to these procedures are made with careful regard for the teacher's developing competences in clinical supervision and his needs at the moment.

Phase 6. Planning the strategy of the conference
In the early stages of working with a teacher, the supervisor alone generally develops the plans, alternatives, and strategies for conducting the conference with the teacher. Later on, if it is advisable, the planning for the conference may be carried out by teacher and supervisor together. If this

occurs, the planning for the conference may be incorporated into the conference itself.

Phase 7. The conference

The conference participants are generally the supervisor and teacher. As need and appropriate circumstances arise, other participants may join them. The conference may on occasion be conducted by the teacher and others, sometimes without the supervisor.

Phase 8. Renewed planning

At an appropriate stage in the conference the teacher and supervisor decide on the kinds of change to be sought in the teacher's classroom behavior. At this point the cyclical nature of the supervisory process asserts itself, and the teacher and supervisor stop the analysis and discussion of the previous lesson to begin planning the next lesson and the changes the teacher will attempt to make in his instruction. The resumption of planning also marks the resumption of the sequences of the cycle.

It should be noted at once that certain phases of the cycle may be altered or omitted, or new procedures instituted, depending upon the successful development of working relationships between the supervisor and the teacher. Once the teacher and supervisor are working well together and the teacher gains understanding about the objectives and processes of clinical supervision, teacher and supervisor may begin to realize certain economies in the cycle. To illustrate, they may for certain purposes omit the planning phase. Or they may telescope some phases in the cycle by performing the analysis of the lesson together and then moving directly to the planning for the next lesson.

On the other hand, the process of carefully working through the phases of the cycle should not be abbreviated prematurely. It is by way of the cycle that the teacher gains an understanding of the rationale for clinical supervision, some of the skills and motivation to participate actively in it, and the confidence to devise his own strategies and continue the process on his own initiative. A central objective of the entire clinical process is the development of the professionally responsible teacher who is analytical of his own performance, open to help from others, and withal self-directing.

This last statement should not be taken to mean that ultimately the teacher can dispense with the services of the supervisor entirely; only very rarely does this occur. In most instances the teacher cannot go on pulling himself up by his own bootstraps. Almost all teachers need the contributions the clinical supervisor and other personnel can make—not continuously, but at appropriate intervals. The "appropriate intervals" for each teacher are determined and re-determined during his career. The teacher himself participates in these determinations. The basis for decision. includes the teacher's skill in analyzing his own teaching, his competence in developing a program of self-improvement, his motivation for working on his own, and the progress he actually makes when working alone.

CHAPTER 2

Rationale for Clinical Supervision

The Condition of Supervision

It was George Bernard Shaw who said, "I am simply calling attention to the fact that art is the only teacher except torture." Shaw has turned a pretty aphorism, but it is only partly true. If art were the only teacher then very few of us would ever be educated. But Shaw does raise an important question: At what cost to the student does the teacher teach? Every generation has said that the cost is too high—there is too much torture and too little learning. To cap it all, someone has said that half of what we learn is wrong—and we don't know which half.

The causes of such a state of affairs in teaching are complex. Perhaps one of the principal reasons why people continue to tolerate this situation is that they do not even begin to dream of the difficulties surrounding the processes of preparing teachers who, though they may not be artists, will not be torturers or incompetents either. These difficulties in educating teachers begin with the teachers' preservice program and often increase while they are actually teaching. This surprising sequence is widely sensed but rarely understood. One of the reasons for the inadequacies of preservice education is the lack of an expertly supervised induction into teaching. One important reason why the inadequacies often increase after the teacher is under contract is that too often clinical supervision is even less available at that point than it was in the preservice phase of his teaching career, and the complexities with which he has to deal—largely alone—increase rapidly in solo teaching.

The Improvement of Teaching and the Inputs of Clinical Supervision
Why has clinical supervision developed so slowly? Part of the answer is undoubtedly found in the subsistence economy governing most schools. Adequate funds are simply not provided. Another brake on the development of supervision has been the generally naive view of educators about what it really takes to improve teaching. An observer from Mars surveying in-class supervision across the nation would have to conclude that educators actually believe that a few short classroom visits made by a supervisor and followed by a conference or a short report to the teacher will actually suffice to improve a teacher's performance. It is also worth noting

that the data usually gathered for the conference consists often of only a few hasty notes or a few impressions—both of dubious value in the supervisory conference.

The profound underestimation of the difficulties teachers face in learning how to teach and in improving their teaching on the job is at the root of some of the major problems in the preservice and inservice education of teachers. The popular assumption is that learning to teach is easy and that the preparation for teaching should therefore be short and simple. The trouble with this assumption is that in a very genuine sense future teachers arrive in college with full-fledged models of teaching already well established in their minds. Their twelve years as students in elementary and secondary schools has provided them with certain models of what teachers are and what they do in class. They have unconsciously learned styles of teaching while being taught, just as they have learned to be parents, or Democrats or Republicans, or law-abiding citizens or criminals while living in a culture in which such models exist.

One consequence of learning about teaching in this most pervasive and persuasive way is that the models learned are learned too well. They are difficult to uproot, to displace, to modify. As a result, future teachers face several difficult tasks. They must first *unlearn* the deeply etched patterns of teaching they arrive with, then select for their own use appropriate elements of the culturally "given" styles of teaching they will consolidate into the new and more effective modes of teaching emerging today. This double task makes the preparation of competent teachers a long, demanding, and expensive operation. The rationale of clinical supervision demands, therefore, that the inputs it contributes to the education of teachers should be equal to the double task the teachers face. This means that clinical supervision itself will be a long, demanding, and expensive process. The rationale also dictates that clinical supervision is much better not done at all than done with inadequate support or with less-than-expert supervisors. Teachers are better left alone than simply tampered with.

The Relationships of Teachers to Supervision

One of the factors affecting the practice of clinical supervision is the unclarified, ambivalent relation of teachers to supervision. Describing this relationship will be useful, and two observations may be made. First, public-school teachers almost unanimously endorse the idea of supervision *in principle*. Second, they often limit severely the supervisory practices they will welcome *in reality*. Teachers tend to exhibit two patterns of response: (1) a kind of emotionalized allegiance to the concept of supervision and (2) a swift and apprehensive rejection of all but a narrow range of approved supervisory activities. The teacher's anxieties are almost universally aroused when a supervisor comes to a classroom as a rater or if the purposes of his visit are unknown. The teachers appear to be wary of the supervisor who comes to make *changes in teaching*. This theme is sounded in a study of teachers in four small districts in California:

> The teachers as a whole saw the supervisor's job as an inspirational, thought-provoking role in which the supervisor takes responsibility to stimulate a broad look at curriculum. . . . These teachers . . . with the exception of four, *rejected specificity* as the most needed problem area for a supervisor to work in. . . . With a single exception among them, the teachers rejected the idea that a supervisor's main job is to make suggestions for changes in teaching.[1]

It would be easy to extend the list of examples, but by and large the research on the teacher's relationship to supervision gives evidence of the following themes—

1. a clear ambivalence about supervision: a dramatic contrast between a strong commitment to the principle of supervision and a stubborn, deepseated distrust of direct supervisory intervention in the classroom;
2. a desire to focus supervision on inspirational leadership and on broad objectives rather than on specifics;
3. a need for a "human relations" orientation in the entire endeavor;
4. a generalized rejection of supervision designed to work *directly* on changes in the teacher's classroom behavior;
5. a need to exert powerful controls over the kinds of supervision practiced in the schools, expressing itself sometimes as a demand for self-supervision or for supervision mainly by invitation;
6. a need of some teachers to seek the protective anonymity of a group through a focus on group work rather than individual programs of improvement.

It is clear that general supervisors themselves have often expounded the virtues of diffuse, group-centered, nonspecific supervision. In doing so, they have effectively barred themselves from many areas of direct action with teachers out of fear of arousing resentment and distrust, only to find themselves still faced with deep, easily aroused, continuing hos-

---

[1]Helen Fisher, "Expectations for Leadership," *Educational Leadership* 16, no. 8 (1959), p. 504.

tility from their teachers. For their part, the teachers are behaving in a very human fashion by trying to earn for themselves the blessings of supervision without any of the discomforts of classroom intervention.

Theory or Rationale for Clinical Supervision?

Dussault has surveyed the literature on supervision in preservice education in order to assess the state of knowledge in the field. He reports that

> . . . an inventory has been made of the knowledge that has been accumulated during the last thirty-eight years in the field of supervision as teaching in teacher education programs. . . . This knowledge consists almost entirely of more or less detailed descriptions of a certain number of entities, phenomena, and relations that have been observed to exist in the field. So it essentially belongs to the natural history stage of an emerging science of supervision as teaching in teacher education programs. As a matter of fact, no scientific theory of supervision as teaching, either all-encompassing or middle-range, has been formulated, and no discovery of laws governing the relations between the entities and/or phenomena of the field have been reported in the reviewed literature.[2]

Although Dussault's conclusions relate only to supervision defined as "teaching in teacher education programs," he could as well have broadened them to include inservice supervision. Further, his observation that supervision is at the stage of natural history seems well founded. One of the characteristics of this stage in the development of a science is that the scientists devote much of their time to collecting and categorizing data and specimens in order to create the data-base for the development of theory and research. The present stage in the development of clinical supervision strongly indicates that its practitioners need above all to gather and systematize their data. A notable beginning in this endeavor has been made by Flanders in the development of systems of interaction analysis of teaching.

The rationale developed in this volume is avowedly at the stage of natural history and places emphasis upon the collection, systematic analysis, and use of data on classroom events. Such concerns for data and analysis may contribute to the formation of theory, but theory building should perhaps wait until systematic practice and the data of supervision

---

[2]Reprinted by permission of the publisher from Gilles Dussault, *A Theory of Supervision in Teacher Education* (New York: Teachers College, 1970; copyright 1970 by Teachers College, Columbia University), p. 105.

are both mature enough to engender and support promising theoretical formulations and related research.

Supervision and the Behavioral Sciences   The role of the clinical supervisor was precisely anticipated by William James in his *Talks to Teachers:* "Psychology is a science, and teaching is an art; and sciences never generate arts directly out of themselves. An intermediate inventive mind must make the application, by using its originality."[3] James is proposing that the teacher must transmute the sciences of teaching into an artistic classroom performance. Even if we substitute "competent" for "artistic," it is evident that few teachers accomplish this transmutation alone. They need the help of colleagues, one of whom is the clinical supervisor.

The rationale for clinical supervision, therefore, casts the supervisor in the role envisaged by James: an intermediate, inventive, trained professional committed to working with the teacher to help him make his own original application of the science available to him, in his own style.

Supervision is not a science, but it is in part committed to science. This commitment follows not from a predilection for science as against art, experience, or intuition, but from a need to inform art, experience, and intuition by science. It might be fair to say that, given the complexities of any professional practice today, whatever relevant science is available is needed to set proper constraints upon the claims of art, experience, and intuition. This is especially so since art is so susceptible to abuse when it becomes cult; experience, when it becomes a claim to universality; and intuition when it becomes superstition.

The advocacy of a partial reliance on science does not derive from any conviction that supervision is at present in possession of a substantial body of general laws and principles drawn from the behavioral sciences —laws and principles directly or by extrapolation useful in the management of the work of supervision. On the contrary, the lack of such laws is only too clearly evident.[4] The necessity for science in supervision derives from other reasons.

First, supervisors need to learn to apply the intellectual rigor and discipline of science in the careful interpretation and use of the sparse and partial findings that *are* available from the behavioral sciences. If any-

[3]William James, *Talks to Teachers* (New York: Holt, 1925), pp. 7–8.
[4]See Morris R. Cohen, "Reason in Social Science," in *Readings in the Philosophy of Science*, ed. Herbert Feigl and May Brodbeck (New York: Appleton-Century-Crofts, Inc., 1953), pp. 663–73. Also Edgar Zilsel, "Physics and the Problem of Historico-sociological Laws," ibid., pp. 714–22.

thing, this is an injunction to practitioners *not* to seize upon anything scientific in the name of science and straightaway make direct applications of it in practice. They are rather called on to employ the scientist's meticulous thought and language and to observe the rigorous limits he sets MB upon his data and his conclusions before they attempt to make practical application of his work. Certainly the disregard of such rigor has opened the door for much pseudoscience in supervision; for example, the painful efforts of some supervisors to teach teachers to use the techniques of behavior modification in the classroom. Second, supervisors need to internalize the standards of evidence and proof that are characteristic of science, as counterweights to tendencies toward uncritical enthusiasms and the formation of supervisory cults, for example, "democratic" supervision.

What help may the supervisor expect from the behavioral sciences? What cautions must he observe in using such help? One answer to these questions is supplied in an article by Gross, entitled "Some Contributions of Sociology to the Field of Education":

> What the sociologist has to offer is basically a series of sensitizing and analytic concepts and ideas based on theoretical and empirical analysis that will allow the practitioner to examine in a more realistic and incisive way the multiple forces operating in his social environment. The sociologist cannot make the educational practitioner's decisions for him, nor can the sociologist's research findings based on one population be applied to any educational population indiscriminately. The practitioner's task is to assess the various forces that have a bearing on the achievement of his objectives, assign them relative weights, and make a decision based on these calculations. The basic sociological contribution is to add to the educator's kit of intellectual tools a set of sociological insights and concepts that will allow him to take account in his decision-making organizational, cultural, and interpersonal factors at work in his environment.[5]

Gross's remarks are equally relevant to the use of other behavioral sciences in clinical supervision. The supervisor must exercise special care in his attempts to apply the behavioral sciences in his professional work, since the ambiguities and reversals of findings in these fields are well known. John B. Carroll provides a striking example of such dangers in his discussion of B. F. Skinner's attempts to apply the findings of his research to the instruction of human beings:

[5]Neal Gross, "Some Contributions of Sociology to the Field of Education," *Harvard Educational Review* 38, no. 2 (1959), p. 273.

. . . many of Skinner's original propositions—deriving from his basic research—were not sufficiently precise to guide the development of programed instruction unfailingly. Where it had been claimed that the
student must construct his own response, a selective response was often
found to be more efficient. Where it had been claimed that reinforcement
must be immediate, it was on occasion found that it could sometimes be
delayed, or even omitted entirely, without affecting the success of the
learning. Where it had been claimed that instruction must proceed in small,
carefully sequenced steps, it was found that the steps did not always have
to be small and that under some conditions it made no difference whether
the steps were presented in a "logical" or in a random sequence.[6]

Nevertheless, in spite of the problems that Carroll points out so clearly,
clinical supervisors must rely upon the behavioral sciences for "sensitizing
and analytic concepts" to strengthen whatever wisdom they may gain
from their own experience. It seems highly desirable, therefore, that they
be well grounded in the behavioral sciences and specialized in one—
perhaps psychology or sociology. With such preparation they may be
ready to evaluate and utilize relevant procedures from the fields of the
applied behavioral sciences.

In sum, the conceptualization of clinical supervision is better represented here by *rationale* than by theory. And rationale itself may be too
ambitious. Perhaps John Blackie's statement of the basis for teaching
captures the sense of the rationale for clinical supervision. His statement,
with *clinical supervision* and *clinical supervisors* substituted for *teaching*
and *teachers*, follows:

. . . there is still much that is not known [in clinical supervision]. It would
not be sensible to let everything remain unchanged until all the facts are
known. That, in any case, is unlikely ever to happen. All that [clinical
supervisors] can do is to found their practice on a combination of their own
experience and intuition, and the knowledge about growth and development and learning which research has made available. If they rely too much
on the former they will certainly miss the advantages that knowledge gives
and they may allow principles to harden into prejudices and insight to be
obscured by dogma. If, on the other hand, they follow too slavishly the
direction of research, their contact with the [teachers] is blunted and they
become transmitters instead of dynamos. Only the combination will really
do.[7]

In brief, clinical supervision is treated here as an applied, practical,
professional operation.

[6]John B. Carroll, "Basic and Applied Research in Education," *Harvard Educational
Review* 38, no. 2 (1959), p. 273.
[7]John Blackie, *Inside the Primary School* (London: Her Majesty's Stationery Office,
1967), pp. 15–16.

Supervision as Continuing Education

A cornerstone of the supervisor's work with the teacher is the assumption that clinical supervision constitutes a continuation of the teacher's professional education. This does not mean that the teacher is "in training," as is sometimes said of preservice programs. It means that he is continuously engaged in improving his practice, as is required of all professionals. In this sense the teacher involved in clinical supervision must be perceived as a practitioner fulfilling one of the first requirements of a professional—maintaining and developing his competence. He must not be treated as a person being rescued from ineptitude, saved from incompetence, or supported in his stumblings. He must perceive himself to be engaged in the supervisory processes as a professional who continues his education and enlarges his competences. This dominant concept is elaborated later in the discussions of the teacher-supervisor relationship and conference strategies.

Interdependence of the Phases of Supervision

The limitations of words on a printed page force us to deal with complex ideas about supervision in over-simplified form—linearly, as it were. We discuss one idea at a time, to be linked to other ideas later. The nature of verbal communication locks us into a process in which we speak unidimensionally about multidimensional phenomena. Thus we must first discuss the relationship of the teacher to the supervisor. Then we may deal with problems in the analysis of teaching. And still later we may examine various strategies to be used in the teacher-supervisor conference.

In spite of these profound linear constraints on printed communication, one might best describe the essential nature of clinical supervision by saying that its effectiveness depends on the interconnections and the interdependence of all its parts. For example, the productivity of a supervisory conference may be greatly influenced by the relationship established between the participants. The nature of the relationship may in turn exert a strong influence on the topics that should be broached or avoided in a conference. As a result, the relationship affects the analysis, which affects the productivity of the conference, which may—in spiral fashion—change the character of the relationship.

In this sense, then, the rationale proposes that the supervisor may go badly astray if he attempts to put into operation any of the suggestions offered here without taking into account the other dimensions of clinical supervision. This is simply to stress the fact that teacher and supervisor are influenced by the totality of the history they create together, not serially by the artificially isolated segments of that integrated history as they are found in a book. Perhaps the nature of this historicity of interpersonal interaction may become more apparent if illustrated by a homely analogy: The doctor cannot focus at one moment on his bedside manner and develop a relationship with a patient, then forget his bedside manner and the relationship to focus on diagnosis, and then base his treatment upon the diagnosis without taking into account the relationship between him and his patient. The success of the treatment may in part depend upon the relationship, upon the kind of knowledge the doctor has gained while establishing this relationship, and the confidence the patient has gained in his doctor.

This is to say that clinical supervision should be studied and practiced, so far as possible, in the full multidimensionality of human interaction.

Supervision as Professional Company for the Teacher

I don't know anything about my fellow teachers. I work from eight to four, and if Miss B Six who teaches down the hall is at home, sick, it may be several days before I hear about it. . . . Teaching is really a lonely profession. Closeted all day with children from whom you conceal your real thoughts and feelings makes teachers "kings of the castle." As a result, they tend to regard any outside intrusion with suspicion. Why is that visitor coming to *my* class, is my immediate reaction when anyone visits me. Of course I smile and welcome the guest. I have learned how to do this with mothers and supervisors. That is the loneliness of a teacher in the classroom.[8]

This loneliness, felt by many teachers, has serious implications for clinical supervision. No rationale for systematic practice can afford to ignore it.

What are the underlying meanings of the teacher's loneliness? First of all, it is not the isolation of a person deprived of human company. Obviously, it is difficult to be alone in a classroom full of young people. Teach-

[8]National Education Association, "Research Memorandum," no. 18 (1963), p. 3.

ers who say they are lonely in school are really referring to the lack of adult professional company in their work. Teaching school is one of the few callings in which the practitioner spends most of his working hours with children. Attempts to introduce more professionals into the classroom have had relatively little effect nationally, and the impact of team teaching has been rather small.

Some of the effects of being deprived of adult colleagues are alluded to in the quotation above. Many teachers feel lonely. Some view other teachers in the same school as strangers. And many more react with distrust or anxiety when supervisors enter their classroom. But other important consequences for teachers who work without adult company often escape notice.

Anna Freud, who was a teacher early in her career and who treated many teachers after she became a psychoanalyst, points out one of the dangers that threaten the schoolteacher:

> . . . working too closely with children fosters a loss of perspective between the child's world and the adult world. The teacher who works with young children only, sees them out of proportion. She gets caught up in the children's lives, loses her adult values, and begins to live in a child's world where everything comes down to the child's size.[9]

Although Freud's observations refer to the effects of isolation from adult company on elementary-school teachers, somewhat similar effects are observed among teachers working with youth of all ages.

As schools are presently constituted, they foster the teacher's anxiety about the entrance of other adults into the classroom. Educators have generally failed to establish firm professional expectations among teachers that other educators *will* regularly and rightfully be present in classrooms, performing a variety of educational functions. As a result, the entrance of adults into a classroom too often provokes a teacher's anxiety and resistance. This failure to build positive expectations and attitudes about in-class supervision creates the curious situation in which many teachers treasure their isolation and hate their loneliness.

The clinical supervisor can help to break down the isolation of teachers in school. He joins them in the classroom, he meets with them in conferences, and he organizes groups of teachers who work together in the supervisory program. In addition, he works with teachers and ad-

[9] Anna Freud, "The Role of the Teacher," *Harvard Educational Review* 22, no. 4 (1952), p. 230.

ministrators for the creation of an institutional climate favorable to supervision. Among the specific objectives he seeks are—

1. the establishment among school personnel of a professional and institutional expectation of competent classroom supervision;
2. the establishment of clinical supervision as a desired and desirable professional service;
3. the establishment of policies, processes, and relationships designed to lower teachers' anxieties about supervision to productive levels.

Ethics in the Rationale of Clinical Supervision

Almost every contemporary vocation calling itself a profession commits itself to a professional morality embodied in a code of ethics. One of the functions of this code is regulation of the relationships between the professional and his client for the protection of the client. The professional association commonly assumes some responsibility for maintaining this social contract in force.

The client is almost entirely dependent upon the integrity of professionals to guarantee competent performance of the vital services he needs, since in most instances only a professional is qualified to pass on the competence of fellow professionals or to evaluate their practice. Thus any attempt to develop clinical supervision as a profession must begin with an ethical commitment that binds the supervisor to the teachers he serves, this commitment being part of his professional self-discipline.

The statements below, dealing with the ethical commitments of supervisors, obviously do not constitute a professional code. Such a code must be *developed*, not given. It becomes manifest as a body of related cases, professional decisions, and ethical practices. All that is sought here is an initial treatment of one important professional problem facing the supervisor: Who are the supervisor's "clients," and what is the nature of his commitment to them?

The supervisor's first commitment is to the dignity and human worth of the teachers he serves, and his first function is the improvement of teaching. When the teacher needs help outside the domain of supervision, the supervisor's duty is to refer the teacher to persons competent to meet those needs. That is, the clinical supervisor is required to limit his work to the domain of his professional competence and not to trespass upon other domains, no matter how good his intentions. Members of all professions live with this problem. For example, the doctor treating a patient who has attempted suicide refrains from lecturing him about the religious and legal implications of suicide.

This is not to say that the supervisor, in dealing with the teacher's teaching behavior, may not draw help and adapt procedures from other professions if he gains enough competence to do so. For example, he may establish rapport by utilizing techniques derived from counseling or he may use techniques of behavior modification derived from Skinnerian psychology. But he does not prescribe physical exercise if the teacher lacks energy in class, nor does he assume the role of marriage counselor if the teacher's work seems to be affected by troubles with his wife.

To put this in still another way, the supervisor's work is specifically related to the teacher's work, and it is limited to this professional domain and its related competences. Even within his own domain, the supervisor's work with the teacher stops when it threatens the teacher's sense of his own dignity or human worth. For example, the analysis of a teacher's classroom behavior stops when the implications of such analysis seem likely to threaten the teacher's security or seriously damage his concept of himself. When such a situation arises, the supervisor tries other modes of working with the teacher or involves other experts in the work.

The supervisor is committed as a human being to the teacher as a human being, but as a professional he is committed to improving the students' learning by improving the teacher's performance. From these priorities it follows, for example, that if the supervisor cannot help a teacher who is seriously endangering the physical or emotional health of his students, then the supervisor is required to call upon the aid of whatever additional resources are necessary to help the teacher and protect the students.

An ethical (and strategic) problem may also arise from conflicts over who will decide what kinds of changes in the teacher's behavior are to become the objectives of the supervisory program. Incompatible views about such decisions may be held by the teacher, the supervisor, the principal, the administrative staff of the school system, and the school community. Obviously no simple formula will solve such problems. Nevertheless, the supervisor does have several strategic options open to him. For example, he and the teacher may study the patterns of the teacher's instruction together, but the objectives for change can be selected in major part by the teacher. Such a starting point has the advantages of insuring relevance and personal meaning for the teacher.

Or the supervisor may be under pressure to work for objectives institutionally derived by a department, a school, or a school system. For example, a systemwide decision may be made to concentrate on more "humane" teaching or on the encouragement of creativity among students. When something like this occurs, the clinical supervisor may find himself faced with a choice between following institutional policy or concentrating on the more pressing needs of the teacher. Or the supervisor himself may consider such large-scale objectives unsuitable for the school system.

In order to be able to deal with the dilemmas involving individual teachers and the values of the administration or community, clinical supervisors need to have a voice in decisions about instruction. The supervisors' participation in decision-making will not in itself invariably solve such dilemmas, but supervisors may on occasion be able to modify broad policies and thus make it possible to take into account the special needs of teachers.

On the other hand, participation in schoolwide or systemwide programs to improve instruction may have great advantages for teacher and supervisor alike. They will have the benefit of professional company, the support of administration and community, and possibly the incentive of their own inclinations.

A fourth possibility is that the supervisor working with a teacher may elect to embark on a program of the former's choosing. Such a point of departure runs the obvious risks of involving the teacher in endeavors to which he cannot or will not commit himself deeply.

Another possibility is that the teacher and supervisor together will analyze the teacher's classroom performance in relation to the students' needs, and on this basis formulate the objectives toward which teacher and supervisor will work.

To examine such possibilities serially is to risk conceptualizing the problem of setting objectives for a supervisory program as though the various alternatives were always irreconcilable. This is possible but far from inevitable. For example, the supervisor might arrange to work on schoolwide objectives with groups of teachers and also to work clinically with individuals. Or he might be able to divide these labors among the corps of supervisors. Or he might be able to begin clinical supervision with a teacher who has already decided on an objective and by working through this problem carefully, establish the basis for their joint participation in such decisions in the future. At that time the two could examine each other's views and take into account still other forces influencing the objectives of their work together.

This discussion of the problem of conflicting, competing, and incompatible objectives is not intended to provide a set of answers. It is, however, designed to make clear the supervisor's need to (1) recognize the possibilities of conflict, (2) avoid conceiving these differences as mutually exclusive or irreconcilable, and (3) develop within himself the professional resources needed to deal with these problems. The clinical supervisor must also—

1. recognize that diverse sets of values impinge upon decisions about what objectives to choose in working with a teacher;
2. examine and develop his own values about goal-setting in clinical supervision;
3. develop within himself the resources of varied and flexible strategies for dealing with these problems;
4. take into account the fact that situational factors may influence the priorities and values affecting decisions about the objectives of clinical supervision.

The Uses of Shared Decision-Making

In the sequences of clinical supervision the teacher and supervisor together make a great many decisions as they determine what aspects of instruction are to be improved and how to improve them. The nature and quality of both the teacher's and the supervisor's participation in these processes are undoubtedly among the most critical factors in the success of the supervisory program.

Decisions about what, why, and how to teach, made by either the supervisor or the teacher alone, even if "correct," tend to interfere with the emerging colleagual relationship. It is not that "two heads are better than one," although often enough they turn out to be if the decision-making process is truly shared and competently developed. The danger is that merely superficial involvement of the teacher may adversely affect his understanding of what he is to do in class and his will to do it. And in the end it is the teacher who will do the teaching. Even if he acts upon the supervisor's decision in good faith, he may truly be unable to carry out the strategies for a plan of action he has not helped create and does not understand.

And the same is true for the supervisor if the teacher makes unilateral supervisory decisions, for clinical supervision is welded to processes that in some of their most important phases involve the teacher and supervisor as a team. As a result, if the supervisor is even in part excluded from the decision, he may be unable to take a productive part in its implementation, in the evaluation of its outcomes, or in other phases of the cycle.

This is not to say that all decisions must culminate in complete agreement of teacher and supervisor about what is to be done. They may agree to disagree and to try one or another alternative. But they must have shared understandings about the decision and its implementation. To require constant agreement is often to force one or the other participant into an empty ritual of compliance. And ritual compliance extracts its own price in alienation from clinical supervision.

It may be useful to take a closer look at some of the likely consequences of full participation and common understandings as a basis for implementation of decisions about teaching.

Let us suppose that the teacher and supervisor together study the former's teaching and together design plans to achieve their objectives. Under these conditions they begin to work within a domain of problems that the teacher himself has helped to define. The goals sought and the processes by which they are to be achieved bear the mark of the teacher's values, needs, and strategies. Even so, however, one cannot safely assume that the teacher's involvement in the improvement of his own teaching will be deeper, more enduring, and more effective simply because he has helped to plan it. The ultimate effectiveness of shared decision-making depends not only upon the form of the process but also upon its ultimate success. It is almost inevitable that at the beginning of clinical supervision the failure of a lesson will create doubts in the teacher's mind about the value of his work with the supervisor. The latter must therefore accept this possibility and see to it that the joint planning does not force the teacher to depart too radically from his customary mode of teaching if it has been successful. On the other hand, a plan can fail in its goal of reinforcing the process of shared decision-making if the changes involved in it are trivial. To set out to seek some inconsequential goal may achieve certain short-term objectives of supervision, but these gains are likely to be washed out in the long run, when the teacher begins to realize that his "success" is only superficial. The supervisor and teacher therefore need to seek safe ground between trivial and overambitious changes in the teacher's behavior.

The Importance of the Cycle in the Rationale

If clinical supervision is a way of helping teachers to improve their teaching, then the cycle of clinical supervision is designed to make that help operative. The cycle is therefore part of a larger strategy to facilitate MB change in behavior. That strategy may be termed *developmental*, in contrast to *episodic* or *discontinuous*. By both its form and its processes the cycle strongly conveys to the teacher the sense that classroom teaching and classroom learning must be worked out, they do not just happen. Both unfold across time, in stages, phases, and occasional regressions. The cycle, being itself developmental, helps to teach the teacher that the learning tasks in which his students are engaged are also developmental.

The cycle also affords extended opportunities for one-to-one interaction. Such a situation offers both the opportunity and the spur for the individualization of the supervisor's program with the teacher.

A common assumption about supervision is that "what takes place during a conference constitutes a fair sample of the teaching that is done by supervisors engaged in professional laboratory experiences."[10] This statement fairly represents what often happens in both preservice and inservice supervision. One must ask, however, whether it does not also reflect the fairly widespread conception that supervision is something one does in a conference. Quite a different position is adopted in the rationale for clinical supervision. The rationale and the cycle postulate the necessity for sequences of supervision that are congruent with the conditions under which teachers can learn. It is apparent that teachers can learn to improve their teaching not only by way of conference, but by learning to take new roles in supervision, by way of a professional relationship with the supervisor, by planning with him, analyzing their teaching with him, experimenting with new behaviors, and, in sum, sharing colleagual help and support in many aspects of their work. Learning theory suggests that such help should be programed, should embody psychologically reasonable sequences and continuities. The cycle provides a vehicle for insuring some of these necessary prerequisites for effective supervision.

The need for continuity of supervision has been stressed in the preceding pages. The teacher needs two types of continuity. The first relates to the sequence of his own learnings, which should be logically interrelated as in any carefully designed learning program. Such a program

[10]Gilles Dussault, op. cit., p. 38.

MB

helps to assure the continuity of learning tasks in supervision. The second relates to the teacher-as-learner. This simply means that the program of learning must be responsive to the teacher's permanent and transient learning states. These states may dictate that at some time, with some tasks, the teacher may forge ahead steadily, "at his own pace." At other times or with other tasks he may slow down, regress, stop trying, or leap ahead. The pace of the program must be continuously related to the pace of the teacher. Both types of continuity are taken into account in the rationale and may be implemented in the cycle.

Learning "Why" in Clinical Supervision

There are many types of learning and many ways in which people learn. Learnings may be affective, cognitive, esthetic, psychomotor. They may, for example, occur by way of conditioning, Freudian psychodynamics, maturation, association, practice, and with or without observable rewards and punishments. Most of the learnings that form the objectives of clinical supervision, however, are learnings characterized by insight and understanding. That is, the teacher should, whenever possible and feasible, not only learn new behavior, but he should understand why he does what he does and why it is better or worse than other things he might do. The cycle, with its emphasis on the close examination of teaching, offers some support for learnings of this nature. Some of the advantages of learning and learning *why* are that they improve the likelihood of transfer, generalization, ready recall at need, and application of learnings in inventive and creative ways.

MB

It has been noted that the cycle offers the teacher peer support and improved opportunities for learning. With such support the teacher may at some point feel ready to try out new roles in the classroom and new techniques of teaching. He may be prompted to try developmental and experimental programs of instruction. The cycle is especially well adapted to such efforts.

The Staff Concept in Supervision

The demands of clinical supervision are too diverse to be satisfied by supervisors alone. The success of supervisors will in large part depend upon their ability to organize and use the resources of others. This problem must be faced by school and university supervisors alike. As a matter of fact, two related problems emerge in the initiation of a clinical program. The first is to develop a corps of adequately trained supervisors— a corps large enough and competent enough to meet the teachers' needs. The second is to organize the collateral staff.

Corps of sup.

The point has already been made that the number of clinical supervisors in many schools and universities is inadequate for the responsibilities they hold. But how many are actually needed? Obviously, the answer to this question must be an estimate rather than a precise and demonstrably defensible number or ratio. Even the estimate will vary sharply from situation to situation. Nevertheless, one might venture to say that in order to supply student teachers in universities with formative rather than merely symbolic supervision, enough supervisors would be needed to provide an average of perhaps five hours a week for each student. If principal responsibility for supervision is the province of a trained, cooperating teacher, then the university supervisor's time should probably be allocated to work with the cooperating teacher, and would vary according to the latter's effectiveness and other important situational factors.

As for inservice supervision, the estimate of the supervisor-teacher ratio required for clinical supervision will vary enormously, being related to the needs of teachers and the program of innovative and remedial instructional activities planned for a school, a department, or a school system. Nevertheless, one might venture to estimate the range as enough supervisors—resident and nonresident in a school—to provide an *average* of three or four hours a week for each teacher. The word *average* is not intended to convey the idea that each teacher in the course of an academic year will have three or four hours of work weekly with a supervisor. The actual allocation of time will vary with each teacher's need.

However, in order to move to consideration of the staff concept in supervision, let us assume the existence of an adequate number of competent clinical supervisors. These supervisors require on occasion the collateral services of other personnel. The collateral personnel might include the following—

1. subject matter specialists in all disciplines—sciences, art, languages, social studies—and specialists in remedial fields;
2. psychologists, psychiatrists, counselors, physicians, and university personnel;

3. specialists in the analysis of teaching; experts in the use and interpretation of data derived from observation instruments; researchers in education, general supervisors;
4. experts in the management of interpersonal relations; administrators, community affairs personnel, program and project developers;
5. specialists in vocational education, compensatory education.

Implementing the concept of the corps and the collateral staff in supervision requires that supervisors change their views of themselves and their work. To begin with, supervisors must define their field of operation not in terms of what they can do to help the teacher improve his instruction, but in terms of what the *teacher needs* in order to improve his instruction. The clinical supervisor may be able to satisfy some of these needs. For others he may require the assistance of the collateral staff. It is obvious that such a staff is only in part resident in the school or school system. As a result, it becomes incumbent upon the system to organize the necessary resources and mobilize them in such a way that they become responsive to the supervisor's needs.

No attempt will be made here to deal with the policies and organizational arrangements requisite for the implementation of the staff concept. It is necessary, however, to discuss the dimensions of the supervisor's perceptions about himself and his work in reference to the concepts of *corps* and *collateral staff*.

The supervisor and teacher both need to learn to view the supervisory program "as one in which many carefully selected staff members possessing extensive resources of talent and experience are integrated into the total supervisory program. . . ."[11] The improvement of instruction thus becomes the responsibility of the corps of clinical supervisors in concert with a broadly defined collateral staff, who also share responsibility for the improvement of instruction. Until teachers and school and univerity supervisors comprehend, accept, and use the whole range of supervisory resources available to them, they will operate at only a fraction of their potential.[12]

The operation of the corps and collateral staff also contributes to a change in the teachers' conceptualization of clinical supervision. Teachers no longer assume that supervisors will make a series of separate and un-

[11]Morris L. Cogan, "Supervision at the Harvard-Newton Summer School," mimeographed (1961), p. 4.
[12]For a more detailed treatment of the operation of supervisors and staff, see Morris L. Cogan's "Clinical Supervision by Groups," in Association for Student Teaching, *The College Supervisor* (Dubuque, Iowa: W.C. Brown, Inc., 1964).

coordinated "visits" at unpredictable and frequently inappropriate times. On the contrary, teachers learn to view supervision as the operation of a set of varied resources supportive of their teaching, brought to bear not according to some random schedule but according to the nature and the occasion of their need for help. It is obvious that such supervision is integral with the concept of the cycle of clinical supervision.

CHAPTER 3

Self-Knowledge: "Set" and Inference

Perception and Judgment

The professional controls required of the clinical supervisor must be constantly operative in his practice. Control in this sense denotes the supervisor's regulation of his professional behavior. Such self-regulation, which constitutes an important part of a professional discipline, depends largely upon (1) the supervisor's knowledge of his own patterns of perception—what he sees, distorts, overlooks, projects, e.g.—and (2) the use he makes of this self-knowledge in forming judgments and controlling his professional behavior.

Working with a teacher in the cycle of supervision, the supervisor sets in motion a chain of events. The process of establishing the teacher-supervisor relationship affects their planning. The planning in turn naturally affects what the teacher does in class, as well as what the supervisor observes in class. Such cause-and-effect relationships are multiplied in each subsequent phase of the cycle. That is, the activities of the cycle represent not only sequential relationships but also—obviously—interactional linkages. It follows, therefore, that if errors are introduced into any phase of the cycle, the entire process is likely to be damaged.

To illustrate the cumulative effects of errors in perception and judgment, we may examine a sequence of four activities in which the supervisor frequently engages: (1) he observes the teacher in the classroom, (2) he studies the transcript of what has occurred in class, (3) he helps the teacher to formulate hypotheses about the teacher's classroom performance, and (4) he joins the teacher in a conference to develop strategies for improving the next teaching session. Let us suppose that the supervisor observes the teacher addressing male students by their first name and female students by the word *Miss* plus their last name. He may later check the frequency of such behavior in the transcript and find that each mode of address occurred sixteen times during a forty-five-minute period. The supervisor may then interpret this behavior as evidence that the teacher is showing sex favoritism. He assumes that the teacher is trying consciously or unconsciously to increase the social distance between himself and female students, and to lessen it between himself and male students. The supervisor may further assume that the students resent this differentiation by sex, that their resentment is interfering with their learning, and that it would be advisable to help the teacher change his modes of addressing students.

In this entire sequence of observing, judging, and acting, the supervisor may have committed certain errors: (1) he may have failed to tabulate occasions on which the teacher addressed female students by their first name, or males by "Mister" plus their last name; (2) he may be mistaken about *why* the teacher does what he does, and (3) he may also be in error about the significance the students attach to these modes of address. If the teacher actually does exhibit these patterns, he may be doing so simply because he feels it is polite to call girls "Miss" and impolite to call boys "Mister." Or he may be using different patterns of address without any conscious rationale, or be imitating British teachers as portrayed in some novels.

To increase the chance of piling error upon error, the supervisor may be overlooking the possibility that these modes of address can be interpreted differently by students of different ages and sexes. That is, the supervisor's judgments about this aspect of the teacher's behavior, about his motives, and about the students' reactions might be partly or wholly incorrect. It is unnecessary to speculate on the painful consequences such a series of errors could have when teacher and supervisor meet to confer about the lesson. It is enough to emphasize the supervisor's need to take steps to minimize such errors. He needs firm knowledge about the effects of his sets, biases, and predispositions upon what he sees, how he responds to these events in the world around him, and how he forms inferences and hypotheses and judgments about them. These tasks require the supervisor's dedicated efforts to understand and modify his own behavior. In this work he also must seek the help of others competent to deal with such problems: psychologists, master supervisors, etc.

Inferential Sets as Sources of Error

Since to err is human, and humans are both numerous and inventive, their errors of perception and judgment are especially rich and varied. People make errors in seeing. If they barely see something, they invent the rest. They see what they want to see. For example, some teachers fail to see errors made on tests by girls, but catch those made by boys. In brief, what people see is in part determined by what is there, and in part by learned tendencies to select what is seen and to modify that. This is to say that the supervisor may exhibit patterns of behavior in what he sees and responds to, what he searches for, what he projects into what he sees, what reassures him or makes him anxious, what he remembers or forgets. These patterns of behavior have been variously called *inferential sets, schemata,* and *perceptual screens.* Such screens may block out some stimuli, bring others into sharp focus, or obscure, magnify, reduce, and change the events perceived.

Several points may be made about such phenomena. The first is that the operation of schemata and inferential sets is powerful, pervasive, and often unconscious. The second is that such sets are almost constantly evaluative. The third is that individuals differ in the speed with which they form judgments. And the fourth is that a person's schemata and his processes of making judgments have been learned originally and may be modified by learning.

We may gain some idea about the nature of errors in perception and judgment by observing a supervisor who is examining the transcript of a teaching session. As he looks at the record, he also recalls the session he has witnessed. Therefore, what he actually scrutinizes are two partial representations of what has happened: his memory—which is not perfect—and a transcript of the teaching, which is inevitably incomplete. To make his processes of analysis even more liable to error, what he perceives, what he sees and responds to, and the interpretations he puts upon what he perceives all depend not only upon what "actually" happened but also upon his own past experience. Furthermore, the events he perceives and the meanings he imposes upon these events all may vary at different times and with the different personal states he experiences: high anxiety, fatigue, pleasurable anticipation, and so forth.

Let us watch a supervisor who is reviewing a videotape record of a teaching session. If his objective is to find evidence about whether or not the students are mastering the objectives set out by the teacher, he will "see" the students' behavior, but little of the teacher's. If, on the other hand, he is looking for evidence about whether the teacher is following the lesson plan, then he may not "see" the students, but he will observe the teacher and may even visualize the lesson plan. He may perceive still other things if he likes the teacher and dislikes the plan, or if he is looking for evidence about the technical skill of the technician who made the videotape record. In brief, what the supervisor "sees" has been influenced by his objectives and his schemata. He sees and interprets selectively, in his own way.

The effects of inferential sets and schemata are clearly demonstrated by the different responses given by individuals who are asked to respond to inkblots and other ambiguous forms used in certain psychological tests.

Anderson and Hunka provide another example of the distortions that may arise from patterns of perception and judgment operating when a supervisor is working with a teacher:

> To the spinster [supervisor], for example, a tall gawky [teacher] who is driving a class either into apathy or distraction by the hesitant dullness of her performance, will be marked up for earnestness and good moral intentions. To the anti-intellectual, on the other hand, an intellectually polished teaching performance will be reduced in value by quibbling, denial and distortion.[1]

It may be useful to examine several interpretations that might be made of the spinster supervisor's behavior. It is possible that she herself, gawky, earnest, and of good moral intentions, may identify so closely with the teacher that her judgment becomes distorted. She therefore judges that a really dull performance is redeemed by earnestness and good moral intentions. On the other hand, let us suppose that the supervisor recognizes her own tendency to identify empathetically with gawky teachers who may also become spinsters with good intentions. Given such self-knowledge, she might gather data from the students to test her hypothesis that the lesson was in whole or part redeemed by earnestness and good intentions. It would not be too unusual to find the students attesting to both the depressing effects of the teacher's dull and hesitant performance and to the redeeming effect of her earnestness and good moral intentions. With such evidence, the supervisor could set to work with the teacher to minimize the hesitant dullness of her performance and to deploy the strength of her earnestness and good moral intentions in the service of the objectives of the instruction.

The point to be made after this hypothetical extrapolation from a simple illustration is not that it is magically easy to remedy a hesitant and dull teaching performance. It is *not* easy. But the homely example may suggest that a supervisor's knowledge about his own behavior, combined with a commitment to testing hypotheses rather than jumping to conclusions may pay off in better supervisory performance.

The effects of distorting schemata are sometimes so painful that people tend to overlook the fact that benign schemata may *help* an individual to see reality clearly and to relate more effectively and satisfyingly with others. For example, if a supervisor learns to recognize his own sensitivity

---

[1]C. C. Anderson and S. M. Hunka, "Teacher Evaluation: Some Problems and a Proposal," *Harvard Educational Review* 33, no. 1 (1963), p. 82.

to hurt, he may also learn to recognize that others are similarly sensitive, or more or less sensitive, or sensitive about other things.

A few vignettes may communicate the power of unexamined and often unsuspected preferences, sets, and schemata over an individual's behavior:

> A supervisor who does not know that he is slightly hard of hearing develops an almost uncontrollable dislike of a teacher who speaks in a low voice.

> A supervisor having no experience of foreign handwriting concludes that a foreign-born language teacher who writes a Z with a bar through it (Ƶ) is "affected," "showing off."

> A supervisor whose own teaching style is tightly controlled and carefully planned cannot stomach a teacher whose style is loose and frequently improvisatory.

> A female supervisor with unattractive legs finds she experiences surges of animosity toward a shapely young mini-skirted teacher.

> A black supervisor has an unshakable belief that white teachers cannot communicate adequately with black students. He finds it impossible to entertain the thought that he himself, by his own reasoning, might not be able to communicate adequately with white students or white teachers.

> In the example above, interchange *black* and *white* wherever they occur.

> A supervisor, formerly outstandingly successful as a teacher in establishing warm personal relationships with students, cannot entertain the possibility that a teacher who is restrained and cool in relating to students may nevertheless be outstandingly successful.

> A supervisor informs a teacher that it is impossible to teach well without a detailed, written lesson plan.

> A supervisor characterizes a teacher who favors corporal punishment as "authoritarian."

> A Catholic supervisor finds it "nauseating" to work with a "hippie" teacher who has a long beard, long hair, and wears sandals on his bare feet. He finds it exhilarating to work with Brother Matthew, a priest who has a long beard, long hair, and wears sandals on his bare feet.

Whose Needs Are Being Served?   Another dimension of self-knowledge relates to an understanding of whose needs are being served when the supervisor makes a judgment about a teacher's request for help. In reference to this problem, Goethals offers several valuable observations:

> Unfortunately, many supervisors do not distinguish between requests for help which relate to their proper supervisory role and concern the profes-

sional maturity of their staff, as opposed to those requests for attention and help which come from infantile needs which if gratified may intensify a person's immaturity. Unfortunately the most pernicious aspect of this is that many supervisors because of their own personality structures are gratified by requests for help without taking the trouble to understand why these requests are made. This can often cause an otherwise competent supervisor to distrust and minimize the efforts of the independently oriented teacher who works well without observation and with a minimum of help from the supervisor. The supervisory helping relationship is thus a two-way situation made up of subtle rewards and complex motives on the part of both people. The supervisor has the responsibility of resolving for himself, with a minimum of distortion, the reasons why he is helping another person as well as why other people are turning to him for aid.[2]

Does the supervisor, for example, recognize that in analyzing a transcript he has made a guess rather than an analysis—because he was tired or because he could not make head or tail out of the transcript? When the teacher asks the supervisor to give a demonstration lesson in class, is it because they both judge that the demonstration is the best way to help the teacher, or because the supervisor somehow—perhaps unknowingly— has steered their discussion toward that end in order to savor the satisfactions he experiences in staging a demonstration lesson? Whose needs will be served?

These vignettes should of course not be viewed as accounts of the Machiavellian strategies of self-serving supervisors. They are rather presented as examples of a large class of very human behaviors whose causes are often unknown and unsuspected. Other phenomena in this class of behavior include "blind spots," prejudices, preferences, dislikes, and distortions, as well as empathies, projection of self into the behavior of others, sympathies, and intuitive understanding of the behavior of others.

The Educated Judgment

The supervisor needs to understand the forces within himself that shape his professional judgments. Otherwise, he cannot learn to make professionally defensible decisions. To clarify the nature of this problem, a few of the forces affecting people's judgments are listed below, with an example of each:

1. *Speed* of judgment
   Example: A supervisor hears a teacher define *hoi polloi* as "the masses." He jumps to the conclusion that she is wrong, since he thinks it means "the aristocracy." He charges her with an error.

2. Racial, ethnic, and religious *bias*
   Example: A white supervisor concludes that a new black social studies teacher cannot do justice to the theme of human rights in the U.S.

3. *Fears* and *anxieties*
   Example: A white supervisor sees the bone handle of a comb sticking out of a black teacher's back pocket and concludes that it is a straight razor.

4. *Interpretation*—the inner meanings of external events
   Example: A teacher in training to be a clinical supervisor is analyzing a transcript of a teaching session before an audience of several professors at the university. He is interrupted by the entrance of an unknown adult who addresses him directly and asks permission to observe the conference. The trainee, a bit shaken by the interruption, and feeling that the visitor should really be answered by the professors, replies: "Are you a professor here or just a student?" (Who will help the trainee to come to terms with the implications of the word *just?* Will he view the teachers he is to work with in this same hierarchical fashion?)
   Example: A supervisor-in-training is conferring with a student teacher who has just completed a unit in which his socioeconomically deprived students have been writing poetry. The conference is at a painful impasse because the supervisor accuses the student teacher of failing to grade the papers or correct errors in grammar and spelling, even on some poems that the supervisor has characterized as "illiterate jingles." At a loss for an answer, the student teacher simply hands the supervisor Kohl's *36 Children,* open at page 136:

   > I read all of the children's papers, commented on them and forgot about marks. . . . Teachers ought to attempt to do the writing assignments they give before deciding upon criteria to judge children's efforts. What would happen to the grading of children's poetry if teachers used examples of their own work instead of Robert Frost or Walt Whitman as models for grading?

   Who will help the supervisor to understand the student teacher? To understand Kohl?
   Example: A supervisor-in-training is asked by a team of professors to comment on what he judges to be the most striking aspect of a lesson they have just observed. The trainee replies that the classroom interaction was marked by too much noise and confusion. The entire group then analyzes a videotape of the session. At the end of the analysis the trainee realizes that what he has perceived as excessive noise and confusion is viewed by others as a very productive session. During the class

period, four student committees had successfully planned the work each committee was to perform in a class project to ascertain the economic and the ecological effects of strip mining in western Pennsylvania. (How can the trainee begin to comprehend the processes by which he perceived only noise and confusion? Does he have a "model" of teaching in which quiet and order are the prerequisites to learning? Does he have a low tolerance for noise? Does he understand the rationale for committee work? Does he "see" classroom processes and fail to see the outcomes of these processes? Who will teach him to make educated judgments?)

The Discipline of Seeing and Judging   How does a supervisor who gains certain insights into his own schemata, sets, biases, and preferences learn to control the behavior that springs from them? How does he separate the schemata that bias his perceptions from those that help him run straight and true? He must first of all *want* to change. It is characteristic of those who are at the extremes—at the far right and far left in their error or their rectitude—that they often tend to perceive their own view as gospel. Such people appear to be rigid, to change only with the greatest difficulty.[3] Another kind of rigidity is often observed in people who are highly "judgmental," who tend to jump to conclusions quickly. They may not hold to their judgments as adamantly as some of the extremists, but they too often persist strongly in their habit of jumping to conclusions rather than walking toward them slowly or postponing them until more evidence is in.

Given the supervisor's imperative need for openness, flexibility, and examined judgments, it might be advisable to screen candidates for their tendencies to judge rigidly or too rapidly. Carefully planned interviews, in combination perhaps with the use of techniques for identifying authoritarianism, ethnocentrism, rigidity, and the like, might prove useful in selecting candidates for clinical supervision.

For individuals in the middle range of judgmentalism, certain procedures may be developed to help them learn to make judgments more deliberately and more rationally and to postpone judgments when postponement is advisable.

Abercrombie reports on an experimental course she taught, designed to help science students understand "some of the factors that had affected their judgment in scientific matters." It is our strong hunch that her procedures may be generally applicable for both cognitive and affective judg-

[3]For a discussion of research on such change, see John P. Kirscht and Ronald C. Dillehay, *Dimensions of Authoritarianism: A Review of Research and Theory* (Lexington: University of Kentucky Press, 1967), pp. 95–126.

ments, since in making judgments the line between the two is often very vague indeed. Abercrombie writes:

> My hypothesis is that we may learn to make better judgments if we can become aware of the factors that influence their formation. We may then be in a position to consider alternative judgments and to choose from among many instead of blindly and automatically accepting the first that comes; in other words, we may become more receptive, or more mentally flexible. The results of testing the effects of the course of discussions support this hypothesis.[4]

She offers valuable suggestions about improving the quality of our judgments, recommending, for example, that we focus on "the *processes* of observing or thinking, as distinct from the results."[5] The wisdom of this suggestion inheres in the fact that the person attempting to improve his decision-making processes first focuses on *how* he makes them and is thus diverted from a preoccupation with the *meanings* of his decisions. The supervisor finds it less threatening to examine his decision-making *processes* than to try to comprehend what these decisions signify to others and to divine what they may imply about his own inner state. It is somehow less painful to say "I went at it the wrong way" than "My decision was wrong." This advantage may be increased if one starts the supervisor's learning process with examples of simple errors of perception—as in proofreading—rather than with the more deeply disturbing kinds of error attributable to unconscious bias, excessive anxiety, etc.

Abercrombie discusses the teaching procedures she employed in helping her students to improve the quality of their reasoning and their judgments. She also proposes some generalizations and hypotheses, many of which may be extremely useful to people concerned with the professional education of clinical supervisors. We present just a few:

> One is more likely to choose a correct hypothesis if one consciously considers more than one possibility instead of "jumping to a conclusion" without considering the evidence for alternative ones. . . . in interpersonal situations the observer influences the other persons he observes. . . . So intimate and indissociable are the relations between the participants in the perceptual act that in some cases we can be said to make our predictions come true, as when he who thinks himself unloved behaves in such a way as to make it difficult for anyone to love him. Such a person is caught in a hopelessly closed vicious circle, because his schemata of people's behaviour are continually reinforced by receiving confirmatory information;

[4]M. L. J. Abercrombie, *The Anatomy of Judgment* (Willowdale, Ont.: Hutchinson and Co., Ltd., 1960), p. 7. Reprinted by permission.
[5]Ibid. (Italics added.)

he cannot be presented with contradictory information until his own behaviour influences people differently. . . . In learning to see, we build up
schemata or assumptions by means of which incoming information is
organized, and by acting on what we perceive, these schemata are con-
tinually checked and modified. No such direct testing by physical manipu-
lation of the outside world is possible for many of our schemata. . . . There
is no check for such schemata other than talking about them, and thus
comparing and contrasting them with other people's. . . . Discussion in a
group does for thinking what testing on real objects does for seeing. We
become aware of discrepancies between different people's interpretations
of the same stimulus and are driven to weigh the evidence in favor of
alternative interpretations. Certain areas of one's private world are com-
pared and contrasted with other people's, and in seeing differences between them it becomes possible to modify our own world if we wish to.
Instead of seeing our own mistakes by contrast with the statements of an
unquestioned authority as in the traditional pupil-teacher relationship,
we see a variety of interpretations of the same stimulus pattern, and the
usefulness of each must be tested in its own right.[6]

Testing Inferences

The supervisor must learn to recognize the springs of his own behavior.
Some of this he can do himself, through reading, study, self-examination.
If he can participate in training sessions for clinical supervisors, his task
is likely to be much easier. In either event, a sampling of assumptions and
strategies that may be useful for these purposes is set out below.

Continued Learning   Since people learn patterns of behavior, it may be
helpful to make an initial optimistic assumption that they can also learn
to (1) recognize some of them, (2) modify them, (3) learn new patterns,
and (4) use these learnings in the control of their own behavior. That is,
having once learned, people do not cease learning.

Cognitive Categorization   Bruner notes that categorizing "an event as a
member of a class and thereby giving it identity involves . . . an act of
inference."[7] Since an inference is involved, people want to know whether
their inference is correct or not. Someone says that the pudding looks good,
but how does he prove it to his own satisfaction? The supervisor feels
that the students looking out the window during a lecture are not paying

---

[6]Ibid., pp. 38, 50, 59–60, 62.
[7]Jerome S. Bruner, Jacqueline J. Goodnow, and George A. Austin, *A Study of Thinking* (New York: John Wiley and Sons, Inc., 1956), p. 17.

attention, but how can he feel "sure"? Bruner proposes "four general procedures by which people reassure themselves that their categorizations are 'valid.' The first is *by recourse to an ultimate criterion*, the second is *test by consistency;* the third is *test by consensus* and the fourth, *test by affective congruence.*"[8]

An old adage teaches us to apply the *test of an ultimate criterion* when it tells us that "the proof of the pudding is in the eating." Or one might apply this test in order to ascertain whether a certain teaching strategy has truly accomplished the objective for which it was designed. Mager provides examples of statements of objectives amenable and not amenable to testing by ultimate criteria. He describes "To be able to solve quadratic equations" as "stated in behavioral, or performance, terms." These are "ultimate" terms in the sense that the person who states the objective must count the objective achieved if a student solves quadratic equations. On the other hand, the ultimate criterion is lacking, says Mager, in "To develop an appreciation for music." He rightly asserts that "since the objective neither precludes nor defines any behavior, it would be necessary to accept *any* of the following behavior as evidence that the learner appreciates music:

1. The learner sighs in ecstasy when listening to Bach.
2. The learner buys a hi-fi system and $500 worth of records.
3. The learner correctly answers 95 multiple-choice questions on the history of music. . . ."[9]

We must note that although Mager's presentation is easily comprehensible, it does sacrifice something for the sake of brevity. Neither behavioral objectives nor ultimate criteria are so easily stated. We do not really know very much about students' ability if we say that they solve quadratic equations. Do they solve them correctly? Can they solve them for x in $x^2 - 4x = 0$? In $x^2 + 3x + 1 = 0$? In the form $ax^2 + bx + c = 0$? How many of what kind of quadratics must they solve correctly? The intention here is not to quibble, but to point out that in the process of setting up ultimate criteria there must be a specification of what will be accepted as "ultimate." As Bruner has said: ". . . There are many categories where it is difficult to specify *the* ultimate criterion against which to check the adequacy of the defining attributes."[10]

[8]Ibid.
[9]Robert F. Mager, *Preparing Instructional Objectives* (Palo Alto, Calif.: Fearon Publishers, 1962), pp. 14–15.
[10]Jerome S. Bruner, Jacqueline J. Goodnow, and George A. Austin, op. cit., p. 18. (Italics in original.)

The *test by consistency* is made by reference to whether an event "fits the context of what has gone before."[11] For example, "I do not believe we can be defeated in war. We have never been defeated before." Bruner cites Cantril's findings on the reactions of the radio audience to *The War of the Worlds,* broadcast by Orson Welles. The listeners, in deciding whether the invasion by Martians "was 'real' or 'theatrical,' used a consistency criterion determined by the set of beliefs that had already been established in their past lives." Some listeners' "preexisting mental sets" were so strong that they immediately took the broadcast as fact. Among these were members of certain religious sects and people who were convinced that an invasion by foreign powers was imminent.[12]

The *test by consensus* is a validation "by people with whose values we identify—what a number of sociologists call a *reference group*."[13] This kind of validation is often provided by groups like "the New York critics," "the compilers of *Who's Who in America*," "the experts in the field," and so forth.

The *test by affective congruence*, in its pure sense, is "the unjustifiable intuitive leap buttressed by a sense of conviction. . . . Such acts . . . are particularly inaccessible to disproof. . . ." They may range from the religious man's strong belief in God to the paranoid's construction of "a pseudo-environment in which the random noises about him are categorized as words being spoken against him."[14] The attempt to validate a judgment by an affirmation of personal conviction may take the form of a sentence like: "X is Y because I believe it is—I am deeply convinced of it." Or it might be expressed in the form: "I just feel it is so —I feel it in my bones." A supervisor might, for example, say to a teacher: "Trust me. This class needs another week of review before they'll be ready for a test."

The concept of affirmation by personal conviction merits careful scrutiny by clinical supervisors—and even more careful use. Its use can of course be questioned if it is applied in support of a judgment or decision made (1) before the available evidence is exhausted or (2) in spite of the weight of available evidence, as in "There is no need to go to the trouble of checking *all* thirty tests. I'm sure that if these three students can't solve the problems, no one in this class can. They all need more drill." Or, "These students did well on the problems because they had just

[11]Ibid.
[12]Ibid., pp. 18–19, cited from H. Cantril, *The Invasion from Mars.*
[13]Ibid., p. 20. (Italics in original.)
[14]Ibid., pp. 20–21.

finished studying them. We both know that by the time the final examinations roll around, they will have forgotten how to do them. They need more drill." Such statements reduce the critical examination of data to a reliance on hunches or experience. Used too often, they erode the rational basis of analysis and tend to establish decision-making processes on the basis of personal ascendance or authority.

Even more perplexing problems are created when the argument by affective congruence is made (1) because for one reason or another no additional data is available or can be secured or (2) because someone has a feeling of "subjective certainty or even necessity."[15] The source of perplexity in dealing with such affirmations is that those who make them expect others to accept them as correct insights. To complicate matters still further, the statements may in reality be true. The last possibility is one that must be faced squarely and seriously. Some people do come up fairly often with "educated insights," and many decisions in education must, as we have noted, be made in the absence of adequate data. To complicate this problem still further, the frequent lack of adequate data often makes it difficult, if not impossible, to test an individual's insight or intuition adequately. But too-frequent recourse to claims of insight or experience or intuition can cause clinical decision-making processes to regress to dependence upon oracles and divination. It is more than merely amusing to note that at the end of a modern treatise on *Behaviour in Uncertainty* the author appends a list of about sixty "Artificial Methods of Divination," ranging from "alectromancy" through "geomancy" to "tyromancy" (divination by cheese).[16]

Teachers and supervisors who make decisions buttressed by claims of subjective certainty must remember that these decisions may be good or bad, but they cannot be used to form the principal basis for clinical decisions. If used too often, such decisions can reduce supervision to superstition. If used at all, they must be made with great caution and accompanied whenever possible by relevant predictions about outcomes that *are* subject to confirmation and that can be tested.

Need for Colleagual Support   Some suggestions have been made for helping the supervisor to understand his own schemata and control his behavior in the light of this knowledge. In this process, however, he needs additional assistance. He needs support when he is brought face to face with some aspects of his own thought and action. In a real sense

[15]Ibid., p. 20.
[16]John Cohen, *Behaviour in Uncertainty* (New York: Basic Books, Inc.), 1964.

the supervisor is learning how great the odds are against his being able to truly understand his own behavior and that of the teachers with whom he works. Beyond this, he encounters in himself unsettling ambiguities, preferences, and antipathies, not to mention nonrational tendencies that may appear to him to be irrational.

What does he make of his own behavior when he learns that in a single conference with a teacher he has five times "settled" differences about the interpretation of data on classroom teaching by abandoning the data and saying "That's simply not so in my experience!" How does he deal with the fact that he consistently focuses on weaknesses with new teachers and strengths with experienced teachers? In conferences why does he regularly talk about four times as much as the teacher?

His principal help in dealing productively with his own behavior usually comes from respected peers and colleagues. Some people can do a great deal about their supervisory behavior by themselves. But the supervisor finds these difficult tasks more manageable when he has the company of peers who are going through the same processes and when he works with experienced supervisors who support the effort and join in seeking understanding. One requirement for programs to prepare clinical supervisors is clear: the need to provide colleagual company and support when strategically appropriate. A carefully supervised internship probably offers the future supervisor his best opportunities to explore his own processes of thought, judgment, and decision in a protected environment and in the company of peers and competent colleagues.

CHAPTER 4

Some Problems of the Clinical Supervisor

Task-oriented Versus Person-oriented Behavior

Some supervisors may exhibit behavior directed principally toward the outcomes of their work. They are deeply concerned about the productivity of their efforts. They want to know what they have substantively accomplished. They frequently try to identify the changes they have helped to bring about in the teacher's classroom behavior. The preoccupation of many contemporary educators with the importance of evaluation and of behavioral change tends to reinforce supervisors in their concern about what they are accomplishing. This task-oriented behavior is further reinforced by the rising pressure for "accountability"—which involves the clear specification of who has done what in education. These pressures on supervisors are intensified in a production-oriented economy that finds it painful to allocate more and more funds tc school systems that may not be at all sure of what they are doing, how, and how well.

At the opposite pole are those supervisors who are more person-oriented. These men and women tend to take the excellence of their interpersonal relationships as the criterion for their performance. They may, for example, maintain that a good relationship is somehow worthwhile in itself—a good thing—and that such a relationship is indissolubly bound up with the improvement of the teacher's performance. Those who adopt this position in its extreme form hold that the better the teacher-supervisor relationship, the greater the chance of teacher change. For them, the possibility that a "hard-nosed" supervisor with poor interpersonal relationships might be highly successful in improving the teacher's behavior is unthinkable. So, too, is the possibility that the best-liked supervisor enjoying the best professional ratings from the teachers he works with could be completely ineffectual in improving teaching. The person-oriented school of thought draws its ideological support from diverse sources, including the celebrated "Hawthorne" experiment, in which researchers at a Western Electric plant attempted to raise the productivity scores of a team of women engaged in assembling relay switches. The research reports state that, although many improvements in working conditions were introduced—better lighting, shorter working hours, etc.—the marked improvement in the team's production records over a five-year period was not attributable directly to these innovations, but rather to the quality of their supervision. The report further states that improvement in production "reflects rather a freer and more pleasant working environment, a supervisor who is not regarded as a 'boss,' a 'higher morale.' " These improvements were attributed more generally to complex factors in which the supervisor played an important role but in which other variables also played a part. In sum, the improvements in human relationships and morale were viewed as being more closely related to increased production than were the physical and temporal changes made in working conditions.[1]

Support for the human relations school of thought also derives from sources as diverse as industrial supervision, client-centered therapy, political democracy, and studies of authority and leadership in group process. Anastasi's review of the bearing of human relations practices on the attitudes and productivity of supervisees may be relevant. Anastasi is writing about supervision in industry, but her ideas should be canvassed for their possible relevance to education:

> Despite the many complexities that beset the study of employee attitudes, one fact that emerges clearly is the importance of supervisory practices. . . . Surveys of the sources of job dissatisfaction have repeatedly shown the behavior of the immediate supervisor to be a major factor. . . . It is interesting to note, too, that some investigators have found group *productivity to be more closely related to the supervisor's attitudes and behavior* than to employee attitudes.[2]

In a discussion of investigations conducted at the Institute of Social Research at the University of Michigan, she says: "A major finding . . . was that the supervisors of high-producing units were more often 'employee-centered,' while supervisors of low-producing units were more often 'job-centered.' " "Employee-centered" is characterized by "a primary emphasis on the human problems of the workers," comprising the supervisor's friendly, supportive behavior and his efforts to protect the workers' sense of personal worth and to permit them considerable latitude in doing their work. Anastasi adds:

> In contrast, the job-centered supervisor places primary emphasis on pro-

---

[1] Elton Mayo, *The Human Problems of an Industrial Civilization* (New York: Macmillan Co., 1933), pp. 77–78.
[2] Anne Anastasi, *Fields of Applied Psychology* (New York: McGraw-Hill Book Co., 1964), p. 141. (Italics added.)

duction itself, seeing that the workers use the prescribed methods and overseeing their work more closely. The more effective supervisors . . . spent less time performing the same functions as the workers and more time in motivating their subordinates, in keeping them informed about policies and in long-range planning.[3]

It is apparent that data drawn from industrial research cannot be directly applied to educational supervision. The differences between supervision in a factory and supervision in a school are enormous. Nevertheless, the two fields may have enough in common to make a critical examination of such industrial research worthwhile for its possible applications in education. The similarities between supervision in industry and in education may be as important as the differences. At the very least, the supervisors in both fields are trying to change human behavior. In such change the relationship between supervisor and supervisee certainly makes a difference.

The first question suggested by the research is whether or not the separation of supervisors into two classes—person-oriented and task-oriented —is inevitable. Are all supervisors in either one or the other class? Do some supervisors exhibit both kinds of behavior? And most crucial: Would an integration of both orientations be more productive in clinical supervision? Although some of the research literature cited makes it appear that supervisors are always cast into one mold or the other, the likelihood is good that many supervisors—perhaps the majority—do exhibit or can exhibit behaviors that fall into both categories. It might be pointed out that this has been observed in many other instances where an attempt is made to categorize human beings into one class or another—authoritarian-democratic, introvert-extrovert, inner-directed versus other-directed, and so forth.

The tentative position proposed for examination here is that the clinical supervisor needs to exhibit both person-oriented and task-oriented behavior in an integrated fashion. Furthermore, it is a good possibility that supervisors who tend to exhibit one type of behavior more frequently than another may learn to exhibit both, although the prognosis would probably be poor for those whose behavior is strongly and predominantly oriented toward either mode of behavior.

In any event, both types of behavior seem to be logically required by the psychological needs of the teacher. At the beginning of the teacher-

[3] Ibid.

supervisor relationship a certain priority is almost inevitably established: the teacher needs to be reassured about himself psychologically before he can wholeheartedly turn his attention to changing himself professionally. To the extent that this is true, there should be a strong initial emphasis on person-oriented relationships in the first phases of the critical relationship, followed in the later phases by appropriate integration of both types of behavior. In our experience, most teachers cannot commit themselves to task-oriented behavior until they feel secure at the deeper, personal level. Furthermore, the processes of clinical supervision touch so often and so closely upon personal sensitivities that personal reassurances must be constantly renewed.

This position might be tested, hypothetically as it were, if one were to imagine the likely effects of either a pervasively person-oriented or task-oriented approach to supervision. Would not the supervisor's strong orientation toward the teacher as person be insufficient for the teacher who needs substantive help in the improvement of his professional tasks? And would not a singleminded concentration on professional tasks be inadequate for all but the most personally secure teacher?

In sum, it seems likely that the psychological needs of the teacher as a person must in most instances be satisfied before he can turn his full attention and efforts to the tasks of professional improvement, and that reassurances of interpersonal security will continue to be needed as teacher and supervisor join in those tasks.

The Scarcity of Dependable Knowledge in Teaching-Learning

In this volume a substantial emphasis is given to the supervisor's commitment to the use of the best data available to him. In the same breath, however, we must also point out that no matter how firm his commitment is, the data themselves are too often infirm and inadequate. The literature of education is full of eloquent testimony to this effect. A recent book of readings on research in instruction prefaces almost 400 pages of text with statements like the following:

> . . . systematic use of reinforcement is a potent tool for modifying behavior. Yet, paradoxically, immediate knowledge of results in programed instruc-

tion—one of the most widely heralded applications of reinforcement principles—fails to facilitate student performance. . . . More research will be required. . . . A section on problem solving and creativity, popular topics among educators, was not included. In addition to being poor research on the whole, studies dealing with problem solving and creativity have not clarified the features of instruction or conditions of learning which lead to the desired outcomes. . . . A section on classroom interaction was rejected because, in our opinion, research in this area has not led to warranted conclusions about features of instructional procedures that facilitate learning. A section on motivation was rejected for the same reason.[4]

A very long list of similar statements concerning the scarcity of dependable knowledge about teaching and learning could easily be compiled. Even the "good" research often proves to be very limited in its applicability to classroom instruction. It is apparent, therefore, that after all we really do not have a very large body of firm knowledge on which to construct an applied science of classroom teaching. How, then, can a supervisor be expected to use "the best data" available and function in a professional field riddled with doubt, ambiguity, anomaly, and confusion? How can he safely traverse such treacherous ground?

The answer to this question lies in the very nature of the profession. All the professions suffer from similar uncertainties. Is it really likely that the practice of medicine—apparently so close to science—is as firmly based in valid knowledge as many laymen believe? So much of diagnosis is educated guess, so much of prescription is on the order of "Take two aspirins and call me in the morning," so much of treatment is powerless to cure, that young men preparing to practice medicine often go through a crisis of uncertainty. And the same ambiguities must trouble the engineers whose bridges collapse and whose dams give way.

Since professional uncertainties seem likely to persist for a long time, the professional supervisor must learn to live with them productively. The key in that sentence is *productively*. We cannot merely go on working, we must work productively. This signifies that we do not make do with what we have, we make the best of it. If our store of useful data is small, we exhaust its resources before we draw inferences, propose hypotheses, or form judgments. Supervisors need to be prepared to live with partial knowledge. As Anastasi has said, "It is evident that there is no simple

---

[4]Richard C. Anderson et al., eds., *Current Research on Instruction* (Englewood Cliffs, N.J.: Prentice-Hall, Inc., 1969), p. vi.

formula for improving supervision."[5] Whatever the problems, the clinical supervisor must learn the controls that prepare him to function well in the midst of them. He will often succeed or fail and not know why. He has to learn that he may be forced to make decisions before he has a watertight rationale for them. Or he may have data too complex to be ordered by reference to the theory and experience he commands. Or he may have so little reliable information to go on that he must refuse to say "yes" or "no" and take recourse in "maybe," "either . . . or," and "perhaps." The psychological and ethical strains of working under such conditions are extreme. Many professionals, however, are able to establish a satisfactory mode of living with them. They simply observe the best and most rigorous safeguards of careful practice they can command. Having done their conscientious best for their clients, and being truly unable to do more, they are thereafter able to work productively without having their physical and emotional energies depleted by the unknowns of their practice.

"To Thine Own Self Be True"

Another necessary control in the discipline of clinical supervision is embodied in Shakespeare's excellent advice, "To thine own self be true." Anastasi deals with the problem in more prosaic but equally cogent terms when she writes that an important variable influencing the supervisor's effectiveness "is the personality and habitual behavior of the supervisor himself. Any sudden change in the supervisor's manner or procedures, such as might occur after a supervisory training program, may be viewed [by the supervisee] with suspicion and distrust." She goes on to add that "supervisory practices that are inconsistent with the supervisor's personality and run counter to his deep-rooted behavior patterns are likely to be superficial and insincere."[6]

All this is probably true, but the supervisor must not, however, yield to the temptation to make life easy by confusing contrived behavior with changed behavior. It is inevitable that the supervisor who attempts to improve his professional behavior will try out new behavior. The control

[5]Anastasi, op. cit., p. 143.
[6]Ibid., pp. 143–44.

that must operate when he does this, however, is that the new behavior he tries out should be congruent with his personality. He should seek change that will be authentic, that will not do violence to what he is, or that will not be simply a facade. For example, he may try to say less, to listen more, and to listen more carefully to the teacher. But if, no matter how hard he tries, his eyes grow glazed when he listens, if he cannot listen attentively, if he can only chain himself to silence and hold his breath until it is "his turn to talk," then he would perhaps be better advised to try to improve himself in other ways.

It is true that the supervisor himself may often not know whether new behavior will prove congruent or unassimilable. In such circumstances he cannot balk at the hurdle and back away. He simply accepts the risks and does what he can to minimize them. Otherwise, he is likely not to change at all.

Integrating Multiple Models of Good Teaching

One hurdle the supervisor cannot refuse to take is the effort he must make to change his views about what good teaching is. Most supervisors have been teachers. Most teachers have consciously and unconsciously constructed a personal model of the good teacher. Such conceptions generally grow by accretion rather than by critical examination and careful testing. The result is that too often the operating model of the teacher-turned-supervisor is pretty much what he himself does well. When teachers become supervisors, these personal preferences generally operate in full vigor, furnishing many of the criteria for viewing the teaching of others.

All this is very human behavior, which makes it very difficult to change. Yet it must change. The supervisor needs to create and internalize multiple models of good teaching. In this context, creating and internalizing are both extremely difficult. Nevertheless, without many and varied *operating* criteria of good teaching, the supervisor generally finds himself trying to help teachers to teach as he used to. Even if he learns to work from a few different models, he is still handicapped in helping teachers to achieve the styles that are personally congruent, since *congruence* here implies that there will likely be as many different ways of teaching as he has teachers to work with.

How does the supervisor learn to work from a conviction that good teaching may take manifold forms? Obviously, a good part of the answer to this question will be found in his professional education. A study of the history of teaching methods, for example, will often illuminate the problem.[7] Another helpful procedure is for the supervisor to study the descriptions of the objectives and teaching procedures of a sampling of modern research studies in which methods are varied, and to try to predict the learning outcomes before he has read them. Or to study the objectives and the outcomes, with the methods masked out, and then to try to match outcomes to methods. If the research studies are well selected, the supervisor is likely to discover for himself that his preferred methods are not always the "best" methods, or that results are ambiguous, or that clearly different methods may be related to significantly different learning outcomes.[8] If the supervisor has competent help in examining and interpreting such research studies, he may be able to break out of a restricted set of teaching models and entertain much more sophisticated hypotheses about the relations between methods and outcomes.

Gaining Knowledge About the Teacher

The proper study of the supervisor is the teacher. Like most aphorisms, this poor variant of Pope's line is at best a useful oversimplification. But the supervisor does in fact need to study the teacher. The larger reason for this is simply that the entire relationship between them is likely to be stronger if it is based on knowledge rather than on ignorance. A subsidiary reason for the supervisor's study of the teacher is that the supervisor requires a wide range of information and a large store of insight about the teacher in order to make a useful contribution to the development of an individualized supervisory program for him. Carefully tuned strate-

[7] A useful essay on this topic is Harry S. Broudy's "Historic Exemplars of Teaching Method," in *Handbook of Research on Teaching*, ed. N. L. Gage (Chicago: Rand McNally and Co., 1963), pp. 1–43.
[8] Two interesting studies that could be used for such exercises are D. M. Johnson and R. P. Stratton's "Evaluation of Five Methods of Teaching Concepts," in Richard C. Anderson et al., eds., ibid., pp. 242–48; and W. James Popham, "Performance Tests of Teaching Proficiency: Rationale, Development, and Validation," *American Educational Research Journal* 8, no. 1 (1971), pp. 105–17.

gies must be designed to achieve individualized objectives in the teacher's professional development. Such programing constitutes part of the meaning of *clinical*, as distinguished from *general*, supervision. The program has to "fit" the teacher.

It would be impossible, and probably not too useful, to attempt to set out an exhaustive inventory of the knowledge the supervisor needs concerning his work with a specific teacher. Perhaps a description of several types of information, plus an illustration of one or two, will serve our purposes better.

The supervisor should be familiar with the preprofessional and professional academic history of the teacher—his major and minor studies, his interests, and his achievements. Such information might pay off in diverse ways. The supervisor might find out that the teacher is teaching physics without an adequate background in mathematics. Or he might learn that he is teaching social sciences in the ninth grade when he has done his major studies in health and physical education.

It is important for the supervisor to have some understanding of how the teacher views his own profession: his perceptions of himself as a teacher, his view of the cardinal objectives of education, his satisfactions, his preferred methods of teaching, and so on. Such knowledge might permit the supervisor to design strategies for helping the teacher to institute some novel methods of teaching. To give a rather simple illustration, the supervisor might be well advised to encourage a teacher with a history of successful participation in team teaching to try to institute some of the practices of the "open" classroom. On the other hand, a similar encouragement might be exactly contraindicated for a teacher who frequently and strongly expresses the view that his students have been spoiled by "Dr. Spock's permissiveness" and need strong doses of strict discipline and corporal punishment.

The crux of these examples is not that they represent subtle insights and inspired planning. They simply demonstrate that the supervisor who has *not* studied the teacher may fall into serious error simply for lack of basic knowledge. How much more productive, then, might it be to become acquainted also with what the teacher views as desirable professional rewards, what he believes are the proper roles and relationships between students and teachers, what he thinks about being required to state the objectives of his instruction in behavioral terms.

In addition, the kind of knowledge we have been discussing here is essential to the supervisor when he begins to set out the objectives for his work with the teacher. He needs to know what the teacher's behavior is at the beginning of the supervisory program in order to be able to assess any changes that may occur afterward.

CHAPTER 5

The Teacher↔Supervisor Relationship

The Domain of the Clinical Supervisor

The proper domain of the clinical supervisor is the classroom behavior of the teacher. That is, the proper subject of supervision is the teacher's classroom behavior, not the teacher as a person. This separation of behavior from the person behaving is artificial but strategically useful. It is designed to persuade the supervisor to limit himself to the domain in which he is professionally trained: to focus on what happens in class rather than to attempt to change the teacher's personality—attitudes, beliefs, needs, and values. On the other hand, the arbitrary nature of this separation is recognized, as are the problems it creates. Furthermore, the division is made with the clear recognition that changes in behavior may eventually, perhaps inevitably, change the person.

In order to facilitate change in the teacher's classroom behavior the clinical supervisor seeks to establish a working relationship and supervisory processes that will enable the teacher to share equal responsibility for the design of the changes to be made. The goals of this partnership are not achieved until the teacher also (1) knows why he is changing his behavior, (2) wants to change it, and (3) derives professional satisfactions from doing so.

What kind of teacher↔supervisor relationship is likely to be most effective in clinical supervision? How may it be described? What kinds of interpersonal processes and practices are most effective and efficient? Do the teacher and supervisor work together as "friends"? As teacher and specialist? As client and therapist? Perhaps the real problem in defining the nature of the relationship will be clarified if we ask several radical questions about it. In his efforts to help the teacher change his classroom behavior, may the supervisor (1) use techniques of Pavlovian or Skinnerian conditioning? (2) use hypnosis or drugs? (3) use explicit or implicit promises of professional advancement? (4) require the teacher to use one or another program of individually prescribed instruction? It immediately becomes evident that the relationship to be established between teacher and clinical supervisor has important consequences—pedagogical, ethical, medico-legal, psychological, and strategic. Let us examine a few types of relationships and their implications for supervision.

The Superior-Subordinate Relationship

If we examine supervision in schools and universities we commonly observe an implicit but fully functioning superior-subordinate relationship generated by institutional hierarchies. Goethals observes that "in education, supervision is usually formulated in terms of a superior attempting to help a subordinate. . . ."[1] This concept is so clearly and powerfully expressed in action, if not in words, that probably no reader of these pages has stopped to wonder whether "superior" refers to teacher or supervisor. After all, "superior" and "supervisor" share the same derivation.

The full list of arguments against the superior-subordinate relationship is too long to be recited here. The teacher is diminished psychologically because he is cast in the character of an inferior. Implicit in such a role are lesser competences, a need for the direction of a superior. As a consequence, the teacher is pressed into assuming certain potentially damaging postures. Many of these are diametrically opposed to his proper professional role in the classroom. A subordinate is not responsible, but the teacher in his classroom *is*, above all, *responsible*. The relationship, therefore, erodes the teacher's sense of professional accountability. The teacher-as-subordinate is dependent when he should be autonomous, diminished by the very process that has been designed to enlarge his powers.

As for the supervisor, his principal profit from such a relationship is the chance to be corrupted by power. Thus the superior-subordinate relationship is considered counterproductive in clinical supervision.

The Teacher-Student Relationship

In the literature of supervision the supervisor is often cast as a teacher, and the teacher as a student. The logic behind this conceptualization of supervision may derive from the fact that (1) most supervisors seek to change the behavior of teachers, (2) changes are learned, and therefore (3) the supervisor assumes the role of teacher, and the teacher that of learner. This conceptualization may be faulty, however, since learning can and does arise from a multitude of other relationships. An additional strategic weakness becomes apparent when the teacher is treated prin-

[1]George W Goethals, "A Psychologist Looks at Some Aspects of Helping," *Educational Leadership* 16, no. 8 (1959), p. 472.

cipally as a learner: learners are too often encouraged to be docile, acceptant, and dependent. To instigate such behavior contradicts precisely the objectives and the rationale of clinical supervision.

Clinical supervision is unlike school teaching in many respects. For example, many teachers will not play student to the supervisor's "teacher." Such a role is frequently rejected by teachers who perceive themselves as competent professionals. Thus the usual teacher-student relationship, with its positions and counter-positions of more knowledgeable and less knowledgeable, more mature and less mature, more experienced and less experienced, may arouse the teacher's resistance. In addition, as supervision is commonly practiced, the temporal and instructional arrangements for "teaching" are lacking: regularly scheduled classes, institutionally allocated time for instruction, an established curriculum, expectations about assignments, and, more important, institutionalized rewards (grades?) for the teacher in the role of the supervisor's student. These circumstances and others like them may make it detrimental for the supervisor to approach his work as though he were a teacher.

This is not to say that the supervisor may not on occasion "teach." Of course he does; so does a mother or a traffic policeman. But this does not imply that mothers or policemen should therefore view themselves principally as teachers. Their principal roles are quite different and quite likely to conflict with the role of teacher. So, too, for the clinical supervisor. He therefore takes great care to avoid assuming the role of teacher often, or letting the teacher assume the role of student too frequently.

The Counselor-Client Relationship

Another stance commonly adopted by the supervisor is that of counselor, with the teacher in the role of counselee. The counseling referred to generally draws heavily upon the techniques of Rogerian client-centered therapy. In recent years many school counselors have become interested in supervision, and many supervisors have been attracted by some aspects of Rogers's work. Dussault has made an extended analysis of the possible utility of Rogerian theory and therapy for a theory of supervision. At the conclusion of his examination he adopts certain Rogerian constructs and concepts for his "middle-range theory of supervision."

The similarities Dussault finds in the results of Rogerian therapy for the patient and the results observed in the research on the supervisory conference are worth noting:

OUTCOMES OF ROGERIAN THERAPY	OUTCOMES OF SUPERVISION AS TEACHING
More realistic and objective perceptions	More reality-oriented, and [attainment of] better understanding of children
Greater congruence between self-concept and real self	Greater correlation between perceptions of ideal and actual own teaching role
Reduction of anxiety and of all sorts of tensions	Decrease in professional anxieties
Increased degree of positive self-regard	Positive changes in self-concept and less depreciation of self
Perception of the locus of evaluation as within oneself	Self decision-making
More acceptance of others	More accepting of other people . . . positive changes in the MTAI[2] scores and more positive perceptions of ideal and actual teachers
Behavior that changes in various ways	Changes in teaching behavior and changes in relationships with pupils[3]

The work done by Dussault indicates some of the similarities and differences between his theory of supervision and client-centered therapy. The Rogerian constructs he builds into his theory include "experience, awareness, self, congruence, contact, positive regard . . . conditions of worth, and empathy."[4]

There are strong arguments against construing supervision as counseling or therapy and then proceeding to apply their concepts, processes, and techniques to clinical supervision. Rogerian therapy is designed to help effect changes in personality. Such therapy deals with the *self* in the profoundest sense: "the organized, consistent conceptual gestalt composed of perceptions of the characteristics of the 'I' or 'me' and the perceptions of the relationships of the 'I' or 'me' to others and to various aspects of life, together with the values attached to these perceptions."[5] But the

[2]Minnesota Teacher Attitude Inventory.
[3]Reprinted by permission of the publisher from Gilles Dussault, *A Theory of Supervision in Teacher Education* (New York: Teachers College, 1970; copyright 1970 by Teachers College, Columbia University), pp. 161–62.
[4]Ibid., p. 116.
[5]Carl R. Rogers, "A Theory of Therapy, Personality, and Interpersonal Relationships," cited in Dussault, op. cit., p. 120.

clinical supervisor deals with classroom behavior and recognizes that this segment of the teacher's behavior arises from the totality of the teacher's self. If necessity demands that the teacher's self be treated at a depth requiring therapy, the clinical supervisor is obligated *not* to attempt to give such treatment but to enlist the help of qualified therapists.

In our view, then, the domain of the clinical supervisor is linked to the level of observable classroom behavior. His work in this domain is governed by his knowledge about the factors influencing classroom behavior.

To summarize, clinical supervision is neither counseling nor therapy. Even if a supervisor were competent to offer such help, there is a strong possibility that a teacher acting the role of client might fall into conflict with his role as a teacher participating in clinical supervision. In addition, the question of the teacher's willingness to participate in counseling or therapy would have to be taken into account. However, the clinical supervisor may, if competent, make a few adaptations from these two fields. The suggestions set out below may be applicable to both teacher and clinical supervisor:

1. They need to have regard for the emotional component in apparently nonaffective behavior.
2. They must comprehend the need of the individual to protect, maintain, and enhance his integrity as a person.
3. They should adopt a nonjudgmental, nonmoralistic approach to their work together.
4. They should maintain a positive regard for each other's views without reference to their "goodness" or "badness." But this regard does not extend to all the behaviors of the individual.[6]

If counseling is taken in the more general, homely sense of simply giving advice, then the supervisor might occasionally and legitimately be engaged in counseling. But such activity within the supervisor's professional sphere is insufficient grounds for referring to him as a counselor—especially in view of the highly specific connotations clustering around the word as discussed above.

The Supervisor as Evaluator or Rater

The supervisor may evaluate the teacher in several different ways. He may make an estimate of the teacher's competence by using a rating instru-

[6]See Dussault, op. cit., pp. 115–28. Although these ideas were suggested by a reading of Dussault's critical interpretation of the work of Carl R. Rogers, responsibility for these statements is, of course, mine.

ment. For example, the supervisor may evaluate a teacher according to the criteria developed by a school system in order to make administrative decisions about tenure or promotion. University supervisors are generally asked to rate the student teachers they supervise.

The supervisor may make another kind of evaluation by taking the individual teacher as his frame of reference. In such an operation the supervisor estimates the teacher's capacity and rates him on the extent to which he realizes his abilities.

Two points must be made here. The first is that evaluation is an almost ineradicable human tendency. It has great survival value. The second is that the supervisor's evaluation, even though made solely to serve the teacher's professional needs, probably cannot be completely separated from normative judgments about teaching in general. This is to say that the teacher is very likely to perceive the supervisor as a person who can and does make evaluations, and an evaluation made by a supervisor may be painful to the teacher, even if it is never communicated to anyone else. The fabric of the teacher-supervisor relationship, therefore, is almost invariably colored by some threads of the rater-ratee relationship, at least in the initial phases of the supervisory program. Indeed, the magnitude of the teacher's anxieties about being rated are very well documented. H. H. Remmers discusses merit rating:

> In general, teachers and their professional representatives in the National Education Association are strongly opposed to [the] use of ratings [for awarding differential salaries]. . . . The opposition of teachers has several bases—the possibilities of favoritism, of lowered morale and efficiency among those "passed over," of interteacher tensions, and, above all, the fact that there are no generally accepted criteria of teacher merit.[7]

How, then, does the clinical supervisor establish a productive, non-threatening relationship with teachers in the face of their understandable anxiety about and rejection of supervisory evaluation, whether evaluation subsists completely within the clinical relationship or whether evaluation is done for administrative rating of teachers? What about the clinical supervisor who is *required* to submit administrative evaluations? Some modern authorities on supervision try to solve the problem by accepting the need for administrative evaluation but playing it down. Lindsey notes that supervisors in teacher education laboratories have "tended to place undue weight on the overseeing, managing, directing

---

[7]H.H. Remmers, "Rating Methods in Research on Teaching," in *Handbook of Research on Teaching*, ed. N. L. Gage (Chicago: Rand McNally and Co., 1963), p. 366. For a powerful expression of teachers' and supervisors' arguments against rating, see "Better Than Rating," Association for Supervision and Curriculum Development, 1950.

and assessing functions and too little emphasis on the guiding, supporting, stimulating and facilitating functions."[8] Others say that there are different kinds of evaluation and let it go at that:

> The teaching function of supervision cannot, manifestly, be fulfilled without some evaluation being made of the supervisee himself or of his teaching performances, or of both. But evaluation made by the supervisor [of future teachers] while he is fulfilling his teaching function is very different from that made while he is fulfilling his evaluating function: it is evaluation as feedback and guide, in contrast with evaluation as judgmental assessment.[9]

Very possibly, but one wonders whether the student teacher can separate the two so neatly.

In sum, the problem of how the teacher and supervisor are to deal with different but coexisting kinds of evaluation lurks under the surface of their relationship like a coral reef under water.

Perhaps the most common solution suggested is to dissociate the clinical supervisor completely from administrative evaluation. This divorce, if the teachers accepted it without reservation or qualm, would certainly do much to clear the stage for clinical supervision. However, it would still leave two problems unresolved. One has already been mentioned: the residue of anxiety that persists because the supervisee knows that human beings (including supervisors) tend to evaluate, and because the supervisor's special training predisposes him to it and makes him especially adept at it. The second unresolved question is: If the supervisor doesn't evaluate for administrative purposes, who will?

The answer to this last question is likely to throw the supervisor—clinical or general—right back into the arena of administrative evaluation. The reason for this is that the other people available for such assessment are likely to be very poorly prepared to do it. The possibility that the supervisor may *have* to do it therefore merits examination.

In our opinion, the role of administrative evaluator today is incompatible with clinical supervision. However, in reality, this is not necessarily the case. For example, if rating *is* inevitable, the teachers may want to trust themselves to the ethically and professionally disciplined clinical supervisor rather than to less qualified personnel. In addition, the problem of rating might be handled by clinical supervisors working with certain teachers for this purpose alone. Or supervisors might serve as the leaders of rating teams.

---

[8]Margaret Lindsey and associates, *Inquiry into Teaching Behavior of Supervisors in Teacher Education Laboratories* (New York: Teachers College Press, 1969), p. 28.
[9]Dussault, op. cit., p. 4.

What are some of the implications of this discussion of evaluation for the kind of teacher-supervisor relationship sought in clinical supervision? They may be summarized as follows:

1. The supervisor should clearly divorce himself from the role of evaluator or rater, unless and until he and the teacher agree that such a role would be productive for both.
2. The supervisor should not attempt to picture himself to the teacher as being without, above, or beyond evaluation.
3. The supervisor should bear in mind that the use of feedback based on sound and convincing data is one of the mainstays of clinical supervision and will strengthen the T ↔ S relationship, even though the teacher may at first have a tendency to distill evaluation from it.
4. The supervisor should seek to establish a relationship calculated to deal with the teacher's residual anxieties about evaluation, a relationship characterized by mutual trust, confidentiality, and confidence.

The "Helping Relationship" in Supervision

Some professions refer to themselves as "helping" professions: social work and supervision, for example. The basis for the use of this term is well stated by Nylen:

> A supervisor talks with a subordinate to help him improve his performance. A teacher instructs and guides a pupil. A friend counsels his companion. Some call it counseling. Others use terms such as teaching, guiding, training, or education. Whatever the term used, there is one common element: one individual is trying to help another.[10]

Nylen holds that the helping relationship reflects fundamental forces acting to influence individuals to change their behavior. This use of the word helping has strong overtones of client-centered counseling. Some of the key conditions considered necessary in the helping relationship are trust, openness, willingness to listen, nonjudgmental manner, support, etc.[11] It is therefore easy to understand why so many educators are impelled to characterize the teacher-supervisor relationship in clinical supervision as a helping relationship.

One of the troubles with interpreting clinical supervision principally as a helping relationship is that most of the satisfactions accrue to the

---

[10]Donald Nylen, J. Robert Mitchell, and Antony Stout, *Handbook of Staff Development and Human Relations Training: Materials Developed for Use in Africa.* (Washington, D.C.: National Training Laboratories Institute for Applied Behavioral Science, n.d.), p. 112.

[11]Ibid., p. 116.

helper. The "helpee" is again cast principally as a "receiver," a person in need, having difficulties. Nor is the role of "helper" entirely without its disadvantages. The supervisor who becomes a professional helper may fall prey to the vices of his virtues. He may get so much satisfaction from being helpful that he may not stop talking long enough to listen carefully to the helpee. Nylen has made an excellent inventory of the pitfalls in the helping relationship:

1. Some helpers become so fond of giving advice that they forget to check the relevance of their advice.
2. The helper may be unaware of resistances in the helpee, who may aver that he has no problems or blame them on someone else.
3. The helper may overpraise the helpee in an effort to establish a good relationship. He may be reluctant to confront the helpee with the hard realities of his situation.
4. The helpee may not relish exposing his problems.
5. People are generally afraid of what others will think of them. The more helpless and inadequate an individual feels, the more likely he is to feel afraid of the opinions of others.
6. People who receive help may lose a sense of independence and become dependent.
7. The helpee may set up defense mechanisms—rationalization, projection, logic-tight thinking, repression, and withdrawal.[12]

In spite of its disadvantages, one cannot dismiss the helping relationship completely in supervision. Supervisors do help teachers, and teachers help supervisors. But the helping relationship should not under any circumstances become the principal dimension of the relationship in clinical supervision.

As soon as a situation arises in which one person needs help and another gives it, a situationally determined hierarchy tends to be established. This hierarchy is characterized by the ascendance of the giver and the subordination of the receiver. To illustrate, if a person needs medical help, the doctor immediately assumes an ascendant position in respect to diagnosis and treatment. The patient (we may hope) receives help. A consequence of needing and receiving the help of physicians is that some patients are reduced to an abject state of dependence that is sometimes almost infantile. Many readers will recognize traces of this feeling of helplessness in their own experience. The dependence of the patient is related not only to his inability to help himself but also to the psychological dependence induced when he does so little for himself and has so much done *to* and *for* him.

[12]Ibid., pp. 79–81, 114–15.

In brief, in clinical supervision it is not more blessed to give than to receive, and neither giving nor receiving should primarily characterize the role of teacher or supervisor. The concepts of teacher, counselor, and helper all denote and connote a hierarchical relationship, and it is precisely this connotation that constitutes the root of our objection to them. In the rationale developed here the superordinate-subordinate relationship is contraindicated; it is simply not right for the job at hand. Such relationships, so strongly implied by words like teacher, helper, and counselor (client-centered or not), greatly influence the perceptions of teachers and supervisors and tend to influence behavior. For example, communication may be channeled toward the teacher's weaknesses rather than his strengths, toward his needs rather than his resources—again highlighting the superordinate-subordinate character of the relationship.

The term considered most appropriate to the rationale developed here is *colleague*.

Clinical Supervision as Colleagueship

In Flanders's discussion of the problems of improving the teacher's classroom behavior he describes both the difficulties of the task and the special nature of the relationship between the teacher and those who participate in efforts to improve his teaching:

> Many teachers would like to improve their own effectiveness. This involves making a change and then deciding whether the change was or was not an improvement. Both steps, verifying change and judging improvement, cannot easily be accomplished by a teacher alone in his classroom. He needs help in circumventing private perceptions. Yet inquiry into a matter that is so personal requires a special kind of partnership if it is to avoid becoming an intellectual, emotional, and spiritual striptease. Personal illusions need not be peeled off, one by one; instead a constructive inquiry into existing behavior and alternatives for change can be planned and carried out.

He goes on to add that the teacher's "self-development is more likely to flourish within the mutual support of a partnership or small action team with work scheduled throughout the year on a regular basis."[13] Flanders's use of the phrases "mutual support" and "a special kind of partnership" are very close to the concepts of *colleague* and *colleagueship* in clinical supervision.

[13]Ned A. Flanders, *Analyzing Teaching Behavior* (Reading, Mass.: Addison-Wesley, 1970), p. 10. Reprinted by permission.

In colleagueship the teacher and clinical supervisor work together as associates and equals, and they are bound together by a common purpose. This purpose is the improvement of students' learning through the improvement of the teacher's instruction, and it does not diminish the autonomy and independence the teacher should have.

This relationship between teacher and clinical supervisor is maintained in force as long as they can work together productively as colleagues. It deteriorates significantly or ceases to exist when either assumes an ascendant role or is accorded an ascendant role by the other. This delicate balance in working together as equals does not imply that teacher and supervisor have similar and equal professional competences. On the contrary, they commonly have dissimilar and unequal competences. This heterogeneity is nurtured in their association and constitutes one of its principal strengths. In clinical supervision the interaction of similar competences at equal levels is generally less productive than the interaction of unequal levels of competence and dissimilar competences. Such productive heterogeneity may be observed when the clinical supervisor, highly competent in observation, the analysis of teaching, and the processes connected with the cycle of supervision, works with a teacher who is more competent in knowledge of the curriculum, his students, their learning characteristics and transient and persistent problems, and the school subsocieties to which they belong.

We must emphasize at once that the role of colleague is not easily or casually assumed. One of the strongest tendencies in human beings in association is the tendency for some to preempt or need ascendant roles. Others assume or need nonascendant roles. In dyadic groups— husband-wife, parent-child, or partnership—the tendency to establish ascendant-nonascendant relationships is especially strong, almost irresistible. In fact, some supervisors reject the role of colleague openly. Others try to fulfill it but fail. These difficulties may arise from a supervisor's need for a superordinate position with respect to teachers. Most supervisors have "risen" from the ranks of teachers. Some gain satisfaction and are enhanced in their self-esteem when they are able to exert power over the teacher or exhibit greater skills. Or it may simply be easier for the supervisor to work from an assumption of superiority, greater wisdom, experience, or training, which may relieve him of the difficult job of trying to analyze the teacher's teaching. The supervisor simply *tells* him what the strengths and weaknesses of his performance are. And some teachers may accept this information gratefully, even if it is not very helpful; doing so saves their time and effort and flatters the supervisor.

In sum, the role of colleague is difficult for teacher and supervisor alike to learn. It may easily be superimposed as a facade over other patterns or relationships. The very competences learned in the process of becoming a clinical supervisor may be used to fortify roles and relationships quite alien to it.

To resist such tendencies and to establish the roles and relationships in which each member may from time to time assume leadership without dominance requires (1) a firm understanding of the rationale for the colleagual relationship, (2) command of the behavior appropriate to it, (3) strong self-discipline in adhering to the concept of colleagueship, and (4) supervision of clinical supervisors by their fellow supervisors.

The rationale for the colleagual relationship derives from a conviction that both the teacher and the supervisor give and receive support: in the colleagueship it is easier for professionals to help each other and at the same time strengthen themselves professionally and personally than it is within the structure of the other relationships commonly recommended for supervision. An observation made by L. C. Wilson and his colleagues bears directly on this point: ". . . teachers are asking not for supervisors to relieve them of decision-making functions, but for an increase in their professional responsibilities as teachers. They are asking, in short, to become participants in supervision rather than the object of it."[14]

The Psychological-Social Level at Which the Supervisor Works

If supervisor and teacher work together, at what psychological and social levels do they interact? The principal phenomena with which they deal are the classroom behaviors of the teacher and the students. The principal goal of supervision is to change the classroom behavior of the teacher so that he can, in turn, change the behavior of his students. The supervisor, therefore, deals with a limited sector of the teacher's behavior. In attempting to bring about changes in that sector, he again limits his domain by dealing with the observable behavior of a teacher who is assumed to be at least minimally healthy— physically, mentally, and emo-

[14]L. Craig Wilson et al., *Sociology of Supervision: An Approach to Comprehensive Planning in Education* (Boston: Allyn and Bacon, Inc., 1969), p. 21.

tionally. If on occasion this assumption proves to be incorrect, then the supervisor enlists the help of qualified experts competent to provide diagnosis and therapy if it is indicated.

To recapitulate, the supervisor may be said to concern himself with behaviors at the manifest level. Speaking figuratively, we may say that he and the teacher deal with behavior at a level close to the surface. They do not discuss the deep-seated causes of such behaviors nor the processes by which they may become manifest. They work directly with the behavior they observe. The supervisor may, therefore, observe that a teacher often expresses a low opinion about his work and about himself, but he will not tell the teacher he has "an inferiority complex." He may note evidence that the teacher tries very hard to succeed, but he will not refer to his "need for achievement." The nonthreatening relationship, the clear understanding about ground rules, the roles and functions developed in the supervisory relationship, and the shared responsibility for its success are all viewed as facilitators of behavioral change.

The question of the "social distance" between teacher and supervisor presents some difficulties. One might be tempted to say that colleagueship implies minimal "working distance," but what about "social distance"? The case for amicable working relationships has been made often and forcefully; it does not require elaborate restatement here. Teacher and supervisor should maintain easy, friendly, professional working relationships. That is in part implicit in the double-headed arrow in *teacher* ↔ *supervisor relationship*. But should they be friends in the social sense? Does it help or hurt the relationship if the two visit each other after working hours, if they seek each other's company socially?

Perhaps the first reply to this question should be: "We don't really know too much about this problem. Let us examine it." To clear the way for this examination, let us simply repeat that a requirement of supervision is good professional rapport. Social friendship, on the other hand, may sometimes interfere with professional judgment. It may be difficult to broach unpleasant realities with a friend. In an attempt to defend against friendship, a friend may become overcritical of another's performance. In brief, role conflicts may develop between friends who are at the same time trying to help each other as colleagues.

Even if social friendship should prove to be an asset to supervision, would the supervisor then be called on to try to become a social friend of all the teachers with whom he works? Put this way, at least one aspect of the problem becomes clear: if social friendship were required for supervision, very few supervisors would be able to establish optimal relationships with their colleagues. In summary, social friendship between teacher and supervisor may on occasion be nonfunctional.

But the professional relationship in clinical supervision should not, therefore, be viewed as cold, distant, or neutral. The close and continued interaction in the cycle of supervision, combined with the importance the work has for both participants, usually generates an intense interaction. This interaction, however, is not personal in the sense that its object is the person, as it might be in an encounter group or in psychotherapy. The target of clinical supervision is not the teacher, it is the teacher's classroom behavior. One does not have to yield one's privacy nor yet invade the privacy of others in order to participate in clinical supervision.

CHAPTER 6

Special Objectives for the Teacher

Self-knowledge and Self-improvement

One of the principal aims of clinical supervision is to help the teacher gain new and more reliable knowledge about himself as a teacher: what he teaches, how, why, and with what results. A more profound and objective perception of himself, in combination with the professional support he gains from the supervisory program, may help him persevere in efforts to improve his teaching. The operation of the cycle of supervision is designed with this end in mind. The clinical analysis of instruction affords the teacher the chance to stand outside himself and learn about his patterns of classroom behavior—for example, how he relates to different students, the operating criteria he uses to evaluate their work, his practices in the use of feedback from students, his style of reinforcement. His increased self-knowledge may encourage him to experiment with new teaching behavior.

The Teacher's Style

The teacher's growing confidence in his ability to improve his instruction is closely tied to the attainment of another objective of clinical supervision: the development of the teacher's personal style of teaching. One problem facing the supervisor in this endeavor is to insure that the new behaviors the teacher tries to develop are congruent with his talents, capabilities, and preferences. The teacher may want to teach by the discovery method and simply not have the flexibility and ingenuity to carry it off. Or he may want to develop the techniques of dramatic reading and lack the talent for doing so.

If the supervisor is to guard against incongruencies in the teacher's style, he must have prior knowledge of the kinds of behavior that are and are not congruent to the teacher. Such knowledge is not readily acquired. The search for it represents one of the continuing themes of the entire program of clinical supervision. In that program the teacher regularly tries out small changes that will constitute a new mode of teaching. But style is occasionally a matter of more substantial change. At certain moments, therefore, the teacher must take the risk of appearing awkward or of failing to carry off a new behavior effectively. The supervisor's function at such times is to help the teacher select behavior that is new but congruent, to contribute wisdom and strategy in planning the change, and to support the teacher throughout the trial period. That is, the supervisor protects the teacher in the change process by minimizing possibilities of failure and by providing support no matter what the outcome.

It is hard to overemphasize the importance of the teacher's adopting novel behavior that is compatible with his established style. The painful and harmful consequences of attempts to perform in ways that are incongruous *and* not technically mastered may be observed when a humorless teacher is blithely encouraged to loosen up and crack a joke, and obediently tries it, with deadly results; or when a frail, unathletic, female English teacher with a piping voice conscientiously attempts to follow her male supervisor's advice to interest the eleventh-grade boys in poetry by reciting "Casey at the Bat" in virile, man-to-man style. It is less funny, but no less destructive, when an uninstructed teacher is urged to use "the discovery method" with her students and has no technique available other than a deadly string of questions that she aims at her students and fires off in a kind of endless inquisition.

No matter what strategies the supervisor may use, he starts from and returns to the process of working within the frame of the teacher's classroom strengths and weaknesses, within the teacher's potential and limitations for professional development. This is not to say that the teacher cannot enlarge his repertoire of classroom behavior. It *is* to say that this enlargement is likely to be bought too dearly if it is not in tune with his own style.

The supervisor is therefore called on to use his resources of insight and technique to help the teacher understand the meaning of "style" and "congruence" and to achieve both at least cost. Methods of achieving this result are the subject of later chapters.

Development of the Teacher's Professional Role

Teachers, like many other Americans, have a strong drive to attain professional status. The literature of education, however, makes it clear that at present the professional status of the teacher is ambiguous. For example, the profession cannot "guarantee competent performance and ethical behavior of practitioners."[1] No matter where teachers may be on the road to professionalism, it is important to note that they and their associations are constantly striving to achieve it. In the following aspects of this effort the supervisor has a contribution to make.

Occupational Specificity   One of the characteristics of modern professions is that they map out and reserve for themselves the domain of their professional service. However, in actual practice they are subject to great temptations to enlarge their territory. The interrelationship of all aspects of man's existence tempts the professional to enlarge his scope, to deal with problems outside his own field. As a result, ministers, rabbis, and priests often feel called upon to behave like psychologists or social workers, the lawyer is under great pressure to serve as a marriage counselor in divorce cases, and the professional soldier often offers advice about problems in the domain of the political scientist.

For teachers, such temptations to become involved in problems outside their field of professional competence are often too strong to resist. As a result, the spinster teacher may offer courses in sex education; the classroom teacher who thinks a student is ill may—with the best intentions in the world—"prescribe" aspirin or other remedies. Some history and English teachers feel impelled to provide instruction in aspects of sociology, psychology, or anthropology—often with very sad results. The clinical supervisor, therefore, has an important function in helping the teacher to comprehend the limits of his professional competence and to remain within them. For example, a history teacher planning to teach a unit on social stratification or the effects of poverty upon school learning should understand the dangers involved in trying to become an amateur sociologist or psychologist. Both the teacher and his instruction may benefit by a suggestion to call in an expert or not to treat the problem at all. So, too, for the English teacher who longs to make a Freudian analysis of Ahab's character.

In addition, the teacher's personal problems of occupational specificity sometimes become involved with decisions about his livelihood, his career, and professional ethics. Any teacher who is asked to give instruction in a subject in which he is inadequately prepared faces a difficult decision. The clinical supervisor is not in a position to suggest acceptance or rejection of

[1] Margaret Lindsey, *New Horizons for the Teaching Profession* (Washington, D.C.: National Education Association, 1961), p. 206.

such an assignment, but he can serve as one of the people with whom the teacher may discuss the professional aspects of such a decision.

Professional and Nonprofessional Roles The problem of professional specificity for teachers is complicated by questions of professional versus nonprofessional roles and functions in the schools. These dilemmas are becoming increasingly acute. Is the teacher a professional decision-maker, or is he a nonprofessional worker who implements decisions made at a higher level? Does he decide about the methods and curriculum he is to use, or not? Will the rapid development of the technology of teaching— programed instruction, computer-assisted instruction, etc.—force the teacher to become a machine tender? Or will it, as Skinner says in an oft-quoted article, free him from the machine:

> If the advances which have recently been made in our control of behavior can give the child a genuine competence in reading, writing, spelling, and arithmetic, then the teacher may begin to function, not in lieu of a cheap machine, but through intellectual, cultural, and emotional contacts of that distinctive sort which testify to her status as a human being.[2]

A good guess would be that some teachers are having machine-tending functions forced upon them. Others are attracted to them as a way of life. And still others are attempting to move beyond them to professional levels of teaching. In all these processes the clinical supervisor is called upon to join the teachers he works with and to concern himself with the development of their classroom roles and functions. The world outside the school also exerts pressure upon the kinds of roles the teacher is to take. Actual reformulation of what the teacher does, however, could be strongly influenced by the innovations the teachers themselves institute. This means that supervisors and teachers can invent, try out, and perfect new models of relationships between teacher and technology, and that these models may later become institutionalized in formal definitions of the professional roles and functions of teachers. Unless enough supervisors are actively engaged in such endeavors, however, the teachers may fail to define their emerging professional domain, leaving that task to others less qualified, or to the hazards of institutional life.

Genuine Professional Competences Technology mastered will not of itself make the teacher a professional; it will merely offer him a better

[2]B. F. Skinner, "The Science of Learning and the Art of Teaching," *Harvard Educational Review* 24, no. 2 (1954), pp. 86–87.

opportunity to become one. In what other ways, then, may the supervisor help the teacher to achieve genuine professional status? The answer is obvious—by helping him to achieve genuine professional competences. It appears that the public tends to seek out and reward the professional rather than the amateur or the untrained practitioner. For important matters people seek the doctor rather than the medicine man, the engineer rather than the steelworker. But at the present moment the public and many educators are not fully convinced that the formally prepared teacher possesses clear-cut, demonstrable professional advantages over subprofessional personnel. This lack of public recognition of the trained teacher's superiority derives from complex causes. For example, the ideal objectives of teaching are reduced in practice to very primitive levels: memorization and the mechanical use of formulas become a substitute for understanding. Difficult instructional tasks are reduced to their lowest terms. Creative writing is graded for "neatness in composition," and the study of mathematics becomes the memorization of the "times tables." As a result, the ideal objectives of teaching, reduced to mechanical and pedestrian learnings, often can be taught fairly well by nonprofessional instructors.

Another reason why teachers today do not generally perform at professional levels is that the collegiate preparation they receive is actually only a first step toward genuine professional competence. The next steps in their education, to be provided on the job, are usually taken alone, without a continuing program or continuing support from colleagues specially trained for this work. In consequence, teachers generally enter the field with a minimum of professional competences, improve these a bit, mostly by their own efforts, for four or five years, and then their performance often tends to level off. As a result, only a small percentage achieve professional competences that are clearly superior to the capability of untrained or only minimally prepared teachers.

It is a fair prediction that for some time to come teachers will continue to be only at the threshold of professional performance when they are certified. Under such circumstances the clinical supervisor is needed to work with teachers and to help them achieve genuine competence. He joins them at a point where they need to fuse theory, study, and practice, and where he can involve them deeply in their own continuing education. At this point, if never before, the teacher must take the role of an equal in the development of his own teaching if he is to achieve the objective of raising his teaching performance to truly professional levels.

Other professional objectives for the teacher are summarized by Champagne, who draws upon his own experience and the writings of Rogers, Combs, Spindler, and others to formulate the supervisor's objectives in working with teachers:

> . . . to clarify and state their role expectations as teachers . . . to perceive the difference between their real and ideal self . . . to develop strategies to diminish the incongruencies between their ideal and real self and between their own perceptions of themselves and others' perceptions of them . . . to evaluate the learning of their students, and of themselves, in a collaborative, rational, open examination of significant patterns and categories of behavioral data . . . to focus motivation for changing behavior and acceptance of change as an element in the instructional environment . . . to learn to deal with their own anxiety and resultant defensive behavior during developmental changes in themselves and in their interactions in order to deal with the students' anxiety and resultant defensive behavior in the interactions, and . . . to enlarge the boundaries of possible professional development during the creation of their own professional identity, an integration of self and profession.[3]

[3]David W. Champagne, "Rationale and Design of the University Phase of an Internship for Instructional Consultants" (Ed.D. diss., School of Education, University of Pittsburgh, 1968), p. 41.

CHAPTER 7

Establishing the Conditions for Clinical Supervision

Anxiety in the Teacher-Supervisor Relationship

Sources of Anxiety No matter what the supervisor's good intentions may be, he should know that "some of the best intentioned efforts to help another person may be deeply threatening to that person."[1] This does not mean that the supervisor *is* threatening. It merely means that he *may be perceived* by the teacher as a source of threat. In fact, the threat may even exist without reference to the supervisor himself, because "the supervisory role and process have psychological impact over and beyond whatever may be the objective dimensions"[2] of the situation. That is, the teacher may view supervision itself as a threat.

For many teachers, the prospect of the supervisor's entrance into the classroom is suffused with danger. It is for this reason that much of the first half of this volume is devoted to the preparation of both teacher and supervisor for the latter's first appearance in class. Both must learn a great deal about each other and about their roles in clinical supervision before they can begin the processes of planning, teaching, observation, analysis, etc., in the cycle of supervision.

Teachers, like other professionals, need to feel that they are competent in their chosen work. Therefore, if they perceive the supervisor as someone who is paid to ferret out incompetence, they must face the discomforting possibility that he will find it or invent it. As a consequence, the first response of a teacher who is expected to change his classroom behavior may be defensive: "What's wrong with it?" To him, teaching is not just "behavior"—something outside himself to be viewed with detachment. On the contrary, unless he feels defeated by his work or cynical about it, his classroom behavior is the heart of his professional self. This is the behavior that helped him to survive the quicksands of his student teaching. He nurtured his behavior, developed his special strengths, and

---

[1]George W. Goethals, "A Psychologist Looks at Some Aspects of Helping," *Educational Leadership* 16, no. 8 (1969), p. 473. Reprinted by permission.
[2]Ibid.

learned to conceal or compensate somehow for his weaknesses. His teaching carried him through the trying pre-tenure years. It gave him job security and a pride in his work. It made him a professional instead of simply a salaried worker. Who, then, will intrude on this universe with talk of improvement?

Another aspect of the problem in the education of teachers is the fact that they rarely accept the professional necessity for constant improvement. "Continuing inservice education" is probably endorsed in principle by most teachers, but that acceptance totters when an observer, a principal, or a superintendent walks into the classroom. One source of teachers' anxiety derives from the circumstances surrounding their education. In other professions the practitioners somehow learn by graduation time that they are at least minimally adequate and must continue studying in order to become even more competent and to keep up with new developments. Many teachers, on the other hand, graduate with the conviction that they are inadequately prepared and that continuing education is designed to help them overcome fundamental inadequacies. Therefore, when the supervisor enters the classroom, he often meets a teacher who is fearful that grave infirmities will come to light, rather than one who is confident in his own powers and anticipates the refinement of already adequate competences.

Under such circumstances the supervisor's first task is to help the teacher understand that clinical supervision is a colleagueship that begins where the teacher is and goes forward from that point. Furthermore, if it should happen, as it sometimes does, that the teacher does in fact exhibit fundamental inadequacies, then he must be confident that the clinical supervisor will be one of his most useful aides in overcoming them and that the supervisor is committed to this task.

The supervisor who enters a classroom for the first time to observe a teacher and class in action may not be aware of the reactions he sets in motion. For example, one teacher may view his appearance as an invasion of academic privacy. The established institutional practice of the school is, after all, still largely a pattern of one adult in one class at one time. Or the appearance of the supervisor may trigger another teacher's real or imaginary fears about certain minor failings: some teachers are simply poor spellers, others make mistakes in recalling dates of historical events, in extracting square roots, in parsing sentences, in balancing chemical equations. Are these weaknesses about to be found out? Although such errors are certainly not symptoms of thoroughgoing inadequacy, the terrors they arouse are real enough for teachers whose standards of excellence are tied tightly to minor or formal criteria. After all, mistakes are what *students* make.

Still other teachers are chronic worriers. They worry about being late to school, or about what the principal thinks, or about whether their students will do well on standardized achievement tests. Some even fret about whether their students will "do well" on IQ tests. So of course they are worried when the supervisor comes to observe. His entrance disturbs the self-doubting teacher. Even teachers who are fairly secure about their competence may nevertheless suffer from residual anxieties about how they will compare with other teachers, about how an unruly student will behave, or about whether they will betray favoritism or prejudice toward some students. These factors about the effects of a single unfavorable incident upon the supervisor's opinion of a teacher spring directly from teachers' firm expectations about one-shot, hit-and-run supervisory visits. The clinical supervisor must set these fears at rest before he makes an observation.

Some teachers establish a formula that "proves" they are competent and therefore should not be supervised in class. The formula often takes the following form:

The university gave me a degree in teaching,
or
I am a certified teacher,
or
I have tenure,
or
I am a professional,

therefore I am proven competent and require no supervision. Are doctors or lawyers supervised in their practice?

These teachers thus take the position that they have no need for supervision and that if they did, they would be professional enough to ask for it. There is no need to repeat the rebuttals to such formulas. It is only necessary for the clinical supervisor to understand that some teachers hold them to be true and are therefore likely to resist supervision overtly or covertly. A conflict is generated when the teacher's conviction about his professional competence collides with his conviction that in-class supervision implies incompetence. This conflict must be resolved before he can participate freely in clinical supervision.

The teacher may see the supervisor as possessing and using certain institutional sanctions, and he therefore often sees him as potentially dangerous. What the supervisor reports about the teacher, says about him, makes known in idle conversation about him, or unwittingly reveals about him may affect the teacher's tenure, his promotion, his salary increments, his career, and his status with administrators, other teachers, students, and parents. These are lethal possibilities. The supervisor cannot defuse them simply by assuring the teacher that he doesn't report, talk, or gossip. He must create a relationship of such trust that the teacher knows he is safe with the supervisor.[3]

Anxiety and Incompatibility   Incompatibility is grounds for divorce in some states, and divorce presumably lowers excessively high anxiety. But teachers and supervisors usually cannot divorce each other. What happens if they prove irreversibly incompatible? The answer is, of course, that they should be divorced. But our topic at this moment is the worries that may plague the teacher before he and the supervisor have had much opportunity to find out about each other. It is these possibilities of mutual antagonisms that may raise the teacher's anxiety to such a pitch that he becomes truly incapable of participating productively in the supervisory program. Such a mental state may generate self-fulfilling anticipatory fears.

The supervisor must know the sources of such fears and take steps to relieve them if he is to establish a good working relationship with the teacher. Some common sources of anxiety are listed here:

1. The supervisor's capricious behavior
   There are generally few external controls over the supervisor's behavior. No one analyzes *his* performance. No one puts a halt to *his* objectionable behavior. In some ways the teacher may perceive him as a loaded pistol on hair-trigger:
   "I just told the supervisor that his pronunciation of *idée fixe* is wrong, and that it isn't *eeday feexay*. He has hated me ever since."

2. The supervisor's unknown criteria for good teaching
   Who can tell what the supervisor thinks good teaching is? In how many unknown ways may he and the teacher differ? What are his ideas about goals, content, and method?
   a. "What will he think if he finds out I'm using a programed text instead of the regular text in algebra?"
   b. "Did he understand that I was only helping the pupils use the dictionary faster when I made them learn to recite the alphabet forward *and* backward?"
   c. "Does he think it's a good idea to have students doing laboratory experiments in teams instead of alone?"
   d. "Does he understand that I am using discovery methods in this social studies unit?"
   e. "Would he want me to try the 'open classroom' methods?"

The problems created when the supervisor serves as a *rater* of teachers are treated in he chapter entitled "The Teacher ↔ Supervisor Relationship."

3. The supervisor's responses to the teacher as person rather than as teacher
   a. "I hear he asked Grace to do something about her oily skin."
   b. "What will he think if he finds out I'm a bartender on weekends?"

4. The supervisor's interpersonal style
   a. "Is he going to order me around?" Or, "I can't stand these guys who always answer my questions by saying, 'Well, what do *you* think?' "
   b. "If he tells jokes about priests, ministers, and rabbis I'll be sick."

5. The supervisor: terminus or tollgate?
   "The besetting danger with those who only criticize is their coming to think books and plays are primarily written for them to pass on; they never suspect that, for the creator, they are not terminus, but tollgate."[4] The teacher may worry about the same danger: Does the supervisor view teaching as designed for him or for the students? An even greater hazard is that the teacher may assume that his safest course *is* to relate to the supervisor as terminus rather than as tollgate.

6. The supervisor as an alien in the classroom
   Teaching at any moment is in part determined by what has gone before. The teacher's behavior is largely influenced by the history of his previous experiences with a class. He is therefore concerned about whether the supervisor will suspend judgments until he too knows the class well enough to understand why the teacher does what he does.
   a. "Does he know that this noisy class just came from a pre-game pep rally in the auditorium?"
   b. "Does he know that this class is the terror of every teacher it has?"
   c. "Does he know that we had to 'drop' *The Scarlet Letter* because two girls in this class are pregnant?"
   d. "Does he know that I've been sick for a week and out of school, and that the substitute left no record at all of what the class did that week?"
   e. "Does he know what kinds of objectives we're shooting for in this class?"

7. Is the supervisor competent? Is he really qualified to work with teachers to improve their performance?
   a. "He's had two courses in supervision. Does that make him a supervisor?"
   b. "What does he know about PSSC physics?"

The Teacher, the Class, and the Outsider   Each class establishes itself as a temporary social system. In each classroom the teacher and students develop rules, standards, customs, and norms of behavior. Whatever the

[4]Louis Kronenberger, "Speaking of Books," *New York Times Book Review*, October 7, 1962, p. 2.

established patterns of a classroom are, the supervisor enters it as an outsider. The teacher may therefore perceive his entrance as a possibly disruptive shock to that system, the more so if the teacher sees himself as the master of his domain.

What happens when a supervisor enters this little kingdom? A subtle revolution may occur. The master is suddenly under the scrutiny of a "superior." The social equilibrium in the classroom is disturbed because teacher and students are instantly aware of the shifts and reversals of roles. To understand completely the drama that is enacted upon the entrance of the supervisor into the class, we must understand that in most schools the students view the teacher primarily as the possessor of power:

> The recognition of the power of the teacher is the predominant feature of the relationship between the teacher and the student. . . . In the classroom the teacher is relatively free, within the general bounds set by administrative policy and control, to direct the group as she wishes. . . . In this way, then, the teacher is in a position of power.[5]

No matter what efforts the teacher may make to mask, reduce, or relinquish his power, he is usually defeated by the unspoken realities of the school. At the beginning of the semester or year he must set in motion the processes by which each unorganized class develops the goals and lifestyle of their newborn society. Thereafter, he must continue the processes by which this entente is maintained in force in order to achieve the central objectives of schooling. In the end he usually must award a grade—fail, pass, middle or high honors. In brief, one of the continuing conditions of most classrooms is the existence of the teacher's power, a condition most teachers and students know with a deep certainty. As a result, the supervisor who enters the classroom is perceived as an unknown, an outsider, an alien, which means that he may be perceived as a threat to the existing social system. One thesis of this book is that the supervisor may gain the competences needed to minimize this threat and may ultimately be admitted to the classroom society as a contributing transient. But he is not likely to achieve acceptance by entering the classroom *before* he has firmly established a nonthreatening relationship with the teacher. Once such a relationship does develop, the teacher can help communicate it to the class.

But the supervisor should not delude himself into thinking that he can once and for all erase the threat he poses initially to the teacher and class. Under the best of circumstances their anxiety may remain dormant.

---

[5]David H. Jenkins and Ronald Lippitt, "Interpersonal Perceptions in the Classroom," in *The Adolescent,* ed. Jerome M. Seidman (New York: Dryden Press, 1953), p. 584.

The supervisor must constantly work to maintain his neutral status if and when he attains it.

Why is it so hard for the supervisor—even if we endow him with all the admirable qualities he needs—to gain acceptance as a nonparticipant in the classroom? From the teacher's point of view the presence of the supervisor in class may represent a challenge to his power. The supervisor may upset the social equilibrium of the class. He comes and goes as he pleases, which may be interpreted to mean that he can override the teacher's power to determine who may enter and leave the classroom.

The students almost certainly perceive the supervisor as a person with more power than the teacher—at least until something happens to change their perception. The teachers often share this view. As a consequence, the supervisor may appear to the class as a functionary who by institutional definition is "higher" than the teacher, "knows more," and is more competent in instructional matters than the teacher himself. It is not too extreme to say that as roles and functions are presently understood in the public schools, the situation created by the supervisor's entrance into the classroom is full of latent mischief for the often comfortable and deeply satisfying position of the teacher, and possibly for the students, in the social system they have already established.

The supervisor's presence may also create a role conflict for the teacher. To the students, the teacher has the authority of knowledge, status, maturity, special competences. But the supervisor appears to have more knowledge, more status, more competence, else why is he there? The teacher and students may therefore view the supervisor as a rival. Unless the teacher-supervisor relationship is structured before the supervisor's entrance into the class, the teacher may feel some compulsion to "recognize" the supervisor by deferring to him, by making it clear that he has greater authority, by asking him for information, or by inviting him to explain some difficult or abstruse problem. Such behavior may trigger a role conflict within the teacher who sees his authoritative status in the classroom as the foundation of his role as teacher. If he believes that his professional authority in class depends upon whether his students attribute to him an encyclopedic knowledge about whatever he teaches, then the presence of the supervisor puts the teacher in the anomalous position of being an authority himself at one moment and being *under* the authority of the supervisor at the next.[6] The teacher's anxieties about

---

[6]William E. Morse, "Anxieties and Role Conflicts in an Interrelated Triangle," in Association for Student Teaching, *The College Supervisor* (Dubuque, Iowa: W. C. Brown Co., Inc., 1964), p. 6.

the possibility of such role conflicts and teacher-supervisor rivalries may create a formidable obstacle to clinical supervision.

The triangle created by the presence of the supervisor in the teacher-class society may have other distressing consequences. When teacher and students are alone, the teacher is at ease with his young audience. The presence of a third party, however, may "force him to change or wobble in the level of discourse he can use with comfort."[7] Furthermore, in the presence of the supervisor the teacher may be under some pressure to demonstrate to him the logic and reason underlying his classroom methods. He may feel less free to work from intuition. That is, the intellectual level and the social mode of his address to students may be constrained by the presence of an analytical adult. When the teacher is the only adult in the classroom with authority, he feels safer, more secure: "Sure of his position, the teacher can lose his own 'awareness of self' and throw himself into the teaching process with an enthusiasm that mobilizes collective sentiments and builds the circular reactive process."[8]

Teachers and supervisors will recognize the possibility of such constraints and discomforts, not the least of which are the teacher's fears about how the students may act because the supervisor is present. This danger may plague the teacher whose relationship with students is good as well as the teacher who has problems. As a matter of fact, relationships between teachers and students today are often so fragile that a "good" class may blow up as violently as one in which relationships are bad. Students in general are less docile today and are more likely to take militant action in school or in class, expressing the dissatisfactions that are born in the school cafeteria, the athletic field, or in the larger society outside. As a result, teachers find students less predictable, even in the best of circumstances. At worst, the classroom may be the arena of a constant battle for even minimal social control. The consequence is that the supervisor's appearance there may be an unsettling event in an already tense and unstable situation. In periods of active conflict in school it is not unusual for supervisors to be asked to suspend their visits to classrooms.

Even in classrooms in which teacher-student relationships are optimal, the presence of a supervisor may be the cue for unexpected and unsettling behavior. An example comes to mind of a teacher of business education who had been working very hard to encourage discussion and student-to-student interaction in a class of girls. The students in business education

---

[7]Dan C. Lortie, "Craftsmanship and Colleagueship: A Frame for the Investigation of Work Values Among Public School Teachers" (address prepared for the annual meeting of the American Sociological Association, 1961), p. 13.
[8]Ibid.

had traditionally been entirely too docile, too uncritical, and too acceptant of ideas proposed by teachers, texts, and future employers. As a result, when the teacher did in fact succeed in getting her students deeply involved in a series of critical examinations of ethical questions relating to employer-employee relationships, she promptly invited the supervisor in to observe the students in their new behavior. When the supervisor entered the classroom in response to the invitation, the students immediately and implacably reverted to their docile, acceptant, noninteractive behavior—"You could almost hear a pin drop." Later, in conversations with the students, the teacher discovered that (1) the girls wanted the teacher "to get a good report" from the supervisor, (2) they believed the supervisor "wanted order in the class," so (3) they therefore tried to guarantee a good rating for their teacher by being as quiet and well behaved as they could—which effectively prohibited lively discussion.

In brief, the students in a class become a society. The introduction of an unknown or an outsider into that society affects it in ways that may cause the teacher to become anxious—or more anxious.[9]

---

[9]Strategies for dealing with these problems and consequent behavior are treated in Chapter 5, "The Teacher ↔ Supervisor Relationship."

PART TWO

The Cycle of
Clinical Supervision

CHAPTER 8

The Preparation of the Teacher for Clinical Supervision

Defusing Anxieties

As has been noted, some teachers are impelled by anxiety about in-class supervision to defuse the dangers they anticipate. They seek safety by whatever means they can devise. Others may relish the opportunity for supervision, but want it on their own terms or not at all. Still others may try to establish a relationship of dependence upon the supervisor, or to imitate him, or to become a disciple or a counselee. None of these relationships resemble those that unite colleagues. The motivations and anxieties impelling teachers to such noncolleagual behavior tend to be greatly intensified when the supervisor observes the teacher in class. It is therefore recommended that the first phase in the cycle of clinical supervision should be a period in which the supervisor does *not* observe, but rather bends his efforts toward establishing the colleagueship, toward helping the teacher to understand the objectives, ethics, policies, practices, and techniques of clinical supervision and his new role in it.

Since the amount of time devoted to these initial tasks is substantial, we must anticipate that this slow induction may raise rather than lower some teachers' anxieties. They may wonder why they are kept poised so long on the diving board. Will the water be that cold? Is clinical supervision so unpalatable that we must first develop a tolerance for it and then a taste—as one might in eating strange foods? Is it so dangerous that we need special safeguards before venturing into it?

The dangers of a quick induction into clinical supervision, however, are too well known to allow us to be tempted to proceed rapidly. It remains, then, to outline the procedures by which those anxieties that are likely to be aroused by a slow and careful induction may be kept at productive rather than destructive levels. These procedures include—

1. the involvement of the teacher in a program in which he may gain some of the competences of clinical supervision;
2. the involvement of the teacher in "safe" observation and analysis by use of—
   a. selected commercial films of teaching performances
   b. microsupervision and simulated supervision

c. condensed and edited versions of typescripts of teaching, and so forth;

3. the participation of the teacher in decisions about the timing and nature of the processes leading to the supervisor's entrance into the teacher's classroom;

4. the explanation and critical study of the implications of clinical supervision for the professional career of the teacher;

5. the exploration and critical study of the roles, relationships, ethics, rights, and responsibilities of the teacher and the supervisor in clinical supervision; (In this area of study an understanding of the relationships among clinical supervisor, teacher, administrators, other teachers, and the Board of Education should be developed);

6. the provision of guarantees to the teacher: assurances of program continuity and duration of supervision;

7. the demonstration that clinical supervision is built around colleagueship and interaction, not around authoritarian intervention.

Establishing Roles and Functions in Clinical Supervision

"Just as in geometry a point cannot be located without describing its relationship to other points, so persons cannot be located without describing their relations to other individuals."[1] This sentence precisely circumscribes the important questions the teacher wants to ask when he begins to work with a supervisor: Who are the supervisor's bosses? What will he tell them about me? The "them" are the Board of Education and school administrators. It is clear that some of these functionaries are in fact the supervisor's superior officers. The teacher therefore wants to know what the supervisor owes to the Board, to administrators, and to the teacher himself. Does the teacher come in a poor third? The answer to these questions must be given clearly, unequivocally, and publicly.

The supervisor's first ethical responsibility is to the educational welfare of the students. His primary professional relationship is with the teachers, and his communication with each of them is privileged and confidential. He does not report to administrators on the work of the teacher unless, as already noted, the teacher poses a genuine and substantial threat to the educational welfare of the students and the supervisor has exhausted all the resources he can call on to help the teacher. In brief, the supervisor honors first his commitment to the public welfare and then his commit-

[1]Neal Gross, Ward S. Mason, and Alexander W. McEachern, *Explorations in Role Analysis: Studies of the School Superintendency Role* (New York: John Wiley and Sons, Inc., 1958), p. 48.

ment to the teacher. His position is very much like that of a doctor employed by the Board of Education to serve the health needs of the teachers. What happens between the doctor and the teachers is a professional matter and is kept in professional confidence. Yet if the teacher has a dangerous disease that might be communicated to the students, then the doctor must advise the teacher about the course of action he should take, and inform the Board of the danger to the students if the teacher does not follow his advice.

Whatever the accuracy of this medical analogy, the principle it illustrates should govern the teacher-supervisor relationship. If it does not, the effectiveness of the clinical supervisor will be severely limited because most teachers, in matters touching their professional competence, trust neither the Board, nor the administrators, nor the supervisor to observe professional conduct without clearly drawn stipulations similar to those above. The teachers' attitude is no more a reflection upon themselves than it is upon other school personnel. It is simply a consequence of the underdeveloped ethical-professional status of public education. If, in fact, the supervisor makes his professional commitments clear and convincing to the teacher, he will have made a beginning in establishing their professional relationship.

But the teacher has still other questions he wants answered before he can put his full professional trust in the supervisor: What are the supervisor's relations with and responsibilities to the individuals with whom he must maintain secondary counter-positions—the members of the Board of Education and school administrators? The supervisor is still linked, even if secondarily, to powerful people in the school system who control it, "run it." The teachers must know what kinds of communication the supervisor will send along these secondary channels and whether these communications will impair or threaten the teacher-supervisor relationship. The teachers' concerns are primarily centered on what the supervisor will say about them, whether he will report formally or informally about them and about their teaching. The problem of formal reporting or rating is discussed in Chapter 5, "The Teacher↔Supervisor Relationship." The teachers' questions about informal communications remain to be answered here.

It seems safe to say that most teachers would not object to being the subject of the supervisor's informal conversation with other school personnel if he were saying something complimentary. On the other hand, teachers have no guarantee that today's compliment may not be tomorrow's disparagement—which could turn into next week's competence rating. No. The relationship necessary for clinical supervision is almost certain to be impaired if the teacher harbors any fear that the supervisor is talking to other people about him. The relationship demands secure professional confidentiality at every point. The possibility of a slip or a "leak" of any kind will almost certainly undermine the teacher-supervisor relationship.

But how does the teacher gain this certainty that the supervisor will always maintain professional confidentiality and professional discretion? One thing is sure: such certainty cannot be nurtured solely by the supervisor's declarations and promises. True, the problem must be discussed openly, especially in the initial stages of the teacher-supervisor relationship, but the teacher's conviction about so crucial a matter as professional confidentiality cannot be built on dialogue alone. It is rather the product of the supervisor's verbal and nonverbal behavior over a substantial period of time. In essence, the supervisor must develop his own history of professionalism through everything he does on the job. For example, the teacher's confidence in the supervisor's professionalism will be weakened if the supervisor is incompetent, if he talks to teacher A about teacher B, or if he discusses A and B with the superintendent or the janitor. The supervisor strengthens his position whenever he demonstrates his competence in clinical supervision. He communicates his professionalism by way of his sensitivity to ethical problems, his strong central concern for the teacher's professional improvement, the meticulous care and control he exercises in confining his practice to his own field of professional competence.

However, even the supervisor's best efforts to build a strong history of professionalism may not be enough to cement his relationship with the teacher. The nature of that relationship must also be explicated, clarified, illustrated, and set out as systemwide policy by the principal representatives of the school system. The recognition and endorsement of the primacy of the teacher-supervisor relationship must be affirmed institutionally and validated by institutional practices.

The teachers, for their part, are bound to the same professional standards as the supervisor and the system. The only difference is that the supervisor should already be in command of and committed to professional standards and roles; the teacher may need help in achieving the same command, in making the same commitments, and in practicing the new roles required in clinical supervision.

Some Suggestions for the First-Phase Program

The clinical supervisor utilizes the first phase of his interaction with the teacher as a period in which the latter can begin to learn about the supervisor's roles and functions as well as his own. But the teacher must make these explorations under conditions of safety and security to himself. The entire first phase of clinical supervision is designed to induct the teacher into supervision in such a way as to provide maximum guarantees of professional security before the supervisor observes his teaching. It follows that the supervisor needs to develop a first-phase *program* rather than simply a few sporadic meetings.

The necessity for a carefully planned program is the more imperative in that the plan has to provide for individual meetings with each teacher as well as for group meetings when group interaction and discussion are strategically appropriate to certain phase-one objectives. Some suggestions for topics that might be incorporated in these programs would include (1) a time-line for the first-phase program, (2) the responsible role of the teacher, (3) public criteria of teaching competence, (4) the benign use of groups in supervision, and (5) encounter groups. Each is treated in this chapter.

A Time-Line for the First-Phase Program

The details of a program to induct teachers into clinical supervision will of course vary with each school and each school system. Nevertheless, an illustrative format may be useful:

1. The summer session
   A school system that conducts summer schools for its students will provide an excellent setting for a supervision institute. Such an institute may be scheduled for a period of two to eight weeks. During these sessions the teachers have opportunities to—
   a. see clinical supervisors in action;
   b. participate in small group discussions of supervisory problems that are of greatest moment to them;
   c. experiment with various roles in the cycle of supervision, serving as observers, content specialists, analysts, process specialists, resource people, and so forth;
   d. engage in simulated supervision;
   e. study and discuss the literature on supervision, reports on research, and innovations in teaching;

    f. become acquainted with the supervisors who may be working with them;

    g. explore ways of getting feedback about their teaching—content, methods, and so forth;

    h. begin to clarify the roles and functions of teachers and supervisors;

    i. examine the concept that the requirements of professional behavior are reciprocal, that they are binding on teachers as well as supervisors in the colleagual relationship;

    j. study special problems of supervision as they arise in the summer session.

2. Regularly scheduled seminar and practice sessions

These can occur during the academic year. During these periods, activities like those suggested for the summer session are scheduled. In addition, they may be utilized as occasions on which groups plan the agenda for the year, begin the study of special problems, etc. Scheduled supervision of individual teachers is of course also in progress during the academic year.

3. Special Saturday sessions and Faculty Planning Days

The Responsible Role of the Teacher

It is in the teacher-supervisor dyad[2] that the teacher learns that the supervisory program is *his*, not the supervisor's. The teacher begins to understand that since it *is* his, he must share the responsibility for insuring that the program develops in congruence with his needs, his objectives, and his competences. If the supervisory program develops in terms of a logic alien to his needs, then the teacher is partly responsible for this failure.

The conversation in the dyad is therefore focused on an attempt to help the teacher express his preceptions about his goals, his problems, and his strengths and weaknesses as a teacher. When these preceptions have been clarified, examined, and given tentative priorities, the teacher and supervisor may formulate the first-phase objectives of the cycle of supervision in assessable form. Such a formulation establishes a base line for their work together. A natural sequel to this first step is for them to explore and set out the steps by which their objectives are to be achieved.

As these first steps are taken, the teacher and the supervisor systematically record their decisions as to objectives and strategies. This record can be referred to or modified, but it remains as an affirmation of their goals, as a signpost giving direction to their efforts, and as a base line

[2]Dyad is used here as a synonym for *pair* or *group of two*.

for the assessment of their progress. In addition, the statement of goals and plans enables the supervisor to anticipate the teacher's needs and to rally appropriate resources and reinforcements for the process of improvement.

It is evident that in many of these early activities the supervisor is taking the initiative in organizing the program and getting it under way. This assumption of initial leadership by the supervisor may tend to increase the severity of a central problem in the colleagual relationship: Who is to be responsible for the maintenance of good morale in clinical supervision? The chances are ten to one that this question will not even occur to the teacher. The teacher "knows" that morale is the supervisor's responsibility, not the teacher's. The hierarchical structure of the schools has taught him this. Yet the concept of the colleagueship demands that the teacher assume an equal share of the responsibility for the maintenance of agreeable and productive working relationships.

If the supervisor and the teacher cannot work their way through to a relationship in which the teacher fully accepts this new role, then the entire colleagual relationship is threatened. If the teacher is a partner in supervision, he must also be an active partner in maintaining the morale of that association. It follows that the teacher needs the opportunity to internalize the attitudes and the competences necessary to support an interacting dyad. He cannot sit back and allow differences or frictions to grow into resentments. He is called on to do something about this deterioration before it affects the supervisory program adversely.

In order to help the teacher assume his new responsibility, both he and the supervisor need to communicate their feelings about the processes they engage in and about the outcomes of these processes. They need to learn to explain rather than to accuse. They must be prepared to make suggestions for resolving differences. They must learn to accept the inevitability of differences and not to bottle up their unexpressed resentments. They can learn to ventilate their feelings by honest examination of the causes for low morale. And since not every difference can be repaired, teachers and supervisors must also learn to control their resentments and discipline themselves to continue to work together productively until their differences are resolved and any rancor is dissipated.

An additional objective of the induction phase of clinical supervision is to enable the teacher to take the first steps toward self-supervision. More immediately, he needs to learn how to continue alone in the processes he and the supervisor initiate. If the teacher does not gain the motivation and the competences to go ahead on his own when the supervisor is not present, he may transform the sequences and continuities of supervision into a set of unconnected episodes. As we have already said, episodic supervision is not usually very effective.

A useful strategy for developing the teacher's autonomy and the competences he needs to continue on his own in his program of supervision is to begin, early in the first phase, to develop in each dyadic and group session clear statements of who will do what before the next session. This procedure is a variant of the written commitment for future action that is built into the lesson-planning sequences. Such expressions of intent may include a variety of tasks—reading or research to be done, the preparation of materials needed for the next session, etc. It is of course equally important that the supervisor also commit himself to future action.

From the activities programed for the pre-observation phase of clinical supervision, certain advantages may accrue to both teachers and supervisors, possibly the most important of which is that they may become acquainted with each other by working together on low-anxiety tasks. Under such circumstances teachers and supervisors have the opportunity to deal with some of their questions and anxieties in relatively "safe" situations. They may handle them symbolically, vicariously. They can, as it were, survey the unknown terrain of clinical supervision from a safe psychological vantage point.

Public Criteria of Teaching Competence

Any task may become intolerable if the criteria for success are unknown to the performer and if failure in the task is painful. One need only consider the appearance of ulcers or neurotic behavior among experimental animals who are severely punished in the performance of tasks in which success becomes increasingly difficult because the researcher keeps changing the operational definition of success.

Few misunderstandings destroy supervisory relationships faster than unrecognized or unresolved differences about the criteria of good teaching. If a teacher has done his best and believes he has successfully taught what he intended to teach, he may be deeply troubled to find that the supervisor believes he has not been successful. It is less painful, but equally confusing, to be commended for what one believes was a poor teaching performance. The message in all this is clear—the teacher and the supervisor must make their criteria of good teaching known to each other.

This process of explanation and clarification may appropriately begin in group sessions, but it must continue in the teacher-supervisor dyad, in which the two may move from the discussion of the general criteria of good teaching to an examination of the specific criteria held by each. This process culminates in the later phases of the cycle of supervision, but areas of agreement and differences should be pretty well developed beforehand in the less stressful atmosphere of the first phase of supervision.

Strategies for dealing with the problem of the criteria of good teaching are of course best developed by teachers and supervisors together. A few suggestions are presented here as illustrations, not as models—

1. discussion of the instruments used to evaluate teaching locally;
2. examination of "Indicators of Quality," an "instrument for measuring school quality by observing the critical behavior that goes on in the classroom. The instrument is based on four characteristics of internal school behavior that are judged basic to quality: *individualization, interpersonal regard, creativity* and *group activity;*"[3]
3. study of books dealing with methods of teaching;[4]
4. reports on the variables in research on students' achievement, e.g., USOE's "Do Teachers Make a Difference?" 1970;
5. analysis of films on teaching;
6. panel presentations and discussion of the criteria of good teaching, etc.

The outcomes of such discussions, or their sequels arising later in the cycle of supervision, may present certain problems of accommodation. If teacher and supervisor are in substantial agreement, the colleagual relationship is safely past one major hazard. On the other hand, the disagreements may be large but manageable, or large and irreducible. In the latter instance, the teacher and the supervisor may still work together very productively if they can agree to accept *some* set of criteria and work within it. After all, differences do not really *have* to be settled always in favor of one or another, as if in a debating class. On the contrary, differences are often productive. If, on the other hand, the differences are not reconciled and no productive work agreement is possible, the best course of action may be to find this out early and make a change in supervisors.

In any event, the study of the criteria of teaching should constitute

[3]A brochure distributed by the Institute of Administrative Research, Teachers College, Columbia University.
[4]E.g., Alice Kaplan Gordon, *Games for Growth* (Palo Alto, Calif.: Science Research Associates, Inc., 1970). Also, Ronald T. Hyman, *Ways of Teaching: Vantage Points for Study* (New York: J. B. Lippincott Co., 1970).

a continuing theme of clinical supervision. Not only do teachers and supervisors gain essential professional knowledge about each other, but teachers may gain some sense of genuine control over their professional destinies.

The Benign Use of Groups in Supervision

Developments in the use of groups to speed institutional change or to solve social and institutional problems resemble a history of cults and fads rather more than they do the evolution of a useful social invention. In fairly recent times we have seen the near-canonization of "group process" in the schools. To group process have been added the "T-group," brainstorming, encounter groups, sensitivity groups, and other group problem-solving techniques. Rogers calls "planned, intensive group experience . . . the most rapidly spreading *social* invention of the century, and probably the most potent. . . ."[5] The tendency to overuse and misuse group processes in the schools is so strong that a discussion of the benign use of groups in supervision may profitably be coupled with a recommendation for benign neglect at appropriate times.

Group processes are not magic, nor are group decisions, solutions, and learnings necessarily better than individual decisions, solutions, and learnings. The kind of group, the kind of leadership, and the kind of tasks attacked are among the multitude of factors affecting the outcomes of group action. For example, a supervisory meeting ostensibly conducted in accordance with the best group practice techniques will alienate the participants if the meeting is used simply to convey information or to discuss trivialities or, worse, to deal with matters of moment to only one or two participants. If the leadership is authoritarian under pretense of being democratic, if it is simply inept, if the participants are too much alike or too different, or lack relevant knowledge or a genuine desire to participate, then group process is obviously likely to be worse than one-to-one process or no process at all.

The implications for group activities are clear: (1) the leaders must be competent, (2) the agenda must be carefully planned, (3) participants must be carefully selected for a balance of homogeneity and heterogeneity

[5]Carl R. Rogers, *Carl Rogers on Encounter Groups* (New York: Harper & Row, 1970), p. 1. (Italics in original.)

in terms of the tasks to be done, and (4) participants must have both the attitudes and competences necessary for productive participation in group meetings.

Even if most of the conditions of good group activity are apparently satisfied, some groups turn out to be unproductive. The group itself sometimes acts as a brake on the pursuit of deeper meanings or better solutions—possibly because of fatigue among some members and excessive anxiety among others. Nor is it unusual for some group members to allow the action and thought of others to become substitutes for their own. It is as though the creative contribution of one participant were perceived by others as being theirs also. Such vicarious satisfactions may reduce some members of a group to the status of enthusiastic seconders of others' ideas or to even more passive pursuits.

However, in spite of the dangers lurking in group meetings, the possibility of productive outcomes may outweigh the risks. The group can serve as a social stimulus and as a source of reinforcement and support. Some individuals do their best thinking in a situation in which they can choose the anonymity of remaining silent or can participate intensely when it pleases them. The group may provide psychological security to some, while arousing anxieties in others. Even those who seem to be withdrawn and nonparticipating may nevertheless be intensely involved.

Teachers working in supervisory groups have the opportunity to accomplish some tasks that would tax the resources of an individual but that can be achieved by a division of labor. (The study of techniques of interaction analysis would be an example.) As an incidental profit, the teachers may gain competences in group process that they can put to use in their own classes.

The use of groups is strongly indicated if teachers and supervisors are to share the values, attitudes, and disciplined understandings requisite to clinical supervision. In addition to the general advantages that may accrue, the supervisors may derive other benefits specific both to the development of morale and to the needs of the supervisory program. For example, supervisors may utilize teachers' groups to form an organizational center designed to relate clinical supervision to other inservice activities of the school and the school system. Without such an organization, the clinical group is likely to become physically and psychologically separated from other school groups and activities. The danger of isolation is especially pronounced during the early stages in the development of the clinical program. In this period the orientation and induction sequences gather momentum. They may tend to overfocus the teachers' attention on clinical problems and detach them somewhat from the larger concerns of the school or school system. Such a development should be anticipated and prevented, if possible, by the organization of a group of teachers specifically charged with responsibility for integrating clinical supervision into the larger fabric of school activities.

The small groups of teachers brought together for induction into clinical supervision may be extremely useful (as a vehicle for) in introducing teachers into some of the roles they will play in clinical supervision. For example, when group members have developed strong working relationships, they may plan lessons together, devise procedures for obtaining feedback from students, and perhaps even observe each other in the classroom. It is obvious that teachers should not initiate such procedures prematurely and that the entire process should be carefully worked out with the help of supervisors. It is equally obvious that the risks may be worth taking if teachers become working colleagues who apply their professional competences to the tasks of improving each other's teaching.

It may be useful to identify a few programs for the improvement of instruction by way of group action designed to prepare teachers for new roles:

1. One of the most carefully designed and critically analyzed programs of this sort is reported in N. A. Flanders's *Helping Teachers Change Their Behavior*. It should be used in conjunction with Chapter 11 of his *Analyzing Teaching Behavior*.
2. Patrick Babin ("Supervisors Look at Themselves," *Instructor Development* 2 [1970]: 1, 3, 6 [New York: General Learning Corporation]) describes a six-week clinic for supervisors. An adaptation of this program might be useful in the preparation of teachers for their role. The activities include:
   a. work on the importance of behavioral objectives, including the use of audiotapes, films, and programed materials to explore the cognitive, affective, and psychomotor objectives of education;
   b. planning for teaching, with stress on activity and realism;
   c. study of microteaching and simulation;
   d. the use of several observation systems.
3. John L. Morgan ("Using the Workshop Approach as the First Stage in Creating a Helping Relationship Between Supervisors and Teachers," paper submitted at the School of Education, University of Pittsburgh) has detailed the plans for a summer workshop designed as the initial step in the development of the teacher-supervisor relationship. Although Morgan's workshop seems crowded for the four days he allots to it, the

format and activities merit study as elements of a four- to six-week program. His program includes—

a. a critical examination of the relationship between teacher and supervisor;
b. a rationale for the workshop approach;
c. objectives for the workshop;
d. an agenda for the workshop;
e. evaluation and feedback instruments for all activities.

The schedule of activities includes the following—

1. an overview of the program;
2. exercises in getting acquainted through nonverbal communication;
3. exercises in getting acquainted by way of verbal communication;
4. provision of feedback about how participants feel about each other;
5. exercises in group problem solving;
6. simulation exercises in which participants take three roles in rotation: teacher, supervisor, observer;
7. division of teachers into two groups, each to set out the objectives for the year's supervisory program (each group's report is negotiated by the participants in both groups until acceptance is reached);
8. discussion of roles of teacher and supervisor;
9. exchange and discussion of progress reports by teachers and supervisors in two groups, cooperatively defining their roles in the program they have designed together;
10. evaluation of the entire workshop.

Elements of Morgan's plan may be adapted for in-school or summer workshops.

Encounter Groups

No treatment of the utilization of groups in the preparation of teachers for their roles in clinical supervision could omit mention of the currently popular encounter groups. In their most publicized formats they range from violent confrontations between groups known to harbor strong resentments against each other to sessions in which the participants seek to communicate important information about themselves largely by way of nonverbal behavior—touch, posture, motion, grimace, etc.

Such encounters are sometimes conducted under special conditions calculated to make it easier for the participants to "let their hair down." Participants may go on a "retreat" to new surroundings, or choose to ignore their institutional relationships or conceal their identities in order to focus on themselves as persons in the here and now. Under such circumstances, it is thought, the individual is free to express himself, to listen, to differ, and to agree. Such freedom, coupled with group techniques for intensifying personal involvement, may facilitate change in behavior.

Rogers formulates his hunches about such group processes as follows:

> A facilitator can develop, in a group which meets intensively, a psychological climate of safety in which freedom of expression and a reduction of defensiveness gradually occur. . . . In such a psychological climate many of the immediate feeling reactions of each member toward others, and of each member toward himself, tend to be expressed. . . . A climate of mutual trust develops out of this mutual freedom to express real feelings, positive and negative. Each member moves toward greater acceptance of his total being—emotional, intellectual, and physical—as it is, including its potential. . . . With individuals less inhibited by defensive rigidity, the possibility of change in personal attitudes and behavior, professional methods, in administrative procedures and relationships, becomes less threatening. . . . With the reduction of defensive rigidity, individuals can hear each other, can learn from each other, to a greater extent. . . . There is a development of feedback from one person to another, such that each individual learns how he appears to others and what impact he has in interpersonal relationships. . . . With this greater freedom and improved communication, new ideas, new concepts, new directions emerge. Innovation can become a desirable rather than a threatening possibility. . . . These learnings in the group experience tend to carry over, temporarily or more permanently, into the relationships with spouse, children, students, subordinates, peers, and even superiors following the group experience.[6]

If even only a few of these hunches turn out to be correct, the utility of group encounters certainly warrants careful examination. Rogers himself says that "it is perfectly feasible to improve communication [among all the individuals and groups involved in education], and it is nothing short of tragic that education has been so slow to make use of this new social invention."[7] Nevertheless, perhaps some qualifications should accompany this strong recommendation. It seems to us that encounter groups are first of all not a unified class or set of activities—there are (1) many varieties of groups, (2) multiple styles of group leadership, (3) innumerable types and combinations of participants, (4) a vast realm of different objectives and special circumstances, and therefore (5) an

[6]Ibid., pp. 6–7.
[7]Ibid., p. 141.

infinity of variables to be put together properly if encounter groups are to be used effectively in clinical supervision. We would therefore recommend that if these groups are used at all, they should be used with the most meticulous care to insure that—

1. the participants prepare themselves for the experience by a study of the literature on encounter groups;
2. the encounter is used experimentally first, as training in process rather than for other important objectives;
3. if participants decide to try the encounter process, it is carried out under the constant guidance of expert leaders; and
4. trained observers are present to evaluate what is happening and to recommend continuation or discontinuance of the process if such action seems warranted.

In the actual operation and assessment of encounter groups in supervision, some elementary precautions should be observed:

1. The responses of individuals drafted into a group are likely to be less favorable than those of individuals who volunteer to participate.
2. The chances are very slight that well-established behaviors will be significantly and permanently changed by short-term treatment, even if it is intensive. Change in professional behavior is usually better managed by way of a program than by way of an encounter. As noted above, however, Rogers is more optimistic.[8]
3. Where strongly held attitudes are in question in a group encounter, it is likely that people at both extremes of these attitudes will be pushed farther out to right and left.
4. The skills and attitudes learned by teachers in encounter groups may be applicable to classroom interaction in the discussion of controversial issues, provided the teachers have had the opportunity to become competent in the theory and practice of group encounters. Otherwise, an amateurish attempt to adapt encounter techniques to the classroom is likely to do more harm than good.

In sum, supervisors attempting to use encounter techniques in the first-phase program to prepare teachers for clinical supervision should perhaps invite both teachers and supervisors to join in the effort for two purposes: first, to examine the pros and cons of an interesting social invention, and second, to become better acquainted with each other under somewhat unusual conditions, as differentiated from the acquaintanceship gained in less highly charged situations.

[8]Ibid., p. 7.

A Note on the Conclusion of the First Phase of the Cycle

The processes suggested for use in the establishment of the teacher-supervisor relationship and the preparation of the teacher for his role in clinical supervision are obviously not terminated when the first phase ends. Most of these processes and activities are naturally continued and elaborated throughout the course of the supervisory program. They are recommended for use as developmental progressions rather than as episodes.

CHAPTER 9

Lesson Planning: Part I

Time and Cost Considerations

Previous chapters have treated some of the problems the supervisor encounters when he initiates the cycle of supervision: establishing the teacher-supervisor relationship and preparing the teacher for his new roles, for example. The present chapter treats the actual joint planning of lessons. All these activities are expensive in terms of time, effort, and money. The economics of clinical supervision therefore generates two important problems. First, is all this elaborate preparation really a necessary prelude to such a simple event as the supervisor's entrance into the teacher's classroom? And second, are the processes of clinical supervision so time-consuming that the entire operation becomes too costly in dollars and in its demands on the energies and time of teachers and supervisors?

The answer to the first question is that the extended processes of preparation for classroom supervision are in fact necessary in order to restructure the traditional relationship between teachers and supervisors. The answer to the question about the human and institutional costs of initiating clinical supervision is yes and no. Clinical supervision *is* likely to be more expensive than other supervisory programs, but it is not really so expensive as it might appear to be at first glance. The real cost is less because every step in the cycle of clinical supervision obviously does not have to be repeated for each observation and for each sequence of supervisory activities with a teacher or groups of teachers. As the new relationship between teachers and supervisors takes form and as they gain skill and confidence in working together as colleagues, entire segments of the clinical process may be combined and telescoped or omitted entirely. The actual supervision emerges from an initial exploratory phase into a more mature operational phase. Economies in shared understandings, better communication, and improved techniques enable the program to pick up momentum. The teacher and supervisor then establish a less time-consuming pace for their work together.

The questions of the pace and cost of clinical supervision are especially important in connection with the present chapter on lesson planning. Lesson planning—especially in the initial sessions—requires a substantial amount of time. Teachers are therefore well within their rights to ask how this planning time is to become available. Where in their crowded schedules can planning time be found? This question is all the more critical because the lack of provision for planning time has been one of the reefs on which many recent innovations in teaching have foundered, e.g., team teaching.

Before attempting to estimate the time needed for planning, it may be useful to specify a kind of time-line for it. The first planning sessions will generally demand substantially more time than those that follow, because they are integral parts of the process of establishing the teacher-supervisor relationships and roles. Once beyond this point, however, the teacher and supervisor can generally complete their planning well within an hour.

In addition, although they will usually work together in several cycles comprising a short series of lessons, they obviously do not continue such cycles without interruption during the year. On the contrary, one set of cycles prepares the teacher for a subsequent phase of work on his own or with other teachers, to be followed after an appropriate period by the resumption of work with the supervisor.

This discussion of the time required for clinical supervision is not meant to create an impression that *present* teaching schedules will in general provide enough time for it. They will *not*. A minimal program of clinical supervision may be implemented if (1) the teachers involved can be inducted into clinical supervision in a two- to six-week summer program and (2) each teacher has a free period of forty-five to sixty minutes at least three days a week for supervision and other professional responsibilities. The availability of more time will of course help the clinical program. Some school systems have made more liberal arrangements for the improvement of instruction by scheduling one free afternoon a week for each teacher and by reimbursing teachers for continuing their programs of clinical supervision after school hours, on Saturday, and on school holidays.

The Role of Lesson Planning in Clinical Supervision

The lesson plan prepared for a single class period or a single day is generally viewed by educators as the basic module of instructional planning. Since the daily lesson plan is so compatible with the episodic, discontinuous supervision common in university programs of student teaching and in the public schools, it is very often treated by supervisors and teachers alike as though it were in itself a sufficient basis for the teacher-supervisor interaction. An opposite view is taken in clinical supervision. The daily plan is perceived as one element in a planning continuum, which originates at the level of what might be called the national charter of American education, develops through state-mandated curriculums, is embodied in local documents—school programs, grade and subject curriculums, and unit plans—and is finally implemented directly in a teacher's daily lesson plan.

One implication of this developmental view of planning becomes readily apparent. Clinical supervisors, although primarily committed to day-by-day, in-class supervision, recognize that the teacher's daily plans must be validated not only in terms of each day's instruction but also by reference to larger educational objectives extending outward to the most important individual and societal goals. This long view of educational design has its consequences in daily planning. In the simplest terms it means that the teacher and supervisor will have to ask themselves whether the daily plan is in tune with the larger plans surrounding it, whether it digresses from them, or even whether it directly contravenes them. This does not mean that the teacher and supervisor embark on a thorough-going critical examination of the aims of education every time they begin to plan together. But it does mean that on occasion they may need to ask whether specific objectives in a daily plan are compatible with larger objectives. For example, does a teacher's plan to have students study outstanding examples of civic disobedience strengthen or undermine the larger unit on civic responsibility?

Perhaps even more frequent than conflicts about a teacher's objectives are differences about methods of achieving objectives. For example, the objective of preserving a way of life called "democratic" is embodied in the curriculum of the public schools and finds expression in a multitude of subobjectives at every level of public schooling. Three teachers, all seeking to further this objective by a study of the Bill of Rights of the Constitution, select three different methods of teaching. The first teacher has the students memorize the Bill of Rights. He tests for achievement by having his students write out portions of the document verbatim, from memory. The second has his class trace the history of human rights; he tests by having the students answer questions on the historical sequences by which these rights developed, were breached, and reappeared. The third teaches his students to examine the problems that arise when two rights conflict with each other, e.g., human and property rights. He tests by asking his students to resolve specific contemporary examples of such conflicts for themselves and to justify their solutions. The supervisor working with all three teachers is likely to differ with one or all about the methods they use, rather than their objectives.

In sum, the clinical supervisor concerns himself with daily planning when he is working intensively with a single teacher. But both he and the teacher seek to validate their decisions about what and how to teach by reference to the larger contexts surrounding teaching. They scrutinize content for its suitability to both immediate and ultimate objectives and for its appropriateness to the students. And they ratify decisions about method in terms that subserve both the short-term and long-term objectives of instruction.

Planning as Prediction

In the lesson-planning processes described in this chapter the teacher and supervisor not only draw up a plan, but they also attempt to predict its effectiveness. They try to test the plan against the multitude of criteria and variables likely to affect its success in class, and try to determine its congruence with educational objectives. *The thoroughness of this antici-patory testing process depends in large part upon the variety and inter-relationships of the criteria and variables the teacher and supervisor have at their command to test their plan.* To put this another way, success in planning is dependent upon the diversity and accuracy of the hypotheses the planners can formulate to predict the outcomes of the students' learning experiences.

For example, many teachers of Latin plan to teach their students to translate Latin into English, only to succeed in teaching them to develop incredible skill in the use of the interlinear translations variously called "trots," "cribs," or "ponies." Other teachers fail to recognize that in teaching biology they succeed best in teaching their students to predict accurately what questions the teacher will ask on his tests.

These illustrations are designed to call attention to the imperative need for teachers and supervisors to elaborate and test their command of hypotheses about effective teaching-learning in order to sharpen the predictions they generate in the planning process. Examples of such hypotheses will be found in the chapters on observation and analysis. Every category of observation may be viewed as a question to be asked in the planning process. For example, in the category dealing with the physical arrangement of the classroom we may ask whether placing the desks in a circle will facilitate or interfere with (1) discussion, (2) individual seat work, (3) the administration of tests, etc.

Overview of the Planning Process

The suggestions made in this chapter provide an overview of the components of the planning process. Each planning session is a unique product of all that has happened before it in the first phase of clinical supervision and in previous planning sessions. It is a product of the history of the teacher-supervisor interaction. The teacher and supervisor develop the plan in their own way. Only three specific recommendations will be offered to them. The first is that they progress from simple to more complex plans as the teacher matures in his planning competences. The second is that they not overdo the planning. Some planning is so extended, so specific, that it drains the teacher of spontaneity and focuses him on following rather than developing the plan in the classroom. The third recommendation is that they not make the plan so thin and so spare that the teacher is committed neither to a course of action nor to expected outcomes.

The Utility of Cooperative Lesson Planning The initiation of the teacher-supervisor planning sessions marks the beginning of in-class supervision. The supervisor can put this occasion to good use. For example, he has an opportunity to work with the teacher, in contrast to simply talking with him. This act of working together in the preparation of a lesson plan helps to convince the teacher that the supervisor really will assume the colleagual role. In addition, it provides the opportunity for the supervisor to help the teacher try out the same role. In the planning process the teacher and supervisor become a team trying to solve a shared professional problem—they are engaged in a campaign to put together the teaching resources and strategies most likely to achieve the objectives of the next lesson. The process of cooperative planning, therefore, serves several important ends: (1) it engages the dyad in work on a professional problem that has significance and utility for the teacher: planning his teaching, (2) it provides opportunities for the teacher to learn about his new role in supervision, and (3) it enables the supervisor to gain valuable information about the teacher's views on the objectives of teaching, his teaching strategies, his perceptions about the students, his choice of the content and experiences to be embodied in his instruction, and the history of his instruction—what has happened before and its relation to what is yet to come.

For the teacher, some of the principal arguments advanced for the utility of written lesson plans are that they—

1. provide a written record of his objectives for the lesson; and they therefore serve as a basis for evaluation and future plans;
2. help him to formulate and assess the effectiveness of the teaching-learning strategies he will use in the lesson;
3. help him to maintain a logical development of ideas and to avoid digressions that may cloud the orderly development of the lesson;
4. keep him from "losing his place" if he does digress for necessary remedial instruction or to pursue an unexpected but possibly rewarding line of ideas;
5. improve the entire planning process by serving as a reference base for future repetitions of the same instruction—permitting the teacher to spend his time on the improvement of the plan rather than on efforts to recall and reconstruct his previous instructional strategies;
6. serve as a ready reminder of the problems, demonstrations, questions, activities, drills, assignments, etc., to be used in the course of the lesson;
7. help him to pace his instruction for optimal use of the time available for the lesson.

The traditional textbook rationale offered for the writing of daily lesson plans seems quite thin. Its weaknesses may derive from the fact that most writers who treat the daily lesson plan seem to conceptualize it principally as a handy and useful device—a kind of daily organizer and prompter for the teacher. Such functions are undoubtedly important, but they have certainly not motivated most teachers to use their plans as important instruments of professional improvement. In addition, the fact that administrators often "evaluate" daily and weekly plans for purposes of rating is not calculated to make the plans very popular with teachers. One writer conveys something of teachers' attitudes toward the whole planning process in the first sentence of his essay on lesson plans: "There are three things that every teacher must face: death, taxes, and lesson plans."[1] We can recall no one—teacher, writer, or supervisor— who grows rhapsodic over the beauties of daily planning. Why has it become so distasteful?

The first reason is probably that writing a daily plan means work, and few people seem to like this kind of work. Perhaps more important, it is

[1]Arthur A. Delaney, "Lesson Plans—Means or Ends," in *Principles and Practices of Teaching in Secondary Schools*, ed. Florence Henry Lee (New York: David McKay Co., Inc., 1965), p. 105.

intimately associated with traditional supervision. For example, it becomes one of the principal exhibits when the supervisor stops in to visit a classroom for a period or part of a period. One consequence of the traditionally discontinuous supervision is that the daily plan ceases to be perceived by the teacher as an integral element of long-term planning. It becomes a daily convenience or a daily chore. Even worse, this isolated entity—a piece of paper without a history or a future—often becomes part of the frail basis for the supervisor's rating of the teacher. It is no wonder, then, that many teachers do as little daily planning as possible. Some of the more cynical keep a carefully prepared full-fledged plan in reserve, to be whipped out and used when the supervisor enters the classroom unexpectedly.

In clinical supervision, however, the entire process takes on a strikingly different character. In the planning sessions the supervisor joins the teacher in an attack on a shared problem. They set out together to find the best way they can devise to achieve the objectives of the teacher's next lesson. This cooperative approach to a professional problem unites the supervisor and teacher and integrates the plan with two interrelated processes: the improvement of the teacher's instruction and the development of the supervisory program.

The plan itself becomes something more than a useful outline for the teacher. Since it is carefully examined and is "worked out" rather than "written," it takes on the character of a set of predictions. It becomes a set of hypotheses about the best way to achieve the objectives of the instruction. The plan is a trial run rather than a road map to be followed. This trial run will be evaluated. What is learned about it in the classroom will be applied in the next conference. And since the cooperatively developed plan is discussed in detail and written out in fairly explicit terms, it provides a stable reference base for future analysis and planning. It becomes a part of the examined record of the program to improve the teacher's instruction.

As for the supervisor, the planning sessions provide him with firsthand knowledge about the teacher's objectives and work patterns. From the supervisor's point of view, his involvement in planning is his introduction to the classroom world of the teacher. He gains new knowledge about the teacher and refines his hunches and his intuitions about how best to work with him.

But what if a teacher maintains that plans are a waste of time, that he teaches better without one? In actual practice, it turns out that a sizable percentage of the teachers who deprecate the written plan actually work from an unwritten plan, often well rehearsed through frequent use. They are therefore understandably reluctant to go through the tedious formalities of writing it all out. The supervisor generally finds that these teachers are quite willing to give cooperative planning at least a trial run after they understand the rationale for it.

There is still another group of teachers, few in number, who believe that the act of writing a plan and having it before them in class inhibits their spontaneity and creativity and dulls their sensitivity to cues from their students. Like many other teachers, they feel that the plan is a promissory note on which payment must be made; they view it as a strait-jacket that prevents them from pursuing interesting and rewarding bypaths with their students. The supervisor working with a teacher who feels very strongly that lesson planning places intolerable constraints upon his freedom to teach may want to follow the procedures described below:

1. Confer with the teacher about his plans, without asking him to write them out.
2. Take notes or make some other type of record that will specify the teacher's objectives and the content and strategies he anticipates for the lesson.
3. Observe the teacher's instruction, secure adequate data about it, and analyze the data. Do this often enough to make possible a good estimate of the level of competence the teacher exhibits.
4. If the teacher seems to be performing at a superior level of competence, the supervisor may—
   a. visit him occasionally to determine whether the teacher is maintaining or increasing his competence;
   b. offer to work with him to strengthen special skills or to experiment with new methods, content, or student roles;
   c. offer the teacher the opportunity to gain supervisory skills that might be used in the program of supervision.
5. If, on the other hand, the teacher's performance appears to need improvement, the supervisor may—
   a. work with him without using written plans; or
   b. ask the teacher to consider the possibility that lack of a written plan is weakening his classroom performance—if the supervisor thinks this may actually be the case—and invite him to try to discover whether written plans would or would not strengthen his teaching.

It is clear by now that the clinical supervisor should not lightly forego the advantages of a written plan. The utility of both the process and the plan—for teacher and supervisor alike—is far too great to be readily relinquished.

Still another strong argument—perhaps the strongest—remains to be adduced in support of careful planning. The written plan, as has been noted, may be viewed as a set of hypotheses relating teaching strategies to learning outcomes. If the teacher adopts this point of view the cooperative writing of a plan ceases to be merely an exercise in which he tries to change yesterday's classroom behavior. It becomes the basis for a process of informal experimentation, a search for the reasons why certain teaching-learning behavior relates as expected to the objectives of a lesson and other behavior does not. Such a plan becomes a search for better hypotheses and a probing for the reasons underlying their superiority. In brief, the lesson plan in clinical supervision becomes one of the basic instruments by which the teacher not only learns to change his classroom behavior but also comes to understand *why* he is changing it. When understanding accompanies change in a teacher's behavior, the teacher is becoming educated, not trained.

Some Elements of the Planning Process

The planning the teacher and supervisor engage in includes their efforts to (1) become more knowledgeable about the students and the instructional resources available, (2) derive and state the objectives in operational form, (3) develop and test the logic of the teaching-learning strategies, and (4) work out the feedback and evaluation processes designed to help the teacher and supervisor understand both the events occurring in the class session and the outcomes of instruction. The teacher and supervisor also try to insure that the plan will be appropriate to the abilities, interests, needs, and previous learnings of the students for whom it is designed.

Deriving the Objectives of Instruction

A discussion of the teacher's objectives in a daily lesson plan is often both a logically and strategically appropriate opening gambit in the planning process. We have already touched upon the problems created by the multiplicity of objectives deriving from various levels and sources— national, state, local, and individual. But still other forces influence the teacher's objectives. These might be termed accidental or institutional pressures extraneous to the teacher's own structure of objectives. They include departmental examinations, standardized achievement tests, the availability of certain textbooks, and the pressures of local militant groups. For example, a history teacher might decide to help his students understand the role played by minority groups in the history of the United States. The supervisor can help him identify the forces leading to this decision. Has it been made because the topic is stressed in departmental tests? in standardized tests? in the available textbooks? because local militant groups want it taught? or because the teacher himself believes the topic deserves to be treated?

In such an examination the forces shaping the teacher's objectives are brought into his conscious and critical view. As a result, his processes of selection may become more rational, more systematic. The accidental, nonrational, and formerly unrecognized pressures influencing his selection of the objectives of instruction may then be examined for their relevance to the primary objectives of instruction.

These efforts to rationalize the teacher's goal-setting activities extend throughout the program of supervision. They should not, however, occupy so much time early in the clinical program that they overshadow or weaken the initial lesson-planning activities. The success of these plans must remain the prime concern of the teacher and supervisor, especially since the teacher may view them as a test of cooperative planning in clinical supervision. One failure may therefore create difficulties in the development of good working relationships between supervisor and teacher.

Stating the Objectives of Instruction

Three major perplexities stand in the way of educators who try to specify the outcomes of their instruction in some operational or behavioral form. The first is that the American school is dedicated to fundamental societal and individual objectives that resist specification. How can the schools assess their contribution to the student's "good citizenship . . . ability and willingness to work . . . general morality . . . health, command of fundamental processes . . . worthy use of leisure . . ."?[2] The second difficulty compounds the first: How does one factor out the school's particular contribution to these grand aims of education, as differentiated from

[2]Educational Policies Commission, *The Central Purpose of American Education* (Washington, D.C.: National Education Association, 1961), pp. 1–2. A review of traditional statements of the objectives of American education.

learnings gained in the home, the neighborhood, and the great world that surrounds both the student and his school? And the third difficulty in measuring the effects of schooling arises when educators try to reduce central objectives to some sort of measurable terms. They really face two dilemmas rather than one. (1) They must relate lower-order behavioral outcomes to higher-order thematic objectives. How does a teacher obtain convincing evidence that the school experiences his students have in his class in U.S. history or civics add an iota to their commitment to a democratic society and individual liberty? And (2) educators must relate lower-order outcomes convincingly to lower-order objectives. Is the teacher justified in assuming that if a child correctly solves problems of simple addition and subtraction on a school test, he will be able to give the correct change to the customers who buy lemonade at his sidewalk soft-drink stand?

One answer to such questions is that we must generally take it on faith that the school and the teacher do make a difference. Another answer is to try to narrow the scope of the school's responsibilities to more manageable dimensions by focusing its efforts on the "central role [of the] rational powers of an individual . . . [upon which] depends his ability to achieve his personal goals and fulfill his obligations to society."[3] The problem of whether it is possible and desirable to make such a distinction between the powers of thinking and the powers of feeling and evaluating is a question beyond the scope of this book. What remains to be treated here is the dilemma the teacher and supervisor face in attempting to state the objectives of instruction in some operational and possibly measurable form.

The Advantages of Operational Objectives   It is readily apparent that efforts to state objectives in operational terms can act as a powerful corrective to widespread tendencies to formulate educational objectives in such broad terms that almost any teacher can teach almost anything and test for almost anything in the name of, let us say, teaching students to be honest or to appreciate literature. The adverse reaction to such global and indeterminate statements of objectives has led to a strong and increasing pressure to have teachers state their objectives in more concrete terms. Some of the advantages and disadvantages of such practices are examined here because they are obviously relevant to the work

[3]Ibid., p. 4. This was the position taken by the NEA's Educational Policies Commission in 1961.

of the supervisor and the teacher when they attempt to set out the objectives of a lesson plan.

The first problem that arises when teachers are encouraged to state their objectives in behavioral form is that a kind of Gresham's law may begin to operate: trivial objectives drive important objectives out of circulation. What happens to instruction when "appreciation of good literature" is related to the number of pages a student reads in the volumes placed on the "good literature" shelf in a classroom?

Another pitfall awaiting teachers who lack competence in articulating behavioral objectives is that they may emphasize the most readily observable behavior rather than the more relevant but less easily observable evidences of learning. Teachers may, for example, observe the students' behavior in the classroom, but ignore out-of-class data. Or they may focus on simple recall when analysis or synthesis is required. For example, the teacher whose intent is that his students should search out the answers to H. S. Commager's question "What have Puritanism and democracy in common?" may try to assess the students' learnings by asking them what century Roger Williams and Cotton Mather were born in. This process of regression becomes even more evident when uninstructed teachers attempt to assess the affective and emotional outcomes of teaching. Their problems are clearly set out by the authors of the *Taxonomy of Educational Objectives* (Affective Domain):

> It was evident to us that there is a characteristic type of *erosion* in which the original intent of a course or educational program becomes worn down to that which can be explicitly evaluated for grading purposes and that which can be taught easily through verbal methods (lectures, discussions, reading materials, etc.). There is a real shift in intent that comes with time. It may be true that it is easier to teach and evaluate cognitive objectives. But we really doubt that this is the whole determining influence. . . .[4]

The difficulties of finding valid indicants of learning—even of cognitive learning—are complicated by the fact that so many of the intended outcomes of education cannot be directly observed. On the contrary, inferences must most often be drawn from observed behavior. It is possible to determine with fair accuracy whether psychomotor behavior is truly learned, because some of it is directly manifest. If a child is to learn to write the alphabet or do a swan dive or play the violin, he may be observed doing it. On the other hand, a teacher may assume that he has

---

[4]David R. Krathwohl, Benjamin S. Bloom, and Bertram B. Masia, eds., *Taxonomy of Educational Objectives: The Classification of Educational Goals*, Handbook II: Affective Domain (New York: David McKay Co., Inc., 1956), p. 16. Reprinted by permission.

taught a student to fulfill his civic responsibilities, but he may never find out whether the student really casts his ballot in local and national elections.

Still another problem in relating the behavior of students to the intent of the teacher is generated by the fact that many students display great virtuosity in exhibiting any behavior that will earn a good grade. A teacher who on one occasion set out to teach a group of highly competitive students to be more cooperative in small working groups was delighted to observe that they began to cooperate very quickly. His satisfaction diminished suddenly when the supervisor pointed out that the students were *competing* fiercely to see who could be more cooperative. If visiting an art gallery is interpreted by the teacher as appreciation of art, some students will dutifully make the rounds of galleries in order to earn a good grade in art. If students "get credit" for handing in book reports, some of them will simply read short digests of books and report on them. Others will plagiarize published book reviews.

All this is not to say that the teacher is to become deeply cynical about either his students or the functionality of objectives stated in behavioral terms. The point to be stressed is simply that behavior itself may be as ambiguous as the answers to an attitude questionnaire. Teachers and supervisors must learn to recognize the extent of the inferences they make in assessing students' learnings and must seek to state their objectives by way of low-inference rather than high-inference criteria whenever possible. Otherwise, the supervisor's program to help teachers state their objectives in behavioral form may end up by glossing over the genuine difficulties of such tasks and eroding the value of the entire program.

The Advantages of Behavioral Objectives   Although teachers and supervisors attempting to state the objectives of instruction in behavioral terms encounter serious problems, the benefits to be derived may repay their efforts. Mager cites the following advantages of objectives carefully stated in observable and measurable form:

> When clearly defined goals are lacking, it is impossible to evaluate a course or program efficiently. . . . There is no sound basis for selecting appropriate materials, content, or instructional methods . . . an instructor will function in a fog of his own making until he knows just what he wants his students to be able to do at the end of the instruction. . . . Unless goals are clearly and firmly fixed . . . tests are at best misleading; at worst, they are irrelevant, unfair, or useless. To be useful they must measure *performance in terms of the goals.* Unless the [instructor] himself has a clear picture of his instructional intent, he will be unable to select test items that clearly reflect

the student's ability to perform the desired skills, or that will reflect how well the student can demonstrate his acquisition of desired information. . . . The student is provided the means to evaluate *his own* progress at any place along the route of instruction and is able to organize his efforts into relevant activities.[5]

Additional advantages may be listed. Unless the teacher works out the concrete outcomes expected of a course of study or a unit, he himself may lose his way or find himself going up some dead-end street as he and his students wander through unknown terrain. A ninth-grade English teacher sets out to teach his students "to appreciate 'The Rime of the Ancient Mariner.'" Not having troubled to translate "to appreciate" into behavioral objectives, he finds himself vaguely uneasy to discover that at the end of three weeks of study his activity-oriented students have (1) carefully plotted the route of the Mariner's ship on the classroom maps, (2) studied the life-cycle of the albatross in great detail, and (3) built a scale model of the Mariner's ship. This example is only one of a large class of ambiguities and misinterpretations that teachers may avoid by becoming competent in clarifying the meanings of their objectives and stating them in appropriate behavioral terms.

Once the teacher is in command of these competences, he has the additional advantage of knowing what student behaviors to reinforce. He can direct positive reinforcement to relevant behavior and avoid rewarding irrelevant and counterproductive activities. Similar advantages accrue to the supervisor who is working with a teacher who clearly states his objectives: the teacher's specification of the behavior he expects from students helps the supervisor to concentrate his observation and analysis on appropriate aspects of both the teacher's teaching and the related behavior of students.

Clearly specified outcomes of teaching also help supervisor and teacher to set priorities of instruction. These priorities, once established, focus the instruction. As Bloom has said:

> There are many possible changes that can take place in students as a result of learning experiences, but since the time and resources of the school are limited, only a few of the possibilities can be realized. It is important that the major objectives of the . . . unit of instruction be clearly identified if time and effort are not to be wasted on less important things and if the work . . . is to be guided by some plan.[6]

[5]Robert F. Mager, *Preparing Instructional Objectives* (Palo Alto, Calif.: Fearon Publishers, 1962), pp. 3–4.
[6]Benjamin S. Bloom, ed., *Taxonomy of Educational Objectives: The Classification of Educational Goals,* Handbook 1: Cognitive Domain (New York: David McKay Co. Inc., 1956), p. 26.

The competences the teacher needs to command in order to translate the general thematic goals of his instruction into behavioral terms are central to his competences in lesson planning. It follows, then, that whenever teachers have not acquired these skills, the supervisor is required to help them do so. This is a task that may appropriately be initiated early in the program designed to establish the teacher-supervisor relationship. It is probably unwise for the supervisor to plunge into lesson planning with the teacher before the latter has at least gained some initial competence in formulating his objectives in behavioral terms.

Behavioral Objectives: An Examined Position   The teacher not only needs to become competent in translating thematic goals into behavioral objectives, but he must also have help in developing an examined position vis-à-vis the use of behavioral objectives. He should become neither a fevered advocate nor a blind adversary of the practice. The fevered advocate of the tangible here-and-now objective often refuses to deal at all with the ambiguities of the general, thematic objective. As a result, he tends to dig himself deeper and deeper into a touch-see-feel-hear-taste world of directionless activities. The blind adversary of behavioral objectives, for his part, often sets out bravely toward grand objectives, only to find himself lost without the direction-testing, relevance-testing services of behavioral feedback. The teacher who has fought his way through to a thoughtfully examined position about both kinds of objectives, recognizing the strengths and weaknesses of both, is fortified in the task every professional faces: relating his own inferences to the best available evidence, which is also often inferential. He must know that the inference-gap that develops in the assessment of the outcomes of teaching-learning processes becomes progressively greater in the cognitive domain as the thematic goals climb from "simple recall of specific and isolable bits of information" through knowledge of methodology, abstractions, and theories, and beyond this stage to extrapolation, application, analysis, synthesis, and evaluation.[7] The inferences that must be drawn in the affective domain are even more open to serious question. The very titles of the principal categories of this domain propel the teacher immediately into the most difficult and complex problems of the outward signs of human learning. He will have to deal with motivation to attend actively and to gain satisfaction in responding, the internalization of values, beliefs, and attitudes, the organization of values into a system, the learn-

[7]Ibid., passim.

ing of "pervasive controlling tendencies," and "the integration of these beliefs, ideas, and attitudes into a total philosophy or world view."[8]

The ambiguity that characterizes some examples of efforts to test for behavioral objectives is readily illustrated in items drawn from the Bloom and Krathwohl taxonomies. If knowledge of specific facts is the objective, then the following test item might represent a fairly low inference level:

The Monroe Doctrine was announced ten years after the

    1. Revolutionary War   3. Civil War
    2. War of 1812   4. Spanish-American War[9]

The gap widens in a question requiring the student to extrapolate: "Contrast the kinds of interpretation one can make from frequency polygons or histograms and smoothed curves drawn from the same distribution."[10] When the objective is phrased as the "production of a unique communication," then we encounter a test question of the following order:

Think of some time in your own life when you were up against a difficulty, something that stood in your way and had to be overcome. Make up a story around this difficulty and tell it to the class.[11]

What complex and possibly dubious inferences must be made in evaluating the behavior one observes when a student makes up and tells a story? Is it really a story? Is it unique, derivative, plagiarized? Does it "communicate"?

When we attempt to appraise the inference-gap in test questions from the affective domain, the entire structure of the relation between teacher's objective and learner's behavior may become very delicate and tenuous. The teacher who commits himself to an objective such as "alertness toward different types of voluntary reading" may have to rely on a question like the following for evidence about what the student has learned:

Directions: The purpose of this questionnaire is to discover what you really think about the reading which you do in your leisure time. . . . There are three ways to mark the Answer Sheet:
    Y means that your answer to the question is Yes.
    U means that your answer to the question is Uncertain.
    N means that your answer to the question is No.

[8]Krathwohl, Bloom, and Masia, op. cit., Appendix A, pp. 176–85.
[9]Bloom, op. cit., p. 17.
[10]Ibid., p. 119.
[11]Ibid., p. 178.

1. Would you like to know much more about the history and development of some type of literature, such as drama or the short story?
2. Are you interested in knowing more about literary awards, such as the Pulitzer and the Nobel prizes?
3. Is there any type of nonfiction, such as biography, travel, or science, which you would like to read more of at present?[12]

If the teacher's objective is to have his students show a "preference for a nutritionally balanced diet," then his evidence about such learning may come from an item like the following:

> To test for this objective the appraisal situation could be set in the school cafeteria during a regular noon meal. The student is permitted to choose his meal freely from a wide range of foods. To limit the number of choices he can make, the student is told that the cost of the meal he chooses cannot exceed a certain amount. When he reaches the end of the serving line the nutritionist notes his choices on a check list. The pattern of choices is then analyzed by the examiner to determine its degree of nutritional balance.[13]

How does a teacher set out to determine whether his students have learned to accord greater value to "respect for the worth and dignity of human beings"? Does he attempt to gather such information by way of items like the following:

> Tom and Bob who know each other only slightly were double-dating two girls who were roommates. A sudden storm made it impossible to go to the beach as planned. Tom suggested going to a movie. After making the suggestion, he realized Bob was without funds. As Tom, what would you do?
> 1. Pay for the party.
> 2. Lend Bob money.
> 3. Leave it up to the girls.
> 4. Get Bob to suggest something.
> 5. Apologize to Bob for making the suggestion.[14]
> (Response number four is keyed to a point of view which the authors of the instrument from which this item is drawn [P. L. Dressel and L. B. Mayhew] call "democratic.")

The items cited above speak very clearly about the weaknesses of the cobwebby inferences spun out by even the most sophisticated test builders in the field. Firm knowledge about such weaknesses in statements of behavioral objectives must be built into the learning sequences of the teachers who are to participate in the lesson-planning processes of clinical supervision. But these teachers must also learn that most thematic state-

---

[12]Krathwohl, Bloom, and Masia, op. cit., p. 115.
[13]Ibid., pp. 146–47.
[14]Ibid., p. 170.

ments of objectives, in turn, are not directly useful as behavioral objectives, nor do they contain within themselves certain essences from which behavioral objectives may be directly distilled. The world of teaching-learning is not that simple.

How, then, does the teacher construct his own examined position about the relation of behavioral objectives to general objectives? How does he deal with this unstable, indeterminate universe of objectives in his own classroom? The beginning of an answer to this question is that he must first learn the strengths and weaknesses of both types of objectives. From this knowledge he may develop a sense of the productive tension existing between the two. He learns that blind adherence to thematic objectives leads him to the most precarious inferences about the relationship between his teachings and the students' learnings. Conversely, a blind addiction to behavioral objectives leads him to the wildest surmises about the relationships between his behavioral objectives and the thematic objectives.

This state of affairs creates two difficult tasks for the teacher: he must master the art of writing behavioral outcomes skillfully and at the same time learn that even with his best efforts he may fail to create logically watertight connections between general goals and the behavioral approximations of these goals. To cap the climax, he is expected to persevere in these trying tasks and at the same time to value their frequently dubious outcomes.

The supervisor's role in this entire process is not simply to help the teacher tolerate this ambiguous situation but to help him find in it a source of increased professional satisfaction as he becomes adept in reducing the ambiguities that emerge when he attempts to develop behavioral objectives that are logically related to thematic goals as insubstantial as "the cultivation of the intellect," "preparation for life in a democracy," or "reading, writing, and arithmetic."

In his attempt to establish his own position about writing objectives, the teacher may find it useful to examine the following tentative generalizations as points of departure:

1. The relationships between thematic and behavioral objectives are usually inferential rather than logically inevitable.
2. Although the teacher commits himself to the use of behavioral objectives for the analysis of his teaching, he remains conscious that their relationship to thematic goals is hypothetical. Such objectives should therefore be tested rather than "established." In figurative terms, the teacher should use behavioral objectives with humility, remaining open to question and ready to change. Alternative and rival hypotheses

(inferences) should be sought and tested. At any given moment, however, the teacher must act on the most scrupulously examined behavioral objectives he can formulate. Otherwise, he is forced to use his intuition about the relationship of students' learning behavior to thematic objectives—a widespread practice with a dismal history and very little future.

3. In order to guard against a preoccupation with one type of objective to the neglect of the other, the teacher should set out the major thematic goals of any large unit of work. The behavioral objectives may then be referenced to the thematic goals in the daily or weekly plans.

4. In the post-teaching conference the teacher and supervisor will examine the transcript of the classroom interaction for evidence upon which to assess (a) the degree of agreement between actual classroom behaviors and the behavioral objectives stated in the plan, and (b) the relationship between stated behavioral objectives and thematic goals.

As for the daily lesson plan itself, the teacher and supervisor will need to check the array of objectives for internal consistency. It is quite possible that two objectives, both consistent with the same thematic goal, may themselves be incompatible if the teacher seeks to achieve both at once. An example is drawn from the experience of a teacher offering combined English–social studies instruction. One of his objectives was to improve the informal, extemporaneous speech of students by helping them to cut down on the number of gross nonstandard constructions used in classroom discussions, for example, "Between him and I," "We could of did it," and "She don't care."

The teacher's second objective was to have the students become so deeply involved in a study of racial integration in the schools that they would (1) master the data and the logical arguments needed to analyze various views about the controversy, (2) use both data and logic in class discussions, and (3) become so deeply involved in the problem that they would express their thoughts vigorously and support them by data and logic during extended classroom discussions of the issue.

Plans were drawn up to achieve these objectives, and the students made excellent gains in eliminating especially barbaric nonstandard expressions from their classroom speech. The preparatory study of school integration also proceeded rapidly, the students showing serious concern about mastering the facts and the logic on both sides of the issue. At an appropriate moment the students launched their classroom discussion. Participation was general, and the students, deploying the facts and the arguments they had mastered, were soon engrossed in an excellent and spirited round-table discussion. At a high point in the exchange one student said: "If this was an integrated high school, a lot of us wouldn't of went to it this September." Upon this, the teacher interrupted the proceedings to remind the students that the auxiliary of the past participle is *have*, not *of*, and that the past participle of *go* is *gone*, not *went*. By the time the teacher had completed his well-meant interruption, designed to recall the students to their study of nonstandard English usage, the discussion had been reduced to ashes.

The collapse of a valuable discussion might have been avoided if the teacher and supervisor had recognized during the planning period that the correction of grammatical errors in speech may under some circumstances be shockingly incompatible with the processes of deeply felt communication about controversial issues. Similar incompatibilities between otherwise worthy objectives may occur when, for example, objectives of music appreciation are confounded with objectives of musical knowledge, or when objectives related to knowledge of science are confused with objectives related to psychomotor skills in setting up laboratory equipment.

In brief, the process of specifying the objectives of a lesson plan must also be a process of examining the teaching-learning logic implicit in the sequence, organization, and interaction of these objectives.

CHAPTER 10

Lesson Planning: Part II

Lesson Planning and the Students

The teacher's daily lesson plan constitutes the design of the sequence of organized experiences for students. The relation of the plan to what has preceded it and to what is to come must therefore be understood by the students. It follows that the plan often embodies strategies designed to help the learners relate one day's activities to preceding learning experiences. It also should provide the students with cues and perspectives about the goals of the work to be done. The teacher and supervisor should therefore include provisions for such perspectives in the lesson plan.

The bond to the relevant "past" of a lesson may be formed in many ways. The teacher may say, "Yesterday we talked about . . ." or "You will remember that . . . ." Sometimes the teacher's bridge to the past kicks it into oblivion and consigns the present lesson to the same place: "For some unknown reason the Board of Education has decided that we must learn the rules for agreement of subject and verb. Let's go on copying yesterday's list of rules and finish the whole job today." The teacher has many ways of connecting yesterday's work with today's. He may invite the students to summarize what they recall of the previous work or to discuss whatever learning problems they may be experiencing. At appropriate times students may be selected to recapitulate the objectives of previous lessons and indicate the likely or necessary next steps. A short diagnostic test or an oral check may serve the same purposes.

The daily plan is of course integral with long-term learning sequences extending over half a year, a year, and longer. Each longer plan should include carefully developed procedures designed to help the students gain a comprehensive overview of the major structures of what is to be learned. This principle of providing perspectives and connections applies also to major subunits and to daily plans.

The practice of providing students with longer perspectives on their work and of stressing and recapitulating the connections among subunits offers substantial advantages to the learners. The comprehensive overview of a course of study and its substructures permits some students to leap across longer spans of learning. Having gained competences a, b, and c, they may, by extra effort or insight, be enabled to move faster through competences *d* and *e* or to make an intuitive leap over them to *f*. The student who has a perspective on the learnings ahead may invent his own ways of achieving them faster. He has the opportunity to integrate learnings that might otherwise remain disconnected. He is able to plan his work better. Above all, the path is open for him to perform self-initiated work. He may use what he learns as a takeoff point for deeper explorations that attract him, or he may digress in productive, idiosyncratic ways from the curriculum he is able to perceive stretched out before him. Thomas Mann says something of this sort in a tribute to the teacher who knows when and how to leave some learning for students to traverse on their own:

> Is it believable that this is the most intensive, splendid, perhaps the very most productive way of learning: the anticipatory way, learning that spans wide stretches of ignorance? As a pedagogue I suppose I should not speak in its behalf; but I do know that it profits youth extraordinarily. And I believe that the stretches jumped over fill in of themselves in time.[1]

It is obvious that the teacher and supervisor engaged in the processes of planning must be as much concerned with the sequences and connections among learnings occurring *across* time as they are with the integrity of learnings in each separate unit of time. Mursell has termed this concept the *principle of sequence: "The sequence of meaningful learnings must itself be meaningful, if authentic results are to be obtained."*[2]

Developing the Written Plan

A lesson plan is shaped by its objectives, by the circumstances of the teaching-learning situation, and by the psychosocial logic of the strategies devised for it. The discussion that follows attempts to treat some of the problems the teacher and the supervisor might work out in the process of writing a plan. The treatment remains, however, illustrative rather than comprehensive.

It is obvious that the objectives of a lesson need to be consonant with each other; so, too, should the *objectives* and the *methods* of teaching. That is, *what* is taught and *how* it is taught should be in accord. Does a teacher teach young children not to scream during play period by shrieking at them not to scream? Does a science teacher try to teach his students

[1]Thomas Mann, *Doctor Faustus* (New York, Alfred A. Knopf, Inc. 1948), p. 57.
[2]James L. Mursell, *Successful Teaching: Its Psychological Principles* (New York: McGraw-Hill Book Co., Inc., 1954), p. 210. (Italics in original.)

to rely upon scientific data for their answers to scientific problems, and then reply to their question about the relationship between cancer and smoking by saying, "Believe me, cigarettes will kill you"? Or does he attempt to teach his students what it means to be a scientist by giving them problems to solve in the laboratory, each problem with its tidy little hypothesis and each with its neatly designed ritual, called an experiment, that takes "precisely 40 or 50 minutes of the class period," and each inevitably successful?[3]

The crucial need to examine the congruence between objectives and methods is never more clear than when one observes a teacher attempting to teach specific cognitive learnings by the *discussion method* so strongly recommended by her supervisor:

> *Teacher*:   How much is 7 times 8, Jim?
> *Jim*:   Fifty-four.
> *Teacher*:   Do you agree, Sarah?
> *Sarah*:   I think it's fifty-four too.
> *Teacher*:   (desperately) How many agree with Sarah and Jim?

Once the question about the relationship between objectives and methods is raised, the teacher can readily understand the need for harmony between them. The supervisor must then be prepared to help the teacher to enlarge his repertoire of methods and to help him understand that the process of making them compatible with objectives is part of the process of constructing the teaching-learning logic of a lesson or a unit.

The introductory activities built into a plan can make a valuable contribution to the students' intuitive grasp of the general nature of the problem they are about to study. These activities are usually intended to serve as motivating devices designed to arouse the curiosity of the student and to get him off to a good start. But they should aim higher than simple arousal of curiosity. Perhaps an illustration will make this point clear.

Two social studies teachers, working separately, each planned to initiate a unit on the role of Australia as a Western power in the South Pacific. The major objective was to have the students study Australia to discover whether it might achieve genuine nationhood in spite of the cultural and geographic anomalies faced by its populations: the aborigines and the English immigrants. One teacher introduced the unit by explaining its objectives, defining nationhood, and describing the geography of the island. The second engaged the students in a discussion about their idea of the meaning of *nationhood* and projected on the screen a set of

[3]Paul F. Brandwein, *Elements in a Strategy for Teaching Science in the Elementary School* (New York: Harcourt, Brace and World, Inc., 1962), p. 11.

colored slides showing the principal geographic features and populations of Australia, together with a picture of newly arrived immigrants. He also displayed to the students a message stick used by the Australian aborigines as a means of communication, an Eton cap, and one of the celebrated wide-brimmed Australian campaign hats. The teacher then developed three concepts around the three symbols. The message stick became a symbol for the culture of the aborigines, the Eton cap represented the English influence the immigrants brought with them, and the Australian campaign hat became a sign of the aspirations for nationhood.

The first teacher's presentation of the problem was principally introductory. The second teacher's presentation not only provided an introduction but also furnished the students with three economical symbolizations of the problem they were to study. The message stick, the Eton cap, and the campaign hat became the three layers of influence at work in Australia. As a result, the students not only understood the objective of the study they were embarking upon but also gained possession of symbolic representations of the major knowns to be applied in their search for the answer to whether Australia might become a Western nation in the Pacific.

The two examples above describe two approaches to the strategies for initiating a unit of work. In the first, the teacher settled for a statement of the objective, a definition of nationhood, and an unfocused verbal picture of Australia—designed to motivate the students to attack the problem set for them. In the second, the teacher engaged the students in a search for the meaning of nationhood and provided pictorial representations of the principal factors of the problem the geography of Australia and the disparate cultures of the population—as well as artifacts representing the three different strata in the population: aborigine, immigrant, and immigrant-becoming-Australian. From these initiating activities the problem emerged and was understood by the students via the concrete, verbal, and purely symbolic learning experiences they had had. The outcomes of this initiating strategy may be listed as follows: (1) the students became interested in a problem set by the teacher, (2) they quickly grasped the major factors in the problem, and (3) they were able to proceed fairly rapidly from the use of concrete symbols to the use of abstractions in their analysis of the problem.

These same objectives and others—perhaps more important—may be achieved by involving the students themselves in planning the instruction. If the students have a voice in deciding *what* to do, this activity in itself is assumed to serve the motivating and problem-structuring objectives of the teacher's initiating activities. These assumptions must, however, be carefully examined by the teacher and supervisor as they develop their initiating activities. Such care is necessary because so many strategies for motivating students and helping them to structure the problems they are to deal with fail on both counts. One of the principal causes of such failure is that the teacher tends to invent strategies related to his own frame of reference rather than to that of the students. What would motivate the teacher may arouse little response in the students. Since few teachers know how to obtain useful evaluative feedback from their students, the majority of teachers are unable to assess the effectiveness of the procedures they have developed to initiate a unit of study. It follows, then, that the supervisor can make a major contribution to the planning by first of all working with the teacher to devise initiating activities appropriate to the students' frame of reference. Once this is done, teacher and supervisor can secure information from the students about the success of their strategies. This feedback should be obtained in the course of the initiating activities and after they have ended. The students' reactions to the introduction of a unit or a lesson may be obtained by assessing their understanding of the problem, how they plan to attack it, and what blocks they anticipate in dealing with it. Such data, like that secured in the course of the unit itself, will often dictate changes in the plans.

In sum, the initiating activity for any teaching-learning unit should not be viewed as a one-shot "gimmick" and nothing more. On the contrary, it establishes continuities with what has been learned before, sets out the structure of the problem to be solved, and helps the student conceptualize his approach to it.

Contingency Planning   Other tasks emerge as the teacher and supervisor attempt to anticipate the development of the next steps in the teaching-learning process. Among these is the formulation of certain contingency plans. Perhaps the first contingency to be kept in mind is the possibility that the lesson may not go as planned. For example, the students may develop their own objectives within the frame of the plan. This means that the plan must incorporate procedures for ascertaining what these objectives may be, how they may be evaluated, and whether or not they merit inclusion in the plan. Additional questions must be dealt with as the teaching strategies take shape in the plan:

1. How may the teacher encourage the performance of self-initiated work by the students? What will be the appropriate response to the girl who wants to paint a picture of the curves generated by the ellipses the class is studying in mathematics?
2. Under what circumstances should the teacher change the plan already

in motion? When the remedial needs of the students demand it? How are these needs to be ascertained? What is to be done if the students become enthusiastic about some important idea that is not really relevant to the lesson? How much will the students' enthusiasm weigh against the dangers of digressing from the developmental logic of the plan?

3. What criteria are to guide judgments about whether unanticipated events should change the course of the plan? What happens when someone in the class studying the problems of water pollution comes in with a newspaper carrying headlines stating that the breakdown of a water treatment plant on Lake Erie is causing the discharge of millions of gallons of raw sewage into the lake?

4. What resources should be prepared for individualized instruction? for group instruction?

5. How is the available time to be allocated in the plan?

6. How will continuities be maintained from one session to another? How will transitions be made between different topics in the plan?

7. Is the teacher really competent to fulfill all the roles demanded of him by the plan? Are these roles congruent with his teaching capabilities?

8. What reinforcement strategies are appropriate to (a) the teacher's personal style of reinforcement? (b) different students? (c) the topics and problems to be treated? (d) the various kinds of behavior the students may exhibit under the circumstances likely to arise in the course of the class sessions?

9. As the plan develops, is it coherent or does it resolve itself into several thematically unrelated topics? For example, is the ten-minute "spelling lesson" related to the thirty-minute "literature lesson" and to the fifteen-minute "grammar lesson"? Is the work on heredity in animals related to the study of heredity in plants and to the phenomena of human heredity?

10. What will the students be doing at each stage in the development of the plan? What behavior will be appropriate for them in the laboratory session? in the discussion session? in the course of a lecture? when they are working alone? What behavior will give evidence that the students understand or do not understand? What behavior will tell the teacher that the students are achieving the objectives of their work? What verbal and nonverbal signals will the teacher look for to tell him how well the teaching-learning process is going?

11. When the unit or lesson is completed, what lines of continuing study will have been opened for the students? Has the study of the Australian aborigine made it more likely that the students will want to learn more about the status of the American Indian in the United States? about Israel and the displaced Arabs? about travel abroad? anthropology? In sum, a lesson plan must be designed not only for the attainment of objectives but for the vistas it may open up to the learners.

It may be apropos to pose a question rarely asked about planning: Should the students be given a plan? If the students have already been involved in preplanning a lesson, the question is not relevant. It applies, however, whenever planning is done without the participation of students.

Involving Students in the Planning Process   It is true that students are often given a topical outline and readings related to the work to be done, especially at the unit level. An outline, however, is not a plan. The question the supervisor and the teacher must ask is: Would it serve any useful purpose to give the students a modified version of the teacher's own operating plan? Topics considered inappropriate for the students would of course be omitted. The modified plan might offer the students new roles in their own education—roles suitable to their interests and abilities. For example, they might discuss the plan in class and gain an overview of some of the objectives and an idea about the teaching-learning sequences. Such a discussion would offer them an opportunity to understand the rationale for the plan and even to contribute to some aspects of it. Students with such understandings become a more integral part of the teaching-learning team than if they are simply the targets of an unknown plan. If they contribute, they are even more intimately a part of the team, and the plan is a little more theirs. Once it is theirs, even if only in part, they are more likely to be committed to its success.

There is no need to elaborate here on the rationale for students' involvement in planning. Our question is simply whether the practice of providing students with a plan and discussing some aspects of it in class might not serve some of the objectives of constructive participation in a shared task. To say that there are apparent pitfalls in such a procedure is simply to ask whether the outcomes might be worth the risks. At the very least, some teachers and supervisors might want to give the suggestion a trial in order to find out what the learning outcomes are when the student assumes some portion of the role of the teacher in planning. And it might be useful to explore whether the assumption of such roles affects the student's attitude toward the schoolwork he approaches in this way.

Preparation of the Teacher for the Conference

The lesson-planning session is not complete until the teacher has been prepared for the role he will take in the supervisory conference to follow. Many teachers anticipate that in the post-teaching conference they will assume a passive role or that, at most, they will be responsive to whatever processes the supervisor initiates. They usually expect to be told how well the lesson plan succeeded. The teacher's expectations about his role in the post-teaching session tend to structure his behavior during and after the actual teaching: he simply does his best to teach well, and then waits to see what the supervisor will have to say.

It is apparent that the enactment of such a role may have detrimental consequences for some teachers. They may fail to examine their own teaching critically, secure in the belief that the supervisor will perform that service. Or they may in all good faith suspend their own analytic and critical faculties and prepare to accept the suggestions of the supervisor and to act on them to the best of their ability. No matter what form the behavior of the teacher may take in these circumstances, the consequences of his assuming a role in which he abdicates professional analytical and critical functions are likely to be detrimental. Every profession requires its practitioners to maintain a careful and objective surveillance of their own professional performance. To relinquish this duty to another may reduce the teacher to the passive behavior of a "trainee," a role inconsistent with professional status.

If such consequences are to be avoided, the supervisor should prepare the teacher for his colleagual role in the conference. The teacher can be helped to understand that he himself must be conscious of his teaching performance, must be analytical in his approach to it. For example, at the end of a planning session the supervisor may ask the teacher if he would like him to gather data on certain aspects of the teacher's behavior in class: Is he reinforcing students' responses appropriately? How does he achieve the transitions from lecture to discussion to small-group work, etc.? With the teacher now focused on his own behavior in a more objective fashion, the supervisor may go on to help him prepare for his own solo analysis. This is part of his preparation for the analysis session in the post-teaching conference. Whatever strategies are used, the objective is to help the teacher to climb out of his own subjective universe as "the teacher" and to observe his behavior and the students' as systematically and objectively as possible. In this way the teacher-supervisor planning process contributes to the development of the teacher's professional perspective on his own work and his sense of responsibility for the improvement of that work.

Outcomes of the Planning Process

A discussion of the outcomes of the planning process is perforce also a discussion of the outcomes of all the supervisor's prior attempts to establish a professional working relationship with the teacher. For the sake of simplicity, however, we shall refer only to the "outcomes of the planning process," trusting that the reader will remember that this phrase is a kind of shorthand.

It seems fair to assume that the most important changes occurring in the early stages of the planning session might take place in the teacher's and supervisor's perceptions of each other as people and in the nature of the relationship they establish. This assumption is based on the probability that both will be trying to find answers to their questions about each other as people and people-in-a-relationship before they can attend to the professional agenda each carries within himself.

Let us assume that prior to the first planning session the teacher has certain expectations about how supervisors will behave. He envisions a superordinate supervisor and a subordinate teacher. The history, present practice, and bureaucratic structure of supervision in most schools conduce to this view. The *clinical* supervisor, however, comes to plan *with* the teacher. They work together on problems of instruction. They develop a rationale, strategies, and tactics for teaching. The plan is no longer the teacher's plan alone. It is in part the supervisor's. Both become involved in and responsible for the teacher's performance. This shared responsibility in planning makes it impossible for the supervisor to say at the end of a teaching session: "You failed to anticipate that the students would not be familiar with the vocabulary they had to deal with." The supervisor will have to say, "*We* failed to anticipate . . . ," etc. The change in pronoun—from "you" to "we"—arises from a genuine colleagual relationship. It is not an editorial "we," nor is it the euphemistic "we" used to sweeten the bitter verb "failed." It is a declaration of partnership with the teacher. And once the colleagueship has become part of a way of life in the classroom, then the supervisor and teacher stop using "you" and "we" as the subjects of their sentences; they begin to focus on behavior rather than person. In sum, if the new role taken by the supervisor evokes such new behavior and new perceptions in the teacher, the outcome may be the establishment of a new relationship that is in sharp contradistinction to the traditional relationship.

Beyond this, the cooperative planning may have other advantages. For example, the formulation of objectives in behavioral form provides criteria for the later analysis of the lesson. During this process and the rest of the session, the teacher is figuratively working his way through his plan. As a result, he has had the experience of a "safe" rehearsal for the next class. Such a rehearsal may make him more secure in the classroom, especially if he has had the chance to remedy a weakness in the plan or refine a strategy that appears to have promise. At the very least, the teacher involved in cooperative planning is learning to approach his work critically and professionally. In that process he may not only change his behavior but learn why he is making the change.

As for the supervisor, in the course of the planning session he has gained valuable insights about the teacher's approach to teaching and about the previous history of the instruction. If the cooperative planning is successful, the process has contributed to restructuring the relationship between himself and the teacher and has formed the basis for the next steps in the cycle of supervision.

But joint planning also has its dangers, which, if actually encountered, hold as much threat for clinical supervision as successful planning holds promise. For example, it is all too easy—and perhaps too human—for the supervisor to contribute too much to the plan itself, so that the lesson becomes his rather than the teacher's. If this situation occurs, it is likely to weaken or destroy the chances for a colleagual relationship to develop, and it may very well strengthen the hierarchical relationship—with the teacher acting as receiver at the low end of the hierarchy.

If the supervisor is too fluent in planning, too ingenious in devising the strategy and tactics of instruction, the teacher may become dependent upon him. In such a case the teacher learns to wait for the supervisor to inject quality into the teaching.

Or the teacher may develop a reluctance to depart from the plan while he is teaching it. His own choices may be constrained by the all-too-visible evidences of the supervisor's part in the plan.

If the lesson to which the supervisor has contributed so much goes badly, he may become a built-in scapegoat for the teacher. Such a failure, attributed by the teacher to the supervisor, can weaken or wreck the newly developing relationship: "Who wants to work with an incompetent supervisor?"

For the supervisor's part, his participation in and contribution to the lesson plan certainly pose a serious challenge to his objectivity in analyzing the lesson when it is taught. If the lesson fails, will the supervisor be able to resist the temptation to make the teacher the scapegoat?

If we acknowledge such perils, and others not touched upon, is cooperative planning worth the risks it entails? It seems to us that the answer must be "yes." To omit cooperative planning may certainly be as detrimental to clinical supervision as to include it. We do not really believe that in facing this question we have a choice between a benign and a dangerous course of action. As usual in the education of professionals, we face a choice of equally dangerous options.

CHAPTER 11

The Observation of Classroom Interaction

Systematic and Informal Classroom Observation

A Definition of Observation   The term *observation* as used here denotes those operations by which individuals make careful, systematic scrutiny of the events and interactions occurring during classroom instruction. The term also applies to the records made of these events and interactions.

Systematic observation of classroom interaction has arrived late in the history of education. What little there is of it has been done by researchers rather than by supervisors. And even the researchers appear reluctant to enter the classroom in order to collect their data about instruction. Rosenshine, in a review of instruments designed for the observation of classroom instruction, reports that "data obtained from direct observation of classroom interaction are seldom collected and analyzed."[1] In support of his statement he cites a finding by Katz, who noted only ten observational studies out of hundreds of research reports filed with the ERIC Clearinghouse on Early Childhood Education since 1960. Rosenshine also cites a survey of forty-six science projects evaluated in a review of science curriculums, in which only one report presented data on classroom interaction.[2]

C. K. Murray has provided a very brief overview of instruments designed to record classroom events systematically. He refers to Horn's 1914 investigation of the behavior of teachers and students during classroom recitation sessions. In an attempt to gather data about patterns of participation in class, Horn devised a seating chart on which he tabulated the teacher's requests for recitation and the students' response. Puckett and Wrightstone elaborated Horn's procedures in the 1920's and '30's. Murray also mentions later research efforts to carry out systematic analysis of verbal and nonverbal behavior in the classroom:

[1]Barak Rosenshine, "Evaluation of Classroom Instruction," *Review of Educational Research* 40, no. 2 (April 1970), p. 279. Copyright by the American Educational and Research Association, Washington, D.C.
[2]Ibid., pp. 279–80.

Verbal behavior:

Anderson and Brewer's work on dominative and socially integrative behavior of teachers (1939).

Lewin, Lippitt, and White's laboratory research on authoritarian, democratic, and laissez-faire styles of leadership (1943).

Withall's research in the measurement of the "socio-emotional climate" of classrooms (1949).

Wright and Proctor's classification system of verbal behavior in mathematics classrooms (1961).

Flanders' widely used systems of interaction analysis of teachers' behavior, together with some of the many variations developed upon the basis of his categories of teacher talk, student talk, and silence (1965).

Oliver and Shaver's observation system, described in their book entitled *Teaching Public Issues in High School* (1966), designed to study two teaching styles characterized by an emphasis on "descriptive information or value judgments."

The Michigan Social Issues Cognitive Category System for the analysis of classroom discourse on social issues (1969).

Nonverbal behavior:

Only two observation systems for nonverbal behavior are found in Murray's listing:

Galloway's nonverbal categories include items for "congruity-incongruity, responsive-unresponsive, positive-negative affectivity, attentive-inattentive, facilitating-unreceptive, and supportive-disapproval" (1968).

Kounin's categories deal with the teacher's "with-it-ness," "overlapping," "smoothness," and "momentum" (1970).[3]

The history of supervisors' practices in classroom observation is short and sad. The entire function of classroom observation was often inadequately conceptualized as evaluation of the progress made by a class or as the diagnosis of serious and possibly disabling weaknesses in the teacher's instruction. The techniques for recording observations were—to use a charitable euphemism—underdeveloped.

In any event, the teachers' general distaste for elaborate observations and their fear of the supervisor's "little black book" interacted with the supervisors' disinclination to become the target of the teachers' hostilities. The result was a lag in the application of modern recording techniques to the practices of supervision.

[3]C. Kenneth Murray, "The Systematic Observation Movement," *Journal of Research and Development in Education* 4, no. 1 (1970), pp. 3–9.

The resistance to systematic classroom observation probably reached a peak in the first half of this century, when some supervisors tried to apply the model of industrial time-and-motion studies to classroom supervision. After this fad for pseudoindustrial efficiency collapsed, the supervisors somewhat apologetically retreated again to practices of making only fragmentary and completely inadequate notes on their observations. Some supervisors have now begun to use interaction analysis systems and audio- and videotapes.

The Importance of Records   The consequences of a lack of adequate records of classroom instruction have proved to be deadly. Without a stable data-base for their work, supervisors and teachers find themselves mired down in fruitless arguments about what did and did not actually occur in the course of instruction. Under such circumstances they waste time and exhaust their energies in trying to arbitrate their often unreliable recollections about the complex events that have occurred in a teaching session. A supervisor can waste a professional lifetime trying to reconstruct a teacher's performance with him by talking about it from recollections. Such data cannot form the foundation of a program to improve instruction.

All this is *not* to say that the problem of observing and recording what happens in a classroom is simple or that it can be solved by the use of audiovisual recording techniques. Kounin summarizes some of the difficulties he and his colleagues encountered in their efforts to obtain complete and objective data on classroom teaching. The list of deficiencies they identified in their observations can serve as a primer for supervisors:

1. An inability to obtain complete records of what happened. In spite of many combinations of divided responsibilities in record taking and synchronization, we were never satisfied that our records contained *all* that happened. We may have recorded, with a reasonable degree of completeness and objectivity, the behavior of one child. But there is more than the behavior of one child to be considered in a study of a classroom. At a minimum, there are activities, props, other children, and a teacher. The behavior of the teacher was especially impossible to record with any satisfactory degree of completeness. Teachers simply have a large behavior volume—they do many different things, in many ways, and direct their behaviors at too many targets to allow an observer to record their behavior with completeness.

2. A tendency to selectively notice and record events that were impressive, contrasting, in line with some pre-existing hypotheses or concerns, intense, or otherwise perceptually outstanding to the point of the exclusion of other mundane and less noticeable events. Thus, if a child was tossing paper airplanes in the air at the back of the room, this event

would be in our notes. However, the notes would contain little description of what the other children were doing.

3. A propensity to include labels, evaluations, judgments, pseudo-inter-
pretations, summaries, and other types of nonobjective and nonde-
scriptive entries. To write that children are "attentive," "well-behaved,"
"disorderly," "apathetic," and the like, is not to provide descriptions of
actual behaviors. These are judgments made by an observer and are
not behavior facts.

4. An inclination to arrive at premature interpretations about the management of children's behavior. An example from the notes: "The teacher
was reading the story with high enthusiasm, changing voice inflection
and 'hamming it 'up' paused, leaned forward in her seat, and visually
swept all the children in the reading group, and said, 'The next part is
a *real* surprise. What do you think he'll find?' looked around suspense-
fully and then . . . all the children were waving their hands to be called
on, including five 'preemies' (children who raised their hands even
before the question was asked). . . ."[4]

When adequate objective data are not available in programs of clinical
supervision, the entire process of supervision becomes distorted. For
example, let us suppose that during the conference following a lesson the
supervisor remarks that some students were not paying attention. Or that
responses made by girls were rewarded, but not those of boys. In the
absence of verbatim records or videotapes, the teacher may simply not
believe that such events and exchanges did in fact occur. He may attribute
the statements to the supervisor's tendency to note negative rather than
positive incidents. Or he himself may remember selectively, often forget-
ting certain events and recalling others clearly. It is only human for both
teachers and supervisors to remember and forget selectively, to project
their expectations, fears, and hopes into classroom events, to magnify
some occurrences, to minimize others, and occasionally to be blind to
events that are outstandingly evident to another observer.

It seems likely, then, that stable data, accepted by both teacher and
supervisor as dependable, convincing, and relevant, will tend to minimize
differences about questions of fact. In addition, it will help to strengthen
the professional relationship between teacher and supervisor and expedite
their work together.

Recording Techniques   It may be useful at this point to examine the
advantages and disadvantages of various recording techniques, including
the use of electronic and mechanical devices, the manual collection of

[4]Jacob S. Kounin, "Observing and Delineating Techniques of Managing Behavior in
Classrooms," *Journal of Research and Development in Education* 4, no. 1 (1970),
pp. 63–64. Reprinted by permission.

data for the various interaction analysis systems, and the records made by the supervisor and other specialists within the classroom itself or from an observation room of some sort.

The electronic recorders—video and audio—have the virtue of accuracy, total recall, and a sort of mindless objectivity biased only by where they are placed in the room and where they are "aimed." Electronic records can be reviewed and referred to readily. When several recorders are used, each can be aimed at a different part of the classroom to secure parallel records of simultáneous events. As a rather simple example, when two videotape recorders are used, one may be focused on the teacher and the other on the students. These separate records may be synchronized and played back at the same time, using a split-screen technique. The utility of such data for the analysis of teacher-pupil and pupil-pupil interaction is readily apparent.

However, the very virtues of electronic recording devices may create problems for the teacher and supervisor who set out to analyze the records produced by them. The comprehensiveness and detail found in an audio-tape, for example, means that making a typed transcription is a time-consuming and expensive task. The nonselectivity of both video and audio records increases the amount of data available but also requires more time for review and analysis—a welcome and salutary problem in supervision, but a problem nonetheless. It also remains to be noted that the sound recorders have certain shortcomings. One microphone seldom picks up all the verbal interaction in a classroom, nor can it "sort out" the speech of several individuals talking at once. Multiple microphones become expensive and create multiple records that must each be transcribed and analyzed separately—also at some expense in time and money. Neverthe-less, electronic recorders provide data that so far surpass the records of human observers in certain respects that they must be utilized in clinical supervision.

Competent observers who take shorthand are sometimes especially useful as recorders of classroom data. The advantage of an observer over the tape recorder is that the former can be specially trained to record selectively, to shift his attention to a prespecified speaker when several individuals are speaking at the same time, and to record only certain types of events.

If data are to be obtained from a pencil-and-paper instrument designed for one of the interaction analysis systems, there can be no substitute for the specially trained observer-analyst. He himself will usually collect the information he needs. He also frequently tabulates, analyzes, and inter-prets it. Untrained personnel, with the best of equipment and intentions, should not play with interaction analysis systems. The chances of gross and possibly destructive errors in supervision are too great to risk.

The well-trained supervisor is for some purposes the best observer available, simply because he knows what kinds of data will be most useful in his work with the teacher and because he is likely to be sensitive to those classroom events integrally related to the plans he and the teacher have formulated. To be sure, his fallibilities remain great, that is to say, "human." Nevertheless, his professional training and his work with and knowledge about the teacher often make him at least *one* of the indispensable recorders of the teaching-learning process.

It should by now be fairly clear that optimal recordings of classroom interaction are probably best obtained by appropriate combinations of electronic recording equipment and specially trained human observers strategically positioned. For the collection of classroom data the electronic recorder has the advantages of indefatigability, accuracy, completeness, and objectivity. The trained human observer, on the other hand, can be aware of many kinds of events simultaneously and can switch the focus of his observation quickly in response to changing circumstances. Certainly, the trained clinical supervisor makes the video camera and microphone seem blind and deaf by his sensitivity to shades of meaning and his shifts of attention in response to them. The strengths of the trained observer become evident when he learns to focus and refocus his observation in response to various events occurring in the classroom. The supervisor's ability to focus rapidly and to sample several verbal and nonverbal exchanges in radarlike sweeps obviously outclasses both fixed cameras and those manned by cameramen.

Perhaps the best answer to the man versus camera-and-microphone question is that each can perform certain important functions in observation far better than the other. Both are necessary if we are to capture the important events of the classroom, and each is incomplete without the other.

The Effects of the Observer on the Classroom

The classroom has usually become a fairly well-established social system by the time the supervisor enters it. Modes of conduct, values, and relationships have been developed. The supervisor, on entering this social system, has to ask himself what effects his actions are likely to have upon it.

Some supervisors assume that the effect of their presence is negligible:

"They soon get used to my being there," or "It's expected," or "After I'm there for fifteen minutes they forget all about me." Such assumptions are probably incorrect. We know that the presence of an observer does have consequences, and a social system is changed by the introduction of observers or instruments of observation. It therefore seems wise for the supervisor to recognize these possibilities and to develop techniques for minimizing the effects of his presence and taking them into account in his analysis of classroom behavior.

As for the effects of the supervisor's presence upon the teacher, perhaps the safest plan is to assume that such effects will occur and to try to identify them and take them into account. Some of the factors influencing teachers' reactions to observation have been discussed previously. That is, some teachers may experience anxiety, uneasiness, or resentment at the entrance of a supervisor into their classrooms. Others may respond with pleasure and a heightened sense of challenge. Still others may experience a kind of productive stimulation deriving from implicit communication with a colleague and the gratifying opportunity to teach in the presence of a knowledgeable professional whose comments would be helpful and whose praise would be a genuine reward.

To put this another way, the teacher may be constrained or liberated when a supervisor is in class. Few remain unaffected. For example, a teacher may achieve a satisfying relationship with his students, characterized by free exchanges in which he and they reveal to each other certain otherwise concealed aspects of themselves—for example, their emotional responses to poetry or their dilemmas about deeply held but conflicting values. The presence of an outsider might make profound changes in such delicate relationships—creating self-consciousness and constraints in the classroom.[5]

In view of such complexities, how may the supervisor deal with the various reactions elicited by his presence in a classroom? It seems likely that his best strategy will be to assess each situation individually, rather than to follow preconceived routines. He can discuss the problem openly with each teacher, attempting to anticipate and to plan his responses to the probable reactions of both the teacher and the students. In some instances it may be helpful for the teacher to discuss with his students the purposes and classroom behavior of the supervisor, seeking to establish him as a neutral, nonthreatening, helpful professional.

If it appears that the presence of the supervisor is likely to have little

[5]Adapted from a research memorandum by Dan C. Lortie, "The Teacher as Craftsman," n.d.

effect or to have positive advantages for students and teacher, then the supervisor may proceed with classroom observation. Even under such apparently favorable circumstances, however, he needs to be constantly alert to the possibility that changes and stresses may develop in the small society that is the classroom. Such alterations arise from a multiplicity of causes—the topics under consideration, problems of interpersonal relations, or circumstances outside the classroom entirely. The content being taught may be explosive—*Othello* and racism, labor-management controversies, or other personal and societal sore spots. Or the relationships within the classroom may change because of disturbing events outside its walls. In any case, even if the supervisor enters the classroom and begins his observations under the best auspices, he may commit serious blunders if he assumes that such favorable situations perpetuate themselves. If, then, the supervisor and teacher do note significant changes in the life of a classroom, they must reconsider and possibly reorganize their supervisory procedures.

It may be wiser for the supervisor to stay out of the classroom entirely at certain times. If he does, he may utilize various techniques as substitutes for personal observation. Such procedures range from the use of multiple, noiseless, remote-control television cameras and recorders to the use of audiotape equipment and one-way observation windows.

If the supervisor is to function as an observer in the classroom, he might be well advised to behave in such a fashion as to cause the students and teacher to perceive him as a *noninteracting* entity in the classroom society. This might mean, for example, that he would seek to limit interaction with students and teacher in class without charging the relationships either positively or negatively. The supervisor might keep *communicative* eye contact at a minimum. He would try to enter the classroom, observe, and leave—all with the least possible communication. Such behavior is the antithesis of initiating conversations with students or encouraging exchanges that they might initiate. In sum, the trained observer is neither friendly nor aloof, neither cold nor warm, but neutral and nonparticipatory in terms of both verbal and nonverbal behavior.

If the teacher and supervisor become convinced that the supervisor's role in the classroom should change, they need to restructure their relationship carefully and communicate it and its implications to the students. Some changes in the supervisor's role may have to be planned *with* the students. The roles the supervisor could assume in the classroom might range from those of colleague-teacher, resource person, or demonstration teacher to occasional participant in classroom work. In some instances the assumption of such roles could supplement or supplant the role of clinical supervisor. It must be borne in mind, however, that they may not be congruent with the role of the supervisor as developed in these pages. A discussion of the probable assets and liabilities of such procedures lies outside our province here. We can only recommend that if attempted at all, they be introduced only after careful thought has been given to the rationale, procedures, and possible consequences of such changes.

The Data of Nonverbal and Affective Behavior

Up to this point we have barely mentioned two universes of data that are central to supervisory practice but that have been fairly consistently ignored in the literature of supervision. The first is the data of nonverbal or kinesthetic communication—communication by body movement. The second is the data about the internal behavior of teachers and students, their mental and affective behavior before, during, and after instruction. Both types of data are required for an understanding of classroom interaction.

It appears that nonverbal communication may at times elaborate or emphasize verbal communication and may at other times contradict it. Torrance corroborates the latter phenomenon in his report of research on the perceptions of students about their teachers' expressed attitudes and "real" attitudes: "From the results reported herein, it would seem that even though teachers say the 'right words' and pupils say that they perceive their teachers as having favorable attitudes, the teacher's 'real attitude' is likely to 'show through' and to affect behavior and emotional reactions."[6]

The neglect of nonverbal behavior in education is general. It extends even to the exclusion of nonverbal (psychomotor) behavior in the Bloom and Krathwohl taxonomies. The basis for this omission is expressed in the *Taxonomy of Educational Objectives* as follows: "Although we recognize the existence of this [psychomotor] domain, we find so little done about it in secondary schools or colleges, that we do not believe the development of a classification of these objectives would be very useful at present."[7] Some first steps are being taken, however, to repair the neglect of nonverbal behavior and objectives.[8]

[6]E. Paul Torrance, "Teacher Attitude and Pupil Perception," *Journal of Teacher Education* 11, no. 1 (1960), p. 101.
[7]Benjamin S. Bloom, ed., *Taxonomy of Educational Objectives: The Classification of Educational Goals,* Handbook I: Cognitive Domain (New York: David McKay Co., Inc., 1956), pp. 7–8.
[8]See Charles M. Galloway, "Teacher Nonverbal Communication," *Educational Lead-*

However underdeveloped the state of speculation, research, and practice may be in the systematic attention paid to nonverbal behavior, the supervisor should be aware of it. First of all, it comprises an important sector of educational objectives: gross and fine motor skills, the education of the hand and body, sensitivity to cues that are heard, seen, felt, tasted, or smelled, and the formulation of dispositions to act or to organize for action.[9] Second, such behavior obviously communicates messages the supervisor cannot afford to ignore. A teacher's position or movement may communicate to the students that he *is with them* (joins a group), *is one of them* (does what the group is doing), *is apart from them* (stands alone facing the group). Some gestures and facial expressions have meanings as unambiguous (or as ambiguous) as words. The supervisor cannot overlook a domain of behavior as important as the nonverbal simply because it is only rudimentarily mapped out. He must observe and record such behavior, even if only with primitive skills and techniques. Can a supervisor ignore the students' secure and confident approach to a teacher? Or their tentative, wary approach? Or their physical avoidance of him when they need help, want company, or want to share experiences, emotions? Data about such behavior, if unnoticed or unrecorded, may seriously skew the meanings of an observation record.

The principal scruples and rigors governing the teacher's and the supervisor's behavior in observing, recording, analyzing, and interpreting nonverbal activity are parallel with those to be observed for verbal behavior: the observer must be alert to nonverbal messages, he must record them in the best notations available to him, he must analyze these data with care, interpret them to the best of his trained ability, use them, and act upon them if he, the teacher, and other qualified analysts are in fair agreement about their significance.

The teacher and supervisor must scrupulously avoid drawing unwarranted conclusions about nonverbal behavior, precisely as they must in dealing with verbal behavior. In this connection it is worth noting that the dangers awaiting the supervisor if he ignores nonverbal behavior also await him if he ignores all but a few categories of the teacher's and students' verbal behavior.

The second important body of data often disregarded by teachers and supervisors is that which concerns the affective behavior of students and

ership 24, no. 1 (1966), pp. 55–63; idem, "An Exploratory Study of Observational Procedures for Determining Teacher Nonverbal Communication" (Ed.D. diss., Univ. of Florida, 1962); and Elizabeth Jane Simpson, "The Classification of Educational Objectives, Psychomotor Domain," *Illinois Teacher of Home Economics* 10, no. 4 (1966–67), pp. 111–44.
[9]Simpson, op. cit., pp. 111–14.

teachers during instruction. It is worth reiterating that such omissions—especially with respect to data on students' affective responses to the outcomes of learning—may represent a neglect great enough to render much of the supervisor's work with a teacher ineffective.

The neglect of affective behavior probably results in part from the current popularity of operationalism and the emphasis on behavior directly apprehended by the senses. The consequent mistrust of the data of internal behavior only indirectly available to the observer is probably caused in part by the fairly common belief that objective data is "hard" evidence and subjective data "soft." The arguments pro and con will not be reviewed here.[10] It seems to us that supervisors must attempt to synthesize both kinds of data because we know intuitively and empirically that we must deal with indicants of internal behavior plus objectively observable behavior, in the same sense that physicians must still make diagnoses and prescribe treatment based on the patient's reports about symptoms and on directly observable evidence about the patient's health. Although feedback about the affective behavior of students and teachers is rarely sought, even by researchers of classroom behavior, it is nevertheless not too difficult to secure. Bloom, for example, has studied the mental behavior of students during class sessions.[11] Data on the emotional responses of students to their instruction may be gathered through case studies, questionnaires, inventories, tests, etc. Krathwohl, Bloom, and Masia, for example, provide examples of techniques for obtaining data about a student's willingness to receive stimuli and pay attention, his satisfaction in responding, and his acceptance of values.[12] These and other methods of collecting data about the affective responses of students in the classroom should be utilized if the supervisor is competent to do so. Some supervisor-researchers have utilized feedback obtained directly from students while a class is in session. Belanger developed a device for these purposes by providing each student in a science class with a push button that he was to press when he did not understand what was being taught. The pupils' "don't understand" responses were visible on a panel of lights on the teacher's desk. When the panel was dark, it was assumed

[10]In this connection an article by Herbert Feigl may be of interest: "The Scientific Outlook: Naturalism and Humanism," in *Readings in the Philosophy of Science*, ed. Herbert Feigl and May Brodbeck (New York: Appleton-Century-Crofts, Inc., 1953), pp. 8–18.
[11]Benjamin S. Bloom, "The Thought Processes of Students in Discussion," in *Accent on Teaching*, ed. Sidney J. French (New York: Harper and Bros., 1954), pp. 23–46.
[12]David R. Krathwohl, Benjamin S. Bloom, and Bertram B. Masia, eds., *Taxonomy of Educational Objectives: The Classification of Educational Goals*, Handbook II: Affective Domain (New York: David McKay Co., Inc., 1956), pp. 107–17, 130–38, 140–45.

that all the students understood what the teacher was saying and doing. The pupils' switching responses were noted on a chart at fixed time intervals. Such data may be keyed into the supervisor's records of the students' and teacher's behavior and other events if the supervisor simply registers the precise time of each of his notations. The data thus obtained might enable the supervisor (and on appropriate occasions, the teacher) to relate the teacher's behavior, the students' behavior, and classroom incidents (the entrance of a messenger into the room, e.g.) to the students' "I don't understand" behavior.[13] Belanger's techniques are admittedly cumbersome, but they could be refined, perhaps by use of (wireless) remote-control apparatus for the switching response. Used carefully, data of the sort collected by Belanger and others in the course of actual instruction may make a significant contribution to the data-base used in clinical supervision. Other techniques of securing feedback about the students' recollections of their responses during instruction are available in the work of Seager; Gage, Runkel, and Chatterjee; and Remmers.[14]

Strategies of Observation

The supervisor and teacher are called on to observe (1) the behavior of the teacher, (2) the behavior of the students, and (3) other events occurring in class. It is with these components that they will ultimately develop their hypotheses about the teacher's instruction and construct the supervisory program for the teacher. What kinds of things do the teacher and supervisor look for in the teacher's behavior? One answer to this question is that the volume and variety of the teacher's behavior are so great as to defy enumeration or categorization. The supervisor and the teacher need to accept and operate within two constraints: (1) they cannot record everything that happens in the course of a teaching-learning session, and (2) they lack the competence to analyze and order the great masses of complex information they *could* collect.

Both limitations, therefore, make it imperative that teacher and supervisor *select* the kinds and amount of information they are to record.

[13]Maurice Belanger, "An Exploration of the Use of Feedback in Supervision," (Ed.D. diss., School of Education, Harvard University, 1962).
[14]G. Bradley Seager, "Development of a Diagnostic Instrument of Supervision" (Ed.D. diss., School of Education, Harvard University, 1965); N. L. Gage, Philip J. Runkel, and B. B. Chatterjee, "Equilibrium Theory and Behavior Change: An Experiment in Feedback from Pupils to Teachers," mimeographed (Urbana, Ill.: University of Illinois, Bureau of Educational Research, College of Education, 1960); and H. H. Remmers, "Rating Methods in Research on Teaching," in *Handbook of Research on Teaching*, ed. N. L. Gage (Chicago: Rand McNally and Co., 1963), pp. 329–78.

The illustrations and categories of observation provided in this volume are only intimations of the vast complexity of the teacher's classroom behavior. There is no definitive inventory of it, only the partial lists that each supervisor must carefully cultivate for himself. This is simply another way of saying that the realm of supervision is at present the realm of the educated, trained supervisor who operates from disciplined intuition in the most difficult and ambiguous reaches of his vocation.

If anything more is needed to complicate this picture, it is the corresponding complexity of the students' behavior. In the classroom, where these two sets of complexities interact, we may observe diverse and puzzling consequences in the students' learning. The teacher's classroom behavior may be related to excellent learning for one child and to catastrophe for another. A fine teaching session with one class may misfire for another. Such phenomena are not too unusual. They have been thrown into high relief these days as some excellent teachers try for the first time to instruct students from socioeconomic and ethnic groups different from their own.

What should be observed in the students' behavior? The teacher and the supervisor must first ascertain what the students feel and know before the instruction begins, what their "entering behavior" is; that is, what the students bring to class. Since such extensive knowledge is—like complete knowledge about the teacher—unattainable, the supervisor and teacher must make maximum use of information available in the students' school records and follow up likely hunches about useful information they may secure in the course of instruction.

The second type of information needed by teacher and supervisor concerns the extent to which the teacher's objectives are achieved. This information may be derived from various kinds of tests, judgments, and techniques of assessment.

The third type of information to be collected relates to process learnings and unanticipated learnings, discussed in a previous chapter.

Phases of Observation

Decisions about what to record are determined by the objectives and needs that develop at various times in the supervisory program. In the first stages of the program, for example, the supervisor often needs to make exploratory observations in which he scans many aspects of the classroom interaction and attempts to become familiar with the general characteristics of the teacher's instruction. In a sense, the supervisor observes in order to learn how the teacher and the students relate to each other as they work together in class. This panoramic view provides important information about the interpersonal relationships that have developed in class, about the students' responses to their learning tasks and to the teacher, and about the teacher's general style of teaching.

The comprehensive overview, carefully checked and rechecked for accuracy, constitutes a useful benchmark and a framework for the planning, development, and evaluation of the supervisory program.

In addition, the teacher may have expressed an interest in securing feedback about problems of special interest to him: patterns of student-to-student interaction, information about his own communication patterns or about the students' responses to certain problems, etc. The supervisor, therefore, may be called on to arrange for the collection of data to serve his own aims and those of the teacher. This task is not too difficult if the supervisor has adequate human and instrumental resources available in the supervisory program. It is probably the analysis of the data and its application in the supervisory program for the teacher that will create the most severe demands on the supervisor. He therefore needs to be careful not to overload himself with commitments to collect and analyze data, especially early in the supervisory program.

As the supervisor and teacher develop the data-base for their work together, they begin to focus more and more sharply on information integral to the teacher's emerging needs in the supervisory program. Let us suppose that the teacher demonstrates well-developed competences in getting students to express their opinions about controversial social issues, but is unaware that occasionally he communicates his own views about an issue by the manner in which he poses his questions, thereby influencing some of the students' replies. He may do this with a double-barreled question like "Why did the Pentagon propose the incursion into Laos, and who at the Pentagon dredged up the idea?" Once the teacher understands that the negative loading on the word *dredge* may tend to elicit a negatively loaded reply from the students, then he and the supervisor may work out a program to eliminate such questions from his repertoire. In the course of these efforts teacher and supervisor would gather data concerning changes in the teacher's question-asking behavior when dealing with controversial issues. They might then (1) tabulate the frequency with which he uses loaded questions and (2) investigate the relationship of loaded and unloaded questions to students' responses. The data to be gathered would then be the teacher's questions and the students' responses. These data would be analyzed for changes in the patterns of the teacher's question-asking behavior and changes in the students' responses.

Sometimes a record of the teacher's nonverbal behavior is required. Such a circumstance might arise if the teacher were trying to increase the student-to-student interaction in discussion and to decrease the number of teacher-student-teacher-student exchanges. The technique devised by the teacher and supervisor for accomplishing these goals might require the teacher first of all to (1) rearrange the students' desks in a circle, (2) ask a question and, while a student is replying, take a seat among the students themselves, (3) remain quiet when the student finishes his response, and (4) indicate by eye contact, facial expression, and the posture of his body that he expects other students to respond. The feedback required by the teacher to assess the outcomes of his new behavior would comprise data on the frequency and sequences of the teacher-to-student and student-to-student statements made during the discussion. The coding would indicate the initiator of a statement, the *responder,* and the sequences of responses. It would then be possible to represent the sequences of (1) teacher-initiated statements, (2) students' responses, (3) *student-initiated statements,* and (4) *teacher's responses.*[15] The data on the teacher's nonverbal behavior would be most appropriately recorded by a videotape recorder or a moving-picture camera, although verbal descriptions might serve in their absence.

With such data in hand the teacher and supervisor could then assess the outcomes of their plan.

The Targets of Observation

Supervisors tend to observe the teacher too much and the students too little. To observe only the teacher tends to create in the observer an unconscious assumption that the teacher's behavior totally determines the behavior and learning of his students. But we know that some students and some classes learn well without much reference to the teacher's competence. Other students and classes learn poorly—equally without much reference to the teacher. It follows from this conception of teaching and learning that the supervisor attempting to gather data that will help him to understand both the teaching and learning processes needs to

[15]Chapter 5 of Ned A. Flanders' *Analyzing Teaching Behavior* (Reading, Mass.: Addison-Wesley Publishing Co., Inc., 1970) is extremely helpful with such problems of coding and analysis.

observe the in-class behavior of teachers *and* students. If he fails to do so, he risks finding himself in a dilemma in which apparently excellent teaching is later followed by wretched learning, or *vice versa*.

The data collected during classroom observation must be detailed enough to permit systematic analysis. It must enable the supervisor to develop hunches and hypotheses about partial causes and partial effects. A statement in the form of "The teaching was (excellent, adequate, or poor)" is incomplete. Furthermore, if said to a teacher, such a sentence (1) simply provides undifferentiated reinforcement for *all* of the teacher's behavior, (2) fails to specify and differentiate between various *kinds, qualities*, and *time segments* of teaching, and (3) fails to relate the teacher's behavior to the students' learning—the latter *also* demanding specification and differentiation rather than treatment as a homogeneous set of events. The supervisor generally needs to deal with statements of the following order: "Such and such specific teaching behavior at such and such times in the teaching session were accompanied by such and such behavior exhibited by such and such students." For example, the supervisor might say, "The use of the brief simulation exercise markedly increased the participation of all the students, and they began to make fewer errors in the set of problems they were working on halfway through the lesson." In effect, both teacher and supervisor need to engage in analysis and interpretation of classroom events, and the data needed to support analysis and interpretation must record the behavior of teacher and students as well as related classroom events.

We are not proposing that the supervisory dialogue between the teacher and supervisor should consist of complete and overstuffed sentences like the examples above. But we are saying that relevant data and carefully qualified analysis will form the foundation of their interaction and the beginning of wisdom—a down payment on sane and rational supervision.

As set out here, the tasks of observation and data gathering appear to be forbiddingly difficult, as indeed they are if carried out to the last letter of these recommendations. The recommendations, however, should be viewed as suggestions for careful professional practice rather than as a set of standard procedures. In addition, it is apparent that not everything is or should be done at once, in a great burst of effort during the first series of observations. On the contrary, the data accumulates gradually and the working hypotheses emerge slowly as the supervisor deepens his knowledge of the teacher. For his part, the teacher learns more about his own classroom behavior *and* begins to know the supervisor better.

CHAPTER 12

Applications of Interaction Analysis Systems in Clinical Supervision

Relating Teacher Behavior to Student Learning

One of the principal obstacles to the development of clinical supervision is the forbidding difficulties the supervisor faces when he attempts to relate the behavior of teachers to the learning of students. The forces that influence learning in school comprise all the variables affecting the behavior of human beings, ranging from factors like their inherited and acquired characteristics, the nature of their society, and the characteristics of their teachers to whether a student's eyeglasses have been ground to the proper prescription. The supervisor is therefore faced with a welter of complexities when he attempts to analyze the teacher's behavior and relate it to students' learning in order to develop an effective supervisory program. The difficulties of these tasks are multiplied by the sparseness of dependable knowledge about the consequences of teaching-learning processes in the classroom. As a result, the supervisor finds he must constantly search for some firm footing of reliable knowledge as he makes his way through the terrain of guesses, hunches, and dimly perceived correlations between teaching and learning. It is no wonder, then, that supervisors are increasingly eager to utilize the relatively firm data and sophisticated analytic techniques available to them in some of the well-developed systems of interaction analysis. As Rosenshine suggests, "Category systems have become very popular in descriptive educational research and in teacher training because they offer greater low inference specificity and because an 'objective' *count* of a teacher's encouraging statements to students appears easier for a teacher to accept than a 'subjective' *rating* of his warmth."[1]

Characteristics of Interaction Analysis Systems

What are some of the salient characteristics of interaction analysis systems? Simon and Boyer describe them as

[1]Barak Rosenshine, "Evaluation of Classroom Instruction," *Review of Educational Research* 40, no. 2 (1970), p. 282. Reprinted by permission.

"shorthand" methods for collecting observable objective data about the way people talk and act. They make possible a relatively simple record of what is happening but they do not record what is being said. . . . They differ from each other in a variety of ways, but all of them code some aspect of behavior. These systems are made up of sets of categories of behaviors. . . . Most of these systems are "content free," that is, they can be used with any subject matter or grade level. They are concerned with how teaching and learning takes place. . . . All of these systems were originally designed for research purposes but they have since found a way into teacher training and supervision.[2]

Flanders seeks to define both the system and the *mode of analysis* in interaction analysis systems:

Classroom interaction analysis refers not to any system, but to many systems for coding spontaneous verbal communication, arranging the data into a useful display, and then analyzing the results in order to study patterns of teaching and learning. Each system is essentially a process of encoding and decoding, i.e., categories for classifying statements are established, a code symbol is assigned to each category, and a trained observer records data by jotting down code symbols. Decoding is the reverse process: a trained analyst interprets the display of coded data in order to make appropriate statements about the original events which were coded, even though he may not have been present when the data were collected. A particular system for interaction analysis will usually include (a) a set of categories, each defined clearly, (b) a procedure for observation and a set of ground rules which governs the coding process, (c) steps for tabulating the data in order to arrange a display which aids in describing the original events, and (d) suggestions which can be followed in some of the more common applications.[3]

McAvoy provides a useful clarification when he suggests that the variables coded in classroom observation "can be defined in one of three categories: *presage, process,* and *product.*" The presage variables relate to the characteristics that the teacher or student brings to the classroom. Process variables refer to the classroom behavior of teachers and students. Product variables are measures of the outcomes of the teacher-student interaction, usually construed as changes in students' behaviors.[4]

---

[2]Anita Simon and E. Gil Boyer, *Mirrors for Behavior: Anthology of Classroom Observation Instruments,* vol. 1 (Philadelphia, Pa.: Research for Better Schools, Inc., and Center for the Study of Teaching, Temple University, 1967), p. 1.
[3]Ned A. Flanders, *Analyzing Teaching Behavior,* 1970, pp. 28–29, Addison-Wesley, Reading, Mass. Reprinted by permission.
[4]Rogers McAvoy, "Measurable Outcome with Systematic Observation," *Journal of Research and Development in Education* 4, no. 1 (1970), pp. 10–11.

The Flanders System of Interaction Analysis

In his Introduction to *Interaction Analysis,* edited by Amidon and Hough, Flanders touches upon some of his early insights and conclusions about the nature of the events recorded in interaction analysis systems. He writes:

> It was . . . during July of 1957, that I first studied a ten-by-ten interaction analysis matrix. It was tabulated from some code numbers collected a few days earlier in an elementary classroom. The purpose of tabulating a matrix was to estimate the amount of interdependence between successively coded statements. . . . The short observation and tabulated matrix had already served its purpose, which was to prove that the interdependence did exist between coded events. . . . The notion that the numbers in certain rows and cells could explain a teacher's influence pattern became apparent only gradually. . . . These insights did not burst into full bloom, suddenly; they sort of crept into the matrix, one at a time.[5]

The conclusions set out at that time were reaffirmed and amplified in Flanders's *Analyzing Teaching Behavior* in 1970:

> Teaching behavior, by its very nature, exists in a context of social interaction. The act of teaching leads to reciprocal contacts between the teacher and the pupils, and the interchange itself is called teaching. Techniques for analyzing classroom interaction are based on the notion that these reciprocal contacts can be perceived as a series of events which occur one after another. Each event occupies a small segment of time, and the chain of events can be spaced along a time dimension. It is clear that the event of the moment influences what is to follow and, in turn, was influenced by what preceded.[6]

This conceptualization of teaching as a chain of related classroom events, coupled with the acknowledged inability of the observer to record everything, leads Flanders to the problem of *"how to select a set of concepts to describe what goes on in the classroom."*[7] His answer to this question has implications for the use of interaction analysis in supervision. Flanders starts by noting that "concepts for thinking depend on our purpose and our predispositions to think in certain ways. . . ." He then goes on to ask, "What purposes guide the analysis of classroom interaction?" He suggests that these purposes are, first, to help "a teacher

---

[5]Ned A. Flanders, Introduction, to *Interaction Analysis: Theory, Application, and Research,* ed. Edmund J. Amidon and John B. Hough (Reading, Mass.: Addison-Wesley Publishing Co., Inc., 1967), p. vii.
[6]Flanders, *Analyzing Teaching Behavior,* p. 1.
[7]Ibid., 2. (Italics in original.)

develop and control his behavior," and second, "to investigate relationships between classroom interaction and teaching acts so as to explain some of the variability in the chain of events."[8] He then turns his attention to a question that is central to clinical supervision: Will helping a teacher develop and control his teaching behavior make him a better teacher? Flanders' answer to his own question is worth quoting:

> So far, at least, there has been no mention of good and bad teaching, making ratings of teaching performance, or suggesting a particular way to teach. We can anticipate, however, that neutrality with regard to teaching behavior is not likely to last. *This is a book about effective teaching. Preferences about teaching behavior should arise rapidly as our understanding of its consequences improves.*[9]

It is important for clinical supervisors to note Flanders' attempt to deal with a question that we venture to express as follows: If a teacher improves his scores in the categories of the Flanders interaction analysis system, will his students' learning improve significantly? Flanders' answer seems to balance precariously between "Yes, it will" and "I hope it will." For example, he writes that his book is about "effective teaching," that the investigation of teaching by way of interaction analysis techniques will provide us with certain useful understandings about the chain of events he selects to investigate, and that our understanding of the consequences of teaching will improve our ability to select important behavior to observe. So far, he has not made the claim that the improvement of a teacher's performance in the categories of the Flanders interaction analysis system will improve his students' learning—either clinically or statistically. Nevertheless, he does make a very strong claim for the importance, the centrality, of his categories to good teaching:

> First, the heart of the matter lies in what the teacher does that influences the educational development of his pupils. Second, of all teacher activities, the most salient are the direct person-to-person contacts and the more indirect teacher-to-class contacts. Third, we start by accounting for events that do, in fact, occur, not what the teacher thinks is happening or what teachers "ought" to be doing. Fourth, the most important concepts are those which are descriptive of the interactive contacts. Other concepts in a field of education simply become less important; these are set aside to be learned and used only after the higher priorities have been satisfied. Fifth, the search is for the *fewest* number of ideas necessary to help a person develop and control his teaching behavior.[10]

[8]Ibid.
[9]Ibid., pp. 2–3. (Italics added.)
[10]Ibid., p. 3. (Italics in original.)

It is obvious from this quotation that Flanders, no matter how modest his statement of the purposes of his interaction analysis system may be, remains deeply convinced of its value for the improvement of instruction. However, the close relationship of this general statement to the substantive and specific clinical effects of the use of his interaction analysis system must be carefully examined by supervisors who may use that system or its many derivatives. Such an examination is made later in this chapter.

Types of Observation Systems[11]

Writers attempting to classify observation systems for the study of classroom behavior have tried to order their data by using various criteria. Simon and Boyer divide such systems into three domains: affective, cognitive, or both. They describe affective systems as those dealing with "the emotional climate of the classroom by coding how the teacher reacts to the feelings, ideas, work efforts or actions of the pupil. The way the teacher responds to pupils determines, in large measure, the affective climate of the classroom." They characterize the cognitive systems as those that "deal with the thinking process itself." They also provide a most important reminder that "every statement carries both a data and an emotional message and in reality these are probably not separable."[12]

A fourth classification, supplementing the three termed *cognitive, affective,* and *cognitive-affective,* would comprise nonverbal or psychomotor behavior, and various combinations of these first four might be subsumed under a fifth class, termed by Meux "multi-aspect" classroom observation systems. He cites Norman E. Wallen's modification of the Flanders system as an example—one among few—that include categories of nonverbal behavior.[13]

C. K. Murray identifies two kinds of observation systems: the "sign" system, in which the observer checks the appearance (not the frequency) of a list of classroom behaviors; and the "category" system, in which "the observer's function is to master the categories of the system and to classify

[11]Two of the best treatments of classroom observation systems we have encountered are Rosenshine, op. cit., pp. 279–300; and Milton O. Meux, "Studies of Learning in the School Setting," *Review of Educational Research* 37, no. 5 (1967), pp. 539–62.
[12]Simon and Boyer, op. cit., pp. 1, 2.
[13]Meux, op. cit., p. 544.

the behaviors exhibited . . . into one of the categories. . . ." The frequency of behavior in each category is noted.[14]

A very useful and heuristic dual classification is suggested by Rosenshine: category systems and rating systems. The difference between the two lies in the magnitude of the inferences each requires of the observer. Category systems are designated *low-inference* systems because they deal with relatively objective behaviors (like the teacher's repetition of students' ideas) and "because these events are recorded as frequency counts." Rating systems, because they deal with less objective phenomena, like "clarity of presentation" or "enthusiasm," require the observer to make a sizable inference and are therefore termed *high-inference systems*.[15]

Many of the low-inference systems seem to derive their categories directly or indirectly from the framework of categories established by Flanders. Still others draw upon the categories developed by Bloom, Krathwohl, and their colleagues in the *Taxonomy of Educational Objectives* (cognitive and affective domains). The work of both groups in general reflects their preoccupation with the actualities of school teaching. Others in the field, however, derive their concepts from a diverse array of sources. Newell and Brown, for example, are working on or have completed observation systems based on such diverse sources as Dewey's "Philosophy of Experimentalism," Gagné's "*Conditions of Learning*," Piaget's "Cognitive Developmental Theory," Herbart's "Theory of Instruction," "Children's Use of Language," and Sylvia Ashton-Warner's "Key Vocabulary,"[16] for example.

Uses of Classroom Observation Systems

It is important to spell out the uses of observation systems clearly in order to assist teachers and supervisors in their efforts to use them appropriately and to help them recognize unwarranted claims for these systems and thereby avoid unwarranted applications of them in practice.

Perhaps the single most important outcome of the use of interaction

[14]C. Kenneth Murray, "The Systematic Observation Movement," *Journal of Research and Development in Education* 4, no. 1 (1970), p. 3.
[15]Rosenshine, op. cit., pp. 280–81.
[16]John M. Newell and Bob Burton Brown, "Theoretical Bases of Observational Systems," *Research Reports* (Gainesville, Fla.: University of Florida, Institute for Development of Human Resources, College of Education, n.d.), p. 13.

analysis systems has been to make some teachers aware of the extent to which their verbal behavior fills the air surrounding the students. The teacher's talk often preempts an incredible percentage of the time available for speech in a class. In their research, Bellack and his colleagues found that for the fifteen teachers whose activity they analyzed "the teacher-pupil ratio of speech is about 3 to 1 in most of the classrooms sampled."[17] Flanders summarizes the cheerless findings of researchers in the decade 1960–70:

> While it is true that teachers talk more than all the pupils combined, from kindergarten to graduate school, the major problem appears to lie not in quantity but in quality. . . . By way of summarizing the current state of affairs in our classrooms, it does not seem very far out of line to suggest that teachers usually tell pupils what to do, how to do it, when to start, when to stop, and how well they did whatever they did.[18]

The research on teachers' talk is fairly consistent in showing that teachers talk about three times as much as all students combined and that much of the talk concerns matters of classroom management or consists of fairly pedestrian kinds of questions. If so, then it will often be advisable for the teacher and supervisor to utilize selected interaction analysis systems to (1) form the basis for their assessments of the quantity and targets of the teacher's talk and (2) develop hunches about the teacher's language patterns in the dimensions measured by some of the observation systems. In Murray's words, "Systematic observation is being used in pre-service and in-service teacher education programs to develop an awareness of the impact of verbal behavior. . . ."[19] Once the teacher and supervisor have decided that certain patterns of the teacher's verbal behavior should be maximized or minimized, then of course an appropriate observation scheme may be employed to furnish information concerning the success of their efforts. This type of feedback-during-training session provides strong support to the clinical supervisor's program for the improvement of the teacher's verbal behavior in class.

Teachers also need to be able to observe their own behavior and understand its relation to the students' behavior. If teachers' understanding derives from analysis and interpretation of such observations, they can, as Flanders says, "use this information to identify patterns of teaching

[17]Arno A. Bellack et al., *The Language of the Classroom* (New York: Teachers College Press, 1966), p. 43.
[18]Flanders, *Analyzing Teaching Behavior*, pp. 13–14.
[19]Murray, op. cit., p. 7.

and then proceed to develop and control their teaching behavior in a continuing program of self-development." He adds that data from interaction analyses are also useful in training programs if they are used as "a pretraining and post-training measure in order to decide whether the participants are learning how to perform particular behavior patterns while teaching their regular classes."[20]

Another dividend from the teacher's training in interaction analysis is that it often enables him to develop some skills and categories useful in analyzing new teaching methods as they come into his view. Such accomplishments are especially valuable at a time like the present, when the reconstruction of curriculum and methods of teaching is a major task facing education.

As for the clinical supervisor himself, he finds interaction analysis systems useful for the objective and systematic feedback they make available about specific aspects of a teacher's classroom behavior. In addition, a knowledge of the research and speculation that form the basis for a well-conceptualized and well-developed system of interaction analysis expands and refines the supervisor's own power to observe, analyze, and interpret what happens in a classroom, and thus constitutes an important element in his professional education. An excellent example of how the supervisor benefits from the work of specialists in the development of interaction analysis systems is found in the report of a research project carried out by Medley and Hill. The researchers undertook to compare and contrast the ten categories of teachers' behavior scored in the Flanders system with the information derived from a system known as OScAR 4V. The fine flavor and utility of Medley and Hill's research are evident in this short excerpt from the conclusions they draw:

> Flanders' instrument appears more sensitive to student behaviors and less able to discriminate teacher behaviors related to substantive content from behaviors related to procedure or management. OScAR is less useful in examining student behavior, but provides more information about how a teacher divides his time between management and instruction, and the quality of both. Both systems seem to measure a number of important stylistic variables of a type with which supervisors and teachers in training are likely to be concerned. Which would be more useful in a given instance would seem to depend on the type of problems which concerned the teacher in question.[21]

[20]Flanders, *Analyzing Teaching Behavior,* pp. 1, 31.
[21]Donald M. Medley and Russell A. Hill, "Dimensions of Classroom Behavior Measured by Two Systems of Interaction Analysis," *Educational Leadership* 26, no. 8 (1969), pp. 822–23.

Some other claims made for the use and study of observation systems are listed here:

1. "A given observational system structures and disciplines the analysis of teaching along some necessarily limited dimensions. . . . It concentrates or focuses sharply on selected aspects of the teaching situation, thereby permitting a depth far greater than that of superficial observation."[22]
2. "This [interaction analysis] category system can be used to study the balance between initiation and response . . . therefore how the teacher statements influence this balance can be studied with this particular set of categories."[23]
3. "The major contribution of interaction analysis may well be that the inferences reached are based on events which can be said to have occurred with a greater degree of certainty than is usually true of classroom observations. In addition, the data are already organized in terms of useful concepts before there is an attempt to make interpretations."[24]
4. "Four major uses of observational systems for the evaluation of instruction are . . . : a) assessing the variability of classroom behavior either within or between instructional programs, b) assessing the agreement between classroom behavior and certain instructional criteria, c) describing what occurred in the implementation of the instructional materials, and d) determining relationships between classroom behavior and instructional outcomes."[25]

It is Meux who points out to supervisors what may be the brightest promise of observation systems: "If categories from several maximally different classroom observation systems . . . are combined in ways not presently observed, teaching strategies might be constructed which are far more effective than those presently used by our best teachers."[26]

Although ratings (rating systems or rating forms) have been deservedly criticized by adherents of counting systems (category systems), Rosenshine draws attention to the possibility of an important and surprising reevaluation of rating systems:

[22]Bob Burton Brown, "Using Systematic Observation and Analysis of Teaching," *Research Reports* (Gainesville, Fla.: Institute for Development of Human Resources, College of Education, n.d.), pp. 1–2.
[23]Flanders, *Analyzing Teaching Behavior*, p. 36.
[24]Ibid., p. 7.
[25]Rosenshine, op. cit., p. 288.
[26]Meux, op. cit., p. 549.

The lack of attention to rating forms is regrettable because recent research using fairly specific items with rating forms has yielded promising results. An estimate of the predictability of rating systems may be obtained by studying the results of seven investigations in which teacher behavior was described using category systems and rating scales. . . . The above results are too varied to attempt to synthesize the findings, but they suggest that ratings are a useful source of information about an instructional program. . . . Perhaps one advantage of rating systems is that an observer is able to consider clues from a variety of sources before he makes his judgment. Even though the low-inference correlates of "clarity" are presently unknown, ratings on variables referring to the clarity of the teacher's presentation were significantly related to student achievement in all studies in which such a variable was used. The results on "clarity" are particularly robust because the investigators used different observational instruments. Furthermore, some investigators used student ratings, some used observer ratings, and the student ratings were given before the criterion test in some studies and after the test in others.[27]

Rosenshine is of the opinion that rating systems and category systems can serve difference purposes and that both may be profitably utilized:

The optimum strategy for research and description may be to use both systems. Rating systems would be used to probe for unknown complexes of variables that appear to be significant correlates of outcome variables; category systems may be used to help identify the specific components of the significant items. In addition, rating forms and category systems which are specific to the instructional program may be developed.[28]

It is apparent that the study of observation systems constitutes an important element in the professional education of the clinical supervisor. The supervisor who is knowledgeable about such systems finds them useful on several counts:

1. The categories defined and illustrated in them become part of his repertoire of diagnostic categories.
2. The techniques used to test the hypotheses developing around the use of these systems can suggest procedures by which the supervisor may test his own hunches after he has made his own analysis of classroom data.
3. The literature of interaction analysis provides the supervisor with cues and clues for the interpretation of classroom data and with relevant models for the interpretation of his own information.

[27]Rosenshine, op. cit., pp. 286–87.
[28]Ibid, p. 288.

4. Some of the work of researchers dealing with interaction systems is ingenious and provocative enough to interest both teachers and supervisors, who may want to attempt an exploratory, in-class application of some of the researchers' ideas about instruction.

The findings of Flanders, Medley and Hill, Rosenshine, and Meux are representative of the best work presently being done on analysis systems. The significance and implications of such contributions to the practice of clinical supervision are manifest. Supervisors should gain from such researchers a knowledge of the special qualities, the limitations, and the promising applications of the present crop of interaction analysis systems.

Limitations and Weaknesses in the Use of Observation Systems

The still unbridged gap between the observed behaviors of teachers and the learning outcomes of students represents a serious weakness in the use of observation systems in clinical supervision. This problem is treated in a recent review of research on the Flanders system:

> The verdict is not in, and is not likely to be in for some time, on the relationship between a teacher's behavior as measured by the Flanders Interaction Analysis (IA) system and pupil achievement. A comprehensive review of the studies relating IA variables to student achievement and attitude remains to be published. There are far more studies, both favorable and unfavorable to IA, than the 12 studies [reviewed here]. If these 12 studies alone are summarized it appears that teacher "indirectness" has a consistent but low positive correlation with achievement, one which is seldom significant at the .05 level. . . . The exact usefulness of IA in predicting pupil achievement remains to be determined.[29]

This message is extremely important for clinical supervisors. It cautions them not to assume that a teacher's "good scores" derived from the analysis of interaction data signify that the students have learned well or that he is a "good" teacher.

Our own view is that it is really asking too much of the interaction analysis systems to expect that the small sample of teacher behaviors utilized in any one system will be closely related to students' learning. The naiveté of such expectations is evident if we remember the com-

---

[29]Rosenshine, "Interaction Analysis: A Tardy Comment," *Phi Delta Kappan* 51, no. 8 (1970), pp. 445–47.

plexity of the teacher's behavior, conjoin that with the vast number of circumstances affecting what students learn, and *then* try to account for learning outcomes by reference to a small array of categories of teacher behavior. Flanders himself carefully avoids such claims. His expectations about the use of IA systems are phrased in very modest terms:

> Teachers can analyze their classroom interaction . . . can use this information and then proceed to develop and control their behavior. . . . The purpose of interaction analysis is to study teaching behavior by keeping track of selected events that occur during classroom discourse. . . .[30]

Clinical supervisors will want to keep in mind the fact that sentences coded, for example, as *direct* or *indirect* influence may be so suffused with other messages from the teacher—apathy, pressure, antagonism, or other affective loading—as to cancel or override the effects of the *form* of the communication. Similar overriding effects may derive from still other uncoded aspects of the teacher's utterances; for example, excessively abstract speech, or lack of fluency in phrasing and rephrasing explanations.

It would appear, in view of these and other complexities of human interaction in class, that the clinical supervisor probably cannot rely on interaction analysis systems to answer his questions about which aspects of the teacher's classroom instruction are principally affecting the students' learning. Still less can he assume that if some good teachers exhibit behavior X, then any teacher who learns to exhibit behavior X will therefore teach well.

Chained and Reciprocal Behavior   This concept forms a central element in the rationale for many interaction analysis systems. It is important for supervisors to note that the behavior viewed as chained and reciprocal is *not* representative of each student's learning behavior. What *is* chained is the behavior of the individuals who become verbally involved in the classroom interaction. Unless each student who speaks represents the speech and learning processes of every other student, the chain is *not* the chain of learning behavior.

We must ask what is happening to all other students when Student A or B or C responds to the teacher or initiates his own inquiry or ideas. What happens when several students talk at once? What is happening to the silent ones, to those who have lost the thread of discussion or are daydreaming, or are far ahead of what is being taught?

[30]Flanders, *Analyzing Teaching Behavior*, Chapter I, passim.

If the chained and reciprocal behavior recorded in an interaction analysis matrix represents a sequence of events, but not necessarily the sequence of events in *each student's* learning processes, then the supervisor has learned a great deal about the teacher but not much about the students in general and even less about each student individually. He may therefore be well advised to use interaction analysis systems to the limits of their potential, but not to go beyond them.

Some Over-Claims for Interaction Analysis Systems

The popularity of IA systems in supervision is growing rapidly. One problem of popularity is that it often breeds overenthusiasm among adherents. This has already occurred in IA circles. One group of enthusiastic "system" builders have fallen into just such a trap. In a discussion of the problems attendant upon the construction of an observation system, they write:

> Items [of observable behavior] developed from a theoretical base must be logically consistent with the theory. It takes considerable skill and effort to formulate operational definitions of relevant behaviors and to build a system which adequately reflects the theoretical framework. The translation of the theoretical statement into one or more observable items is the first, and often most difficult, task in instrument development.[31]

Yet one of the authors of this statement recommends that teachers construct their own systems on a do-it-yourself basis: "Once teachers have mastered several available observation systems and have used them to deal effectively with [certain problems], they are likely to want to try their hand at the development of their own observational systems. Staff-made systems can be used to study highly detailed aspects of teaching which are untouched by established systems, enabling observational feedback to focus on local needs and interests."[32] There may be an occasional staff of teachers competent to develop their own systems, but, with a few such exceptions, to invite teachers to develop a "local" theory and local instruments may be to invite disaster.

Some supervisors, enthusiastic about the use of IA systems, become overdependent upon them, using the categories of one or two favorite systems as the sole sources of diagnostic information about a teacher's performance. Such procedures, though they may occasionally hit the mark,

[31]Newell and Brown, op. cit., p. 7.
[32]Brown, op. cit., p. 4.

cannot be expected to substitute for the extensive repertoire of categories of observation the clinical supervisor needs in his work. As Flanders has said:

> Classroom interaction analysis systems seek to abstract communication by ignoring most of its characteristics. For example, a category such as "teacher asks a question" is used to code many different statements, provided they are all questions. Once the same code symbol is used for all of these statements, the differences among them are ignored and lost forever. Yet this loss is offset by keeping an accurate record of the number of times that a teacher attempts to solicit verbal expression from the pupils, which is the characteristic common to all statements with this code symbol. This process is sensible only when keeping an accurate record of teacher questions is crucial to some investigations. This procedure makes no sense at all when what is lost by the process is more important than what is gained.[33]

[33]Flanders, *Analyzing Teaching Behavior*, pp. 29–30.

CHAPTER 13

The Analysis of Teaching

The sequences of the cycle of clinical supervision discussed so far have included (1) the processes by which the teacher-supervisor relationship may be established, (2) the preparation of the teacher for his colleagual role, (3) the lesson-planning processes, (4) the strategies of classroom observation, and (5) the accomplishment of the observation itself. Following the observation, the teacher and the supervisor separately examine the records and analyze them in preparation for the conference. (Later on, when the teacher has become more competent in the clinical cycle, the analysis may be done cooperatively.)

Objectives of the Analysis

The objectives of the supervisor's analysis of the events of the classroom interaction are—

1. to assess the extent to which the students have achieved the objectives set out in the plan;
2. to identify unanticipated learnings;
3. to identify critical incidents that occurred in the class;
4. to order the data on the students' behavior in a fashion that brings into focus those aspects of their behavior that seem likely to relate in an important sense to what they learn or do not learn;
5. to identify salient patterns in the teacher's behavior;
6. to relate important terms the teacher uses in his plans to his behavior in class (This is an attempt to ascertain the behavioral correlates of key ideas expressed by the teacher in his plan. For example, what does the teacher *actually* do when he attempts to engage the students in what he calls in his plan "a free and open discussion among students," or precisely what does he do when he sets out to "provide rapid reinforcement in a question-and-answer session"?);
7. to develop the data-base upon which the supervisory program will be developed (These data might include, for example, the teacher's short- and long-term objectives, the major patterns of his style, etc.).

The supervisor's assessment of the extent to which students achieve the objectives set out in the lesson plan is based upon both direct and indirect evidence about their learning, including data derived from the record of classroom events and from extra-class sources. The former type of data might include students' answers to questions, problems, and tests; their in-class performance or nonperformance of the behavioral objectives set out in the plan; and verbal and nonverbal indicants of affective learnings. Evidence bearing on the achievement of stated objectives but obtained outside of class might be derived from systemwide tests, cumulative records, observation of out-of-class behavior, spontaneous testimony proffered by students, interviews with them, and the testimony of competent observers. The base line for measures of "entering behavior" will often be the students' performance on diagnostic tasks, in addition to other diagnostic data available to the teacher. (Nothing is more disconcerting to the teacher and supervisor than to discover tardily that the learning exhibited by students in class had been achieved prior to the lessons in which they were supposed to learn it.)

In most schools, data concerning students' entering behavior is rather limited. It is generally represented by brief anecdotal records and the results of testing programs. Most of this information is related only to very narrowly defined first-level cognitive learnings. Data about affective learnings is hard to come by and often very limited. The information the supervisor and teacher derive from a sequence of analyses of classroom events will therefore augment the scanty sources available to them.

Process Outcomes

The supervisor engaged in analyzing the transcripts of teaching-learning sessions should also identify two commonly neglected sets of outcomes termed *process-learnings* and *unanticipated learnings*. A definition of process goals is provided by Heathers:

> *Tool skills* include the whole array of communication skills used in reading, listening, writing, and speaking. They include skills in computation. They include the techniques of observing, manipulating, and measuring things. It should be noted that the classical Three R's are tool-skill subjects. . . . *Problem-solving thinking or inquiry* is generally considered to be the core of the educational process and the chief mark of the educated person. It is the route of understanding and the basis for invention, planning, interpretation, and criticism. In formal education, problem-solving thinking is not focused on learning to deal with practical problems of everyday living. Instead, it deals mainly with intellectual problems within the academic setting of a discipline. Yet these problems must still be real in the sense of being testable. . . . *Self-instruction, or self-direction in acquiring and using knowledge,* is the essential partner of problem-solving thinking. A teacher cannot do the thinking for his students. The student himself must learn to

identify and analyze problems, gather relevant information, develop and test plausible solutions, and evaluate outcomes. Motivation to learn for the joy of learning is a prime requisite for self-instruction. . . . *Teaching the student to evaluate his work by employing criteria of mastery* may seem not to belong in a list of the process goals of education. But anything that is only partially learned is of little use either in dealing with practical matters or as a stepping stone to further learning.[1]

Other educators have addressed themselves to what Heathers has called "process" learnings. Perhaps the most widely cited thesis on the subject is Bruner's on learning how to learn: ". . . it is indeed a fact that massive general transfer can be achieved by appropriate learning, even to the degree that learning properly under optimum conditions leads one to 'learn how to learn.' "[2] One of the underlying significant aspects of *process outcomes* is that they comprise many of the important learnings often submerged in the tide of simple cognitive learnings purveyed under the title of "content."

The inventory of process learnings might well include outcomes such as the student's learning to know himself as a learner, to be responsible for his own learning, to make better choices, to perform self-initiated work, to be receptive to new ideas, etc.

In this book we extend the definition of process outcomes to include unanticipated and/or unintended learnings. The world of the unanticipated is, almost by definition, often a mad mad world. For example, a teacher intends to teach Latin, and a student learns to want to be an archeologist. A long line of English teachers sets out to teach the appreciation of poetry, and crowds of high-school boys learn to dislike it. Hosts of girls learn that they are not likely to be good at mathematics and physics. Legions of small children learn to be docile in school. And so on, unexpectedly. Long exposure to programed instruction may teach students that learning comes in small bits; other students may learn to outwit the teaching machine. An anthropologist has stated that many students learn to give teacher what teacher wants, even if it is wrong, rather than to stick to their own right answers. A teacher once tested this theory in a mathematics class in which the students were learning about squaring numbers and extracting square roots. In a series of quick bursts of questions and answers in unison from the class, he established a pattern of correct answers to "What is the square root of 4? 25? 36? Then he asked

---

[1]Glen Heathers, "Notes on the Strategy of Educational Reform" (unpublished paper, 1961), p. 24. (Italics added.)
[2]Jerome S. Bruner, *The Process of Education* (Cambridge, Mass.: Harvard University Press, 1960), p. 6.

for the square root of 9. When the class chorused "3," he shouted incredulously, "What??!!" and the class instantly shouted "81!" Apparently they had learned to give teacher what teacher wanted, right or wrong.

The data about process learnings and unexpected learnings are generally not tapped in the analysis of classroom interaction, possibly because supervisors have not learned to look for them, or—much more likely—because they have learned *not* to look for them. In view of the importance of these types of learnings, it is clear that clinical supervisors need to be specially trained in order to be able to look for and identify them.

Some useful strategies may be employed to sharpen the supervisor-analyst's eye for these phenomena. He should learn to observe the students' behavior very carefully, without forming hunches or drawing inferences. In such objective, open-minded observation the students' behavior takes shape simply as *behavior*: the students talk, write, read, listen, whisper, and leaf through the dictionary. The most likely inferences to be made from these data are that the students are learning to talk, write, read, listen, whisper, and leaf through the dictionary. Note that we do not say that they are learning to look up words in the dictionary.

Now let us suppose that we observe the students cheating, doodling, writing short answers, shuffling their feet, receiving candy when they answer correctly, and checking their answers to multiplication problems. It is then a fair inference—worth testing—that they are learning to cheat, doodle, write short answers, shuffle their feet, expect candy when they answer correctly, and check answers to multiplication. People learn what they do. The appropriate strategy, then, is to view with naive eyes what students *do* in the classroom, without making assumptions about what they are *supposed to be learning*. The insights derived from such clear-eyed observation may be startling. For example, if young students are giving short answers in programed instruction while they are studying reading and arithmetic, the chances are good that they will be learning the characteristics of short-answer instruction and how to write short answers. And the chances are even better that they are *not* learning how to compose long answers nor how to write correct sentences in answers to drill or test items. They are more probably learning to recognize correct answers than to create them. In brief, the supervisor needs to entertain many diverse hypotheses and to scan the record of classroom events for process learnings and unexpected learnings as well as for planned and anticipated learnings.

The problems the supervisor encounters in his analysis will be simplified if both he and the teacher engage in this study. In addition, the teacher will become aware of entirely new kinds of learnings. As he gains competence in dealing with them, he may begin to specify them, to anticipate them, and—more important—to teach for appropriate process outcomes. In all probability the kinds of information the teacher and supervisor will need in order to identify these outcomes will not become evident through the customary feedback apparatus of tests and class discussions. The new types of data will probably demand the use of different techniques: "rap sessions" for the students, small-group interviews, attitude questionnaires and open-ended questions to be answered. The students themselves will have to become involved in the search for process outcomes in classroom instruction.

Critical Incidents and Pattern Analysis   The objectives of analysis also include the identification of (1) critical incidents occurring in the class and (2) patterns in the teacher's behavior—patterns likely to be significantly related to the students' learning. *Critical incident* refers here to teacher behavior occurring only once or, at most, occasionally. The term *incident* is used to emphasize the distinction between *single* or *occasional* behavior and *patterns* of behavior.

A critical incident is usually some single action by the teacher that is likely to have a strong and lasting effect upon students' learning, upon their affective relation to their learning, or upon their relationship to the teacher. *Patterned behavior* refers to a set of similar behaviors appearing often enough in the teacher's repertoire to constitute a predictable element of his classroom behavior. "Critical incident" and "pattern" will be treated again later in this chapter.

A major objective of the analysis is to ascertain the principal characteristics of the teacher's teaching—its strengths and weaknesses, its quality, its distinctive substance and structure. In this sense both critical incidents and patterns constitute elements of the teacher's classroom behavior and conclusions about it should be drawn most carefully and deliberately. The process requires time, repeated observations, repeated analyses, and meticulous scrutiny of emerging hypotheses. These hypotheses will of course be further tested in the supervisory conference, when the teacher expresses *his* perceptions about his own teaching and considers those of the supervisor. This process of cross-checking hypotheses should also be pursued with the help of other supervisors, behavioral scientists, and individuals qualified by experience and insight to venture into this field. Some examples of a supervisor's thoughts as he develops his working hypotheses about the characteristics of a teacher's classroom behavior may clarify the ideas just set out here:

1. I think that this teacher times his reinforcements well and uses them appropriately.
2. I find good evidence that he appears to be task-oriented. He avoids and resists digressions, and minimizes unavoidable interruptions and intrusions by outsiders who enter the room. He sticks to his plan. However, I have yet to observe him release tension or change pace in class. Does the interaction of these behaviors strengthen or weaken the learning processes? Could these patterns be related to my presence in class?
3. So far this teacher has not asked a question requiring more than recall of a simple fact, the spelling of a word, or a *Yes* or *No* answer.

It may be useful to observe that such speculations and working hypotheses are also expressed by the teacher in his analysis of his own teaching and in supervisory conferences. As the teacher gains proficiency in these supervisory tasks, he also begins to *reconstruct* his perceptions about his teaching. As a consequence, when teacher and supervisor formulate their plans to improve a teaching pattern or deal with a critical incident, they are thereby integrating the processes of planning, observing, and analyzing into the developing supervisory plan.

The Context of Analysis

The context of analysis in clinical supervision is the totality of significant and relevant information available to the supervisor and teacher: the students' behavior, the teacher's behavior, and events in the world in which they work. This comprehensive and complex view of the phenomena the supervisor deals with is presented because the world of teaching-learning is indeed complex and is better approached cautiously rather than confidently. Each student is a world of his own; so is each teacher. Each class is a constellation of worlds; and around all these is the universe surrounding the classroom. Every individual brings to class his whole self, of which a portion becomes visible in class. Each person in class interacts with the others in it, and they all interact with the universe around them. If we try to illustrate the variety and complexity of the factors affecting each student's learning, we get a picture something like the following:

Each student's learning is related to—
1. his ability to learn;
2. his store of experience;
3. his attitudes toward the content to be learned (like-dislike, etc.);

4. his relation to the teacher;
5. his relations to other students in the class;
6. his relations to people outside the class;
7. his response to stimuli impinging on the class; and
8. his state at the moment of learning: mental (is mentally fatigued), physiological (has a hearing defect), physical (is rested), emotional (is, in love with the girl in the seat behind him), etc.

And each of these factors interacts with the teacher's—
1. ability to teach each student;
2. experience in teaching;
3. attitudes toward the content to be taught;
4. relation to each student;
5. relation to the groupings that students form;
6. response to outside stimuli entering the class;
7. relations to people outside the class (his wife is threatening to leave him); and
8. state at the moment of teaching: mental (is alert), physical (is rested), emotional (is afraid she won't), etc.

And each of these factors interacts with what the world outside the classroom does (the town won't buy books for the schools or build laboratories, etc.). When we understand that the students' learnings may at any time be significantly affected by the interaction of such factors and that the supervisor's function is to find out what the students have (or have not) learned, and why, and do something to improve that learning, then we may understand why the supervisor must develop his working hypotheses about students' learning within the context of the relevant information available to him. Perhaps it is lucky that the information available is limited, or we might have very few supervisors. On the other hand, an awareness of the complexity of the context of teaching-learning may persuade supervisors not to oversimplify their analysis, not to commit themselves too readily to oversimplified cause-and-effect hypotheses. It hardly needs to be repeated that analysis of classroom interaction is finally intuition based on informed and disciplined reason.

Kinds and Levels of Analysis

Three kinds of analysis are commonly performed in clinical supervision: (1) the solo, full-fledged analysis performed by the supervisor, (2) the solo analysis carried out by the teacher, and (3) the truncated analysis done cooperatively by both in the conference.

Following his observation in the classroom, the supervisor performs the full-fledged analysis of the transcripts and records, which amounts to a comprehensive effort to identify the structure of the teaching-learning events that have occurred in class and to develop some working hypotheses relating the teacher's behavior to students' learning. The supervisor engages in the full-fledged analysis for several reasons. First, a careful and complete diagnosis is a professional requirement. A painstaking study of the classroom may protect the teacher against a supervisor's premature inferences about the events that have occurred in class. Second, the full analysis reduces the chances that the supervisor will overlook certain occurrences, jump to unwarranted conclusions, or make other errors in diagnosis.

The careful solo analysis represents one of the major instruments by which the supervisor may gain knowledge about the teacher as he is in class. The amount of prudent care the supervisor displays in getting at the best answers to the question "What is this teacher?" is a measure of his concern to approximate the truth insofar as he can discern it. And these "best approximations" of the meaning the teacher's behavior has for his students' learning constitute one of the foundation stones of the supervisory program. The full-fledged analysis provides part of the basis upon which the supervisor's working hypotheses are developed.

The supervisor's analysis of the classroom interaction furnishes him with some intimations of the structures of the teacher's instruction. The solo analysis, therefore, prepares the supervisor for some of the contingencies that may arise in his conference with the teacher. For example, it is very probable that the teacher will, in *his* analysis, formulate some working hypotheses about how certain aspects of his teaching relate to students' behavior. He may open the conference by saying, "I think my techniques for getting the three research committees to work in class were effective. They were really finding the correct answers to their question about who determines the policies the U.S. armed forces pursue in Vietnam." In order to be able to respond knowledgeably and strategically to statements of this nature, the supervisor must have command of the data and alternative interpretations of classroom events. The strategic appropriateness of the supervisor's response to such an overture will depend in part on the care with which he has performed the full-fledged analysis prior to the conference.

Above all, the full-fledged analysis contributes to the form and character of the supervisor's intuitions about the relationships that may exist among the events occurring in classroom interaction.

The teacher's solo analysis should serve many of the same purposes as the supervisor's: to prepare the teacher to take a constructive leading role in the conference, to help him search out the structures of his own teaching, to enable him to think hypothetically about his own behavior and its relationships to students' learning, and to form the data-base for his own program of professional self-improvement. His review of the record of the teaching-learning sequences in his class may also enable him to study his behavior more objectively, from a record rather than from his recollections. Perhaps most important of all, the analysis offers the teacher an opportunity to amplify his colleagual role in a new dimension. He may learn that the proper study of the teacher is teaching —and he may learn to relish that study and persevere in it.

The *truncated analysis* is the analysis that teacher and supervisor perform together in the course of the conference. Its aims and procedures are treated in the chapter on the conference.

Processes and Procedures of Clinical Analysis

Critical Incidents   The identification of critical incidents should be given important priority in the analysis. By definition, the critical incident demands attention because it is likely to impede desired learnings in some striking fashion. To illustrate: if a teacher, in an outburst of anger, strikes a student in a school or community in which physical attack and corporal punishment are expressly and strongly taboo, his action—even if it is an isolated incident—may have serious and possibly irreversible consequences for the students' learning. Such an aggression—experienced or witnessed—may produce indelible aftereffects on the students and their relationship to teachers, school, and the subject under study when the incident took place. ·

Sometimes a minor classroom problem suddenly turns critical. A teacher with a history of minor problems of classroom discipline suddenly sets in motion an ill-advised program "to restore order." He demands the students' instant and full compliance with an inflexible set of rules and harsh penalties: "Stand up for every recitation, no matter how short." "Do not speak unless called on." "Absolutely no whispering." "If any student is disorderly, the whole class will stay after school," and on and on. As a result, the students grow mutinous, then defiant. They launch a campaign of resistance: they scrape chairs constantly; stand up to recite, remain silent for a long pause, then answer with a monosyllable, and subside slowly into their seats. They drop books on the floor in a slow trickle or in cascades. They write slogans on the blackboard: "Mr. Butts is nuts." "Down with ifs, ands, and Butts." And the breakdown of discipline accelerates rapidly.

No supervisor can ignore such events. The students' alienation resulting from a teacher's aggressive attack may have serious learning consequences. A breakdown of discipline can hardly ever be repaired. Therefore, the supervisor must in his analysis be alert to identify such negative critical incidents and to help the teacher cope with their already visible or future consequences. To fail to do so is to risk intolerable damage to students and teacher.

Neither can the supervisor in his analysis afford to overlook a critical incident likely to have favorable and propitious consequences. A teacher may help his students to achieve some sudden insight, with lasting effect: they experience the catharsis of tragedy, gain a strong sense of the power of mathematics, feel the deep resonances of poetry, or come face to face with love, hate, pity, cruelty, or their own humanity. The teacher whose students have such an experience, even if only once, should have the supervisor's help in recognizing the occasion and assessing its effects.

In addition, the supervisor may be able to help the teacher formulate reasonable hypotheses about *why* he achieved such results, and the teacher may be able to change a critical incident into a pattern.

On the other hand, the supervisor must guard against a tendency to find "critical incidents" in every nook and cranny of the classroom. Too many such incidents can transform a supervisory program into a series of crisis interventions.

Patterns of Teaching   Human behavior is in part predictable. Predictability implies *patterns*. Thus Lewin studies patterns of aggressive behavior, and Linton refers to the tendency of human beings to form aggregates as a "universal human pattern." Words like *personality*, *society*, and *culture* all imply patterned behavior. And if so much of human behavior is patterned, then the behavior of teachers is also in part patterned.

If a teacher exhibits such consistency in his behavior, then certain advantages may be gleaned for clinical supervision by a process of pattern analysis. First of all, we have learned that a pattern identified and documented by data from a teaching session carries conviction. The teacher learns, for example, that what the supervisor refers to as the teacher's "social distance from students" does not refer to a single or occasional or accidental behavior. It is, instead, a phenomenon that becomes visible in the teacher's customary placement of himself in relation to the class, in the regular use of certain exclusive terms like *you*, or certain inclusive phrases like *all of us*. Such patterns merit the attention of the teacher as an important and consistent aspect of his classroom behavior. The pattern helps make sense and order out of what may otherwise be a confused mass of data in the record of classroom interaction. A teacher may want to learn about and modify patterns if he perceives them to be related to important themes in his teaching.

The identification of a pattern will often dissuade the teacher from focusing on trivial matters and help him to concentrate on more significant behavior. In this sense, pattern analysis achieves two additional useful objectives: it saves time, and it focuses the teacher on analysis rather than on a defense of his own behavior.

Perhaps a few examples of patterns may convey some sense of their use and significance in the clinical analysis of teaching. In order to accentuate the patterns and make them more readily identifiable by the reader, the following sequences derived from classroom records have been extracted from longer contexts and on occasion modified in order to throw the pattern into higher relief.

A teacher is in process of teaching his students to arrive at critically examined generalizations about the characteristics of American folk heroes, real and fictional. A portion of the discussion in a ninth-grade English class follows:

1. *Student 1*:   Our heroes are usually honest.

2. *Student 2*:   Jesse James stole from the rich to give to the poor.

3. *Student 3*:   So did Robin Hood.

4. *Teacher*:   (going to the blackboard where he has written a list of characteristics the students have suggested) Since a robber obviously *can* be a hero, we had better cross "honesty" off our list of characteristics (erases the word).

5. *Student 4*:   Abraham Lincoln came from the common people.

6. *Teacher*:   So we can say that one characteristic of the American folk hero is humble origin.

7. *Student 5*:   Billy the Kid . . .

8. *Teacher*:   (interrupting, with enthusiasm) Yes! A great gunfighter!

9. *Student 6*:   Andrew Jackson was a great fighter, too. He came from the common people and fought for their rights.

10. *Teacher*:   Look on page 237 in your text and you will find proof of that. Now we've had characteristics of common origin, love of common people, personal bravery, and so on. Now Andrew Jackson . . . .

Such exchanges took place several times in the course of the lesson. The period had started well but had ended in inattention and disorder. Now let us analyze the fragment of dialogue reproduced here in order to illustrate some of the processes in an attempt to identify teaching patterns and to formulate working hypotheses about their relationships to students' learning.

We shall start by asking the reader to accept certain assumptions. First, that the fragments of interaction juxtaposed in the dialogue above are representative of what occurred in the lesson as a whole. And second, that they are further representative of the teacher's behavior throughout the year when he attempts to engage his students in discussions designed to teach them to make a critical examination of generalizations. If these assumptions are accepted, we may proceed to ask two questions: (1) What are the long-term patterns of the teacher's behavior when he seeks such objectives as we have stipulated? and (2) What learnings are the students likely to achieve under the impact of such patterns?

Having agreed to assume that each single instance of teacher behavior in the excerpt above is characteristic and is therefore repeated throughout the year, we may try to indicate some of the sequences of analysis in which a supervisor is making an attempt to formulate first approximations of patterns.

Patterns of Teacher's Behavior   For our first analysis we start with what seems to us to be a useful oversimplification and its corollary: "People tend to learn what they practice." The corollary is: "People are not likely to learn what they do *not* practice." Therefore, for each pattern exhibited by the teacher, we attach a working hypothesis and a corollary, as follows:

TEACHER'S PATTERN NO. 1

Takes students' contradictory claims and settles them.

Corollary: Students are not likely to learn how to settle contradictory claims.

Data
Student 1:   Our heroes are usually honest.

Student 2:   Jesse James stole from the rich to give to the poor.

Student 3:   So did Robin Hood.

Teacher: (goes to the blackboard, erases "honesty" from the list of heroes' characteristics) Since a robber obviously can be a hero, we had better cross honesty off our list of characteristics.

TEACHER'S PATTERN NO. 2

Formulates a generalization from a student's suggestion.

Corollary: Students are not likely to learn the competences needed to generalize from specific instances.

Data
Student 4:   Abraham Lincoln came from the common people.

Teacher: So we can say that one characteristic of the folk hero is humble origin.

TEACHER'S PATTERN NO. 3

Interrupts students and completes their sentences.

Corollary: (The reader is invited to try to state his own working hypothesis about students' learnings under such a teaching pattern.)

Data
Student 5:   Billy the Kid . . .

Teacher: (interrupting) Yes! A great gunfighter!

TEACHER'S PATTERN NO. 4

Provides evidence for students' unsupported claims.

Corollary: Students are not likely to learn the competences needed to adduce proof for unsupported claims.

Data
Student 6:   Andrew Jackson was a great fighter, too. He came from the common people and fought for their rights.

Teacher: Look on page 257 in your text and you will find proof of that.

TEACHER'S PATTERN NO. 5

Summarizes discussions designed to teach students how to arrive at critically examined generalizations.

Corollary: Students are not likely to gain skill at summarizing discussions of critically examined generalizations.

Data
Teacher: Now we've had characteristics of humble origin, love of common people, personal bravery, and so on.

We may now turn to an analysis of students' behavior patterns and the likely learning outcomes of those patterns.

STUDENTS' PATTERN NO. 1
Students' sentences tend to be short and are shorter than the teacher's sentences.
Data: Students average 8 words per utterance to teacher's 17.

Likely Learnings: 1) Students will be likely to learn to make short responses in this teacher's class. 2) They will be likely to learn to speak less than the teacher in this class. 3) They will not be likely to learn to make long responses.

STUDENTS' PATTERN NO. 2
Students' claims tend to be only claims, without empirical or logical evidence.
Data: See Items 1, 2, 3, 5, 7, and 9 in the dialogue.

Likely Learnings: Students will be likely to learn to make claims without offering evidence to support them in discussions in this class.

Still other patterns may be discerned in the interactional structure of the discussion.

INTERACTION PATTERNS

1. Students interact more often with the teacher in discussion than with each other.
2. No student offers an objection when the teacher alters the student's statement.
3. No student defends or amplifies his own statements.
4. No student questions or challenges the teacher's assertions.

Data: Examine items in the dialogue.

Likely Learnings: Rephrase the patterns, ad lib.

The patterns indicate that the students have very probably learned more about the teacher than about the characteristics of American folk heroes or about how to participate productively in group efforts to make a critical examination of unsupported generalizations.

We may also venture a guess that if the teacher in the transcript is representative of many other teachers these students encounter, then the learnings and nonlearnings gained in interaction with these teachers may tend to generalize to other classes and, for some students, to their lives outside of school.

As we have seen in the example above, the supervisor engages in the formulation of working hypotheses. These hypotheses should be made at the lowest level of inference. That is, the inference-gap should be as small as possible, and the inference should be as logically close to the data as possible. In an example from the excerpt, the inference (pattern) is a statement that the teacher "summarizes discussions designed to teach students how to arrive at critically examined generalizations." The pattern "summarizes discussions" is inferred from this sentence (a set of sentences): "Now we've had characteristics of humble origin, love of common people, personal bravery. . . ." The inference made by the supervisor is considered minimal because the three examples were furnished by students, not the teacher, and the generalization was made by the teacher, not the students. The inference also states that the discussions the teacher summarizes are "designed to teach students how to arrive at critically examined generalizations." This portion of the inference is not inferential at all; it derives verbatim from the objective stated by the teacher himself. The supervisor may therefore make a strong claim that he is working with minimal inferences.

But it is too easy and too tempting to go beyond this limited analysis. A larger inference could be drawn if the supervisor were to hypothesize that the teacher seemed to perceive his role to be that of the active, initiating, clarifying agent, the judge. Or, in another inference, the supervisor might see the students principally as responders rather than initiators, as vessels to be filled rather than as learners who need to solve problems and practice making generalizations, and so on. Even for this higher level of inference a fair argument could be made from the data.

At a still greater remove, the supervisor might hypothesize that this teacher is authoritarian, or that he is insecure and therefore seeks to compensate by dominating the class and making decisions. . . . This sort of facile psychologizing and pseudoanalysis should be avoided at all costs. It leads to increasingly larger and more precarious inferential gaps.

In the example of pattern analysis just completed, the reader was asked to assume that each numbered statement represented a pattern of teacher or student behavior. That is, he was asked to assume that each numbered statement in the excerpt fairly represented other similar statements that would be found in the transcript. As the supervisor reads and rereads the transcript, he forms tentative hypotheses about the significance of each statement (behavior). In effect, he gives each statement a name or classifies it tentatively as a specific kind of teacher or student behavior.

The individual items are then studied for connections or similarities. When the classifications have been examined critically, revised, and checked for homogeneity of items, the categories in which the most frequent behaviors occur may be classified as patterns. However, a category may contain as few as four or five items and qualify as a pattern if the behaviors exert a significant effect upon a teaching session or upon a portion of it.

Another example of pattern analysis may be helpful. The following description of an elementary science lesson is freely adapted from pages 84–86 of *A Sourcebook for Elementary Science*, by E. B. Hone, A. Joseph, and E. Victor. The dialogue is fictitious. The reader may want to identify patterns in the dialogue before he reads beyond it.

ELEMENTARY SCIENCE

An elementary teacher is conducting a lesson on plants as living things. The students have had several long sessions in which to observe 24 similar potted plants: 8 pots are upright and the plants are growing upward; 8 pots are lying on their sides and the plants are growing upward; 8 pots are suspended upside down with the soil held in the pots by a cover through which the plants protrude, all curling up around the pots and growing upward. In addition, the students have had good opportunity to observe closely a transparent display in which about 20 irregularly cylindrical seeds have been planted. These seeds are oriented at 20 different angles from the horizontal—some pointed up, some down, and some sidewards. Each seed has sprouted a root, and all the roots point down. The objective of the lesson is to teach the students to observe carefully and to formulate original scientific generalizations about the growth of the plants.

1. *Teacher*: Now that we've all had a chance to examine all these potted plants, would you tell me what you noticed about them?

2. *James*: Some are hanging upside down. They're funny.

3. *Teacher*: What's funny about them?

4. *James*: They're sick.

5. *Marie*: They *look* OK. How do you know they're sick?

6. *James*: Look how they're twisted up.

7. *Albert*: So are these laying down. They twist up.

8. *Frank*: They're not sick. All the leaves are green.

9. *Teacher*: Are they, Carol?

10. *Carol*: Sure. They're OK. They're just trying to get air.

11. *May*: There's air all around. Why do they twist *up*?

12. *Frank*: They're looking for sun. They can't get sun if the leaves are laying face down, so they curl up.

13. *Teacher*: That's very good, Frank, especially because we learned that

plants need sun. Now, boys and girls, how about these seeds? (moves to the seeds planted in the transparent display) What do you observe about *them*?

14. *James*:   They all got tails.

15. *Teacher*:   (recognizing Fred): Fred?

16. *Fred*:   They're not tails. They're roots.

17. *Helen*:   They're sick. They're all going down instead of looking for the sun. They're sick.

18. *Teacher*:   Helen must have looked very carefully because she noticed that the roots all grow down. That's right, Helen. Are they all sick, too?

19. *Billy*:   I guess the leaf parts go up for sun but the root parts go down for water. There's wet down there at the bottom.

20. *Teacher*:   That's very good observing, Bill. Very good. And you gave a reason, too. That's fine. Now can anyone tell us again the things we've learned about roots and leaves, so I can write out on the board the things we've discovered?

PATTERN NO. 1
Teacher offers opportunities for student to respond to student.

Data: See exchanges 5 to 4; 6 to 5; 7 to 6; 8 to 7; 11 to 10; 12 to 11; 17 to 16.

PATTERN NO. 2
Students talk more often than teacher, in the ratio of 13 to 7 utterances.

PATTERN NO. 3
Teacher's reinforcement is selective, in that she intervenes in the discussion when students have voiced a correct surmise.

Data: See sequences 13 to 12, 18 to 17, and 20 to 19.

PATTERN NO. 4
Teacher's reinforcement is rational in that she rewards and explains *why* the rewarded statement is correct.

Data: See sequence 13 to 12. ("That's very good, Frank [reward] because we learned that plants need sun [reason for reward].") See also 18 to 17; 20 to 19.

PATTERN NO. 5
Students express themselves in plural, compound, and complex sentences, often rationalized by evidence supplied for an assertion.

Data: Statements 2, 5, 7, 8, 10, 12, 16, 17 and 19 are either plural, compound, or complex sentences. Statements 8, 10, 12, 17 and 19 all offer reasons for claims.

None of the statements made here are meant to imply that these patterns are the only ones that might be identified. On the contrary, it would be very unusual if analysis of a transcript did not generate varied and conflicting views. In this same sense, any single pattern may generate multiple hypotheses about the learning consequences related to it. The identification of a pattern is only the beginning of a search to relate the teacher's behavior to the students' learnings. An inference about students' learnings may be entirely false, or it may relate in different ways to different students' learnings and on different occasions. For example, in the dialogue above, on American folk heroes, the teacher's practice of providing evidence to support students' claims made in a discussion may be interpreted as depriving some students of any motivation to learn how to defend their assertions. On the other hand, for students who for some reason are already motivated to learn techniques of empirical and logical support for their ideas, the same teacher may be providing a brilliant and instructive demonstration of various techniques useful in argument, discussion, and debate. Pattern analysis is not the answer to the question of how the teacher's behavior may be related to the students' learnings. It is only what appears to be one reasonable way of beginning the search for that answer.

The limitations of space on a book page prevent us from setting out in sequential form the relationships we hypothesize to exist between patterns and learnings, but perhaps a schema and a parallel example may illustrate the relationships useful in analysis (see Figure 1).

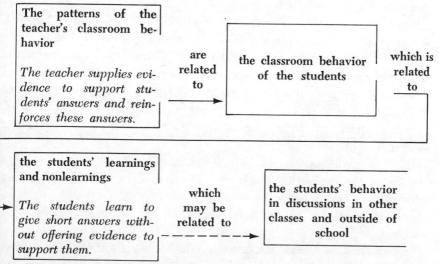

Figure 1   EVIDENCE AND INFERENCE IN PATTERN ANALYSIS

The virtue of pattern analysis is that it helps the teacher and supervisor to make sense and order out of the welter of classroom data. Without such help, they often resort to anecdotal accounts of what happens in class, or to a canvassing of the classroom data for something worth noting.

The search for the links between patterns and learning is a charm against "impressions" about the lesson; it is a sort of insurance against undisciplined intuition and unconscious selection.

Some Objectives and Outcomes of Pattern Analysis

The objectives of pattern analysis are of course intended to be compatible with both the comprehensive objectives of clinical supervision and the several specific objectives of clinical analysis.

Pattern analysis is first of all an instrument designed to help the teacher and the supervisor comprehend the major structures and outcomes of the teaching-learning process. One outcome of the process is organized evidence. Another is the development of inferences about the structures, processes, and outcomes of classroom teaching-learning. This evidence and these processes often convey to the teacher a sense of objectivity and rationality that help to convince him that he is dealing with a system of supervision oriented toward his behavior as a teacher, rather than toward himself-as-person. This sense of order and rationality helps to allay excessive anxieties of teachers who cannot otherwise find a secure base on which to work with supervisors.

Pattern analysis complements other methods of developing an approximation of the teacher's characteristic classroom behavior. It provides the supervisor with a clearer view and thus a better understanding of the classroom world in which students and teacher live. He is better equipped to work within the realities of a specific classroom, and he therefore runs less risk of losing touch with the teacher and the students. In brief, pattern analysis constantly reminds the supervisor that lessons are taught for students, not for supervisors.

The process of pattern analysis serves the teacher's needs by helping him assess the degree to which the objectives of instruction are being achieved. It further helps the teacher to identify differences in the outcomes achieved by different students and by different methods of teaching.

Pattern analysis generally seems to reinforce strongly the other security-giving procedures developed for clinical supervision—the establishment of the $T \leftrightarrow S$ relationship, for example. In this sense, pattern analysis contributes to the security the teacher may need to try out new kinds of behavior, new curriculums, and perhaps even new relationships with students.

Forming and Checking the Working Hypotheses A working hypothesis is defined as a theorem not yet proved. This expression is used purposely to emphasize the tentative and speculative nature of the hunches and the hypotheses the clinical supervisor deals with. He rarely has hold of a truth, a demonstrated verity, but rather has commerce with partial truths, with likelihoods, fair chances, and probabilities. He must therefore be constantly vigilant against falling into the errors of certainty. Pattern analysis has proven to be persuasive and convincing to so many—and not least to clinical supervisors. For this reason they must learn about the sources and kinds of errors they are likely to fall into.

The first trap is the tendency to make premature inferences. The clinical supervisor who has made many observations and toiled through long analyses and conferences becomes an inference-maker, a formulator of working hypotheses. Such activity is at the heart of the profession. The supervisor is trained to have very extensive knowledge of items and categories of classroom behavior. And all these items and categories must resonate, must come to the surface when relevant, when the supervisor studies the events of the classroom. The more encyclopedic his knowledge and the more sensitively he responds to his data, the more carefully he must guard against the premature identification of a pattern or a critical incident. It is a temptation to jump to a conclusion: doing so saves so much time and labor. For such errors there is no easy remedy. Only professional discipline and commitment to the tenets of professional practice will help the supervisor to avoid them.

A companion piece to the overhasty inference is the "favorite" pattern. Review enough transcripts, and you cannot help being struck by the frequency with which teachers use the word *I*. It proliferates like crab-grass. Analyze the *I* long enough, and it begins to emerge as a substitute for a thousand more appropriate words in the teacher's lesson:

I agree with = You are correct.

I think you should get back to work = We're wasting time, we should get back to work.

I want quiet = Please be quiet.

I can't go on with the work = Those of us who want to work can't.

I'll give you an "A." = You've earned an "A," and so on.

When the teacher tabulates the number of *I*'s, he is often overwhelmed by the teacher-centeredness of his instruction. He wants to change the pattern. What is more, the supervisor can help him. And so the cycle of supervision goes into high gear, with everybody satisfied. But there may be a good-sized fly in the ointment. It *is* true that many teachers use *I* frequently. But is it true that every teacher who uses *I* frequently is teacher-centered? No. A teacher can use *I* and still by a thousand other more persuasive signals tell his students that he and they are one, are together, and that the *I* is an unconscious mannerism without much meaning. Or again, if *I*' *is* abused, is it more important than other patterns, or is it simply easier to demonstrate and to treat?

Other favorite and often prematurely identified patterns cluster around whatever happens to be popular at the moment in educator's jargon, especially in misused technical terms:

He exhibits a pattern of *operant conditioning.*

She's very *nondirective.*

That's a *democratic* pattern.

His *superego* is superactive.

Lots of evidence that he sees himself as a *father figure.*

No question but that he's *charismatic.*

She's *open* and runs an *open class.*

Good medicine for premature and facile inference-making is iron self-restraint. Regular therapeutic seminars and workshops for clinical supervisors are helpful also.

Another common weakness of clinical supervisors is a tendency to work with one pattern at a time. Some supervisors identify a pattern and then treat it in isolation, as though it alone were the major determinant of a teacher's strength or weakness. The trouble with such a procedure is that in most instances a major characteristic of a teacher's performance develops not from the action of one pattern, but from the *interaction* of several. Naive analysis often stems from an oversimplified perception of teaching, which leads to a reliance on single-factor hunches about what affects a teaching performance. For example, one may analyze an entire lesson and attribute the students' learning to the adequacy-inadequacy of the teacher's plan or to the cold-warm interpersonal relationships established between the teacher and the students. But only when all other factors are nullified or overpowered by one single factor can such a single-factor hypothesis be entertained—and such situations are certainly not common.

The effectiveness of the teacher in class is more often determined by a complex interaction of patterns, and a complex analysis is therefore required. In such an analysis one might find that the teacher's ability to communicate to his students the fact that he genuinely cares about them as learners interacts with his commitment to and command of his subject, and also with a strong talent for inductive teaching. This interaction produces an effect upon students that overrides the equally interacting patterns of excessive use of lecture, few rewards, and complete absence of a sense of humor. The interacting patterns generate learnings of the highest order among his students. An analysis focused on any single pattern would not shed much light on the reasons for such outcomes.

A simpler example: A teacher who communicates with students at a high level of abstraction and imagery may be effective or not, depending upon the interaction of his communication patterns with the students' vocabulary and upon his ability to motivate them.

Some Tests of Working Hypotheses

1. Check the frequencies of observed behaviors in several teaching sessions rather than in only one.
2. Arbitrarily divide a typescript into two parts. Form hypotheses on the evidence in one part and test for their presence in the other part.
3. Test working hypotheses with the teacher during the conference.
4. Collect and take into account data from several sources—
   a. feedback from students;
   b. analysis by other supervisors; and
   c. analysis by behavioral scientists.
5. Use several media for gathering data. Make an analysis of both verbal and nonverbal behavior.
6. Use well-developed interaction analysis systems whose categories are closely related to your working hypotheses.
7. Try to create alternative hypotheses from the same data, and check them.
8. Review the data that does not "fit" your tentative patterns.
9. Analyze "who did what" in addition to "what happened."
10. Ask whether your analysis arises from your own strong reactions to behavior that may not produce the same reactions in students. For example:
    a. Do you have a low tolerance for noise, or is the class really noisy?
    b. Is the teacher's voice too low to hear, or is the tape a poor one? Or were you stationed too far from the teacher in class? Or are you slightly hard of hearing?
    c. Does the teacher exhibit a pattern of excessive physical contact with young children, or are you uptight about physical contact?
    And so on through your store of self-knowledge.
11. Try the following sequence:
    a. Analyze the data on students' behavior *first*.

   b. Analyze the data on students' learnings in the following categories: cognitive, affective, psychomotor, and unanticipated learnings.
   c. Relate these learnings to the objectives of the instruction.
   d. Analyze the teacher's behaviors.
   e. Form hypotheses about the relationships between the teacher's behaviors, students' behaviors, and learning outcomes.

The touchstone of clinical analysis is the examination of patterns of classroom behavior in interaction, in their relatedness and synchrony. This is simply a way of saying that we are likely to succeed better in the work of supervision if we avoid dealing with a facet, a part, or a pattern of behavior in isolation. The significance of the part—its meaning for the clinical supervisor—is rarely evident within the part itself. The part gains its meaning from its place, relationships, and interaction in the totality of classroom behavior.

The Place of Intuition in Analysis

Intuition plays an important role in the analysis of teaching-learning. We have no option about *whether* or not to depend upon intuition, only about *how* to use it. Intuition is, as Bruner puts it, the left hand—the dreamer. Order, lawfulness, and science are the right hand. The "scientist and the poet do not live at antipodes, and . . . the artificial separation of the two modes of knowing cripples. . . ."[3]

> One thing has become increasingly clear in pursuing the nature of knowing. It is that the conventional apparatus of the psychologist—both his instruments of investigation and the conceptual tools he uses in the interpretation of his data—leaves one approach unexplored. It is an approach whose medium of exchange seems to be the metaphor paid out by the left hand. It is a way that grows happy hunches and "lucky" guesses, that is stirred into connective activity by the poet and the necromancer looking sidewise rather than directly. Their hunches and intuitions generate a grammar of their own—searching out connections, suggesting similarities, weaving ideas loosely in a trial web. . . . We have learned too that the "arts" of sensing and knowing consist in honoring our highly limited capacity for taking in and processing information. We honor that capacity by learning the methods of compacting vast ranges of experience in economical symbols— concepts, language, metaphor, myth, formulae. The price of failing at this art is either to be trapped in a confined world of experience or to be the victim of an overload of information.[4]

[3]Bruner, *On Knowing: Essays for the Left Hand* (Cambridge, Mass.: Harvard University Press, 1962), p. 2.
[4]Ibid., pp. 3–4, 6–7.

All we can add is that the clinical supervisor's intuitions must be based on a disciplined examination of the phenomena with which he deals, that his intuitions—his working hypotheses—must be generated from the widest relevant knowledge he can master, and that these hypotheses must remain vulnerable to every question and every bit of information.

Nonverbal Behavior in Clinical Supervision

In the literature of supervision, nonverbal behavior receives too little attention. The question of its place in supervision and in the improvement of instruction is slighted. Reasons for this neglect are varied. Some educators simply ignore nonverbal behavior, possibly because it is extremely resistant to analysis. Others maintain that the teacher's influence is expressed principally by way of oral communication and that analysis of nonverbal activity would add little of real value. Such an assertion appears to be well supported by the sheer volume of teachers' speech—surely everything that needs to be said must be said in all that talk! Still others believe that verbal and nonverbal speech are so highly correlated that to interpret verbal communication is to interpret the nonverbal messages accompanying it.

Our own view is that the study of nonverbal behavior is important to supervision, for at least four reasons:

1. If we assume that nonverbal communication does in fact closely mirror verbal communication, then the nonverbal may provide useful clarification when oral communication is unclear, doubtful, or ambiguous, as indeed it often is.
2. There is no doubt that nonverbal behavior is on occasion at variance with or even contradicts verbal behavior. If so, then it may again be important for the clinical supervisor to find the means to decipher the "best" meaning or the "real" intent of dissimilar messages communicated simultaneously via two different systems.
3. Nonverbal behavior may amplify verbal communication and add meanings to it. Gesture and facial expression surely add emphasis and emotion to spoken language, making the meaning richer and more evocative.
4. Nonverbal communication *may provide important data in the absence of spoken communication.* Students who are silent much of the time in class may yet be communicating volumes if we can only decipher their *silent* messages. Teachers, too, are on occasion silent, but they may communicate clearly and forcefully by way of posture, facial expression, and body movement.

Such possibilities as these are rendered plausible by our own experience as a supervisor. No one really doubts that people communicate nonverbally. Obviously, we often read both kinds of messages clearly. The difficulty arises because we read and understand both at once in a swift, complex, but largely unconscious synthesis. It will repay supervisors' efforts to learn this second language. Nonverbal communication exists, and the clinical supervisor must work with it—carefully, cautiously, patiently, and with wisdom. He cannot ignore it. Who could safely ignore the message sent by a student who "replies" to a teacher's criticism by making a sour face, by pointedly turning away, or by bursting into tears? As Birdwhistell warns us, "to focus exclusively upon the *words* humans interchange is to eliminate much of the communicational process from view, and, thus, from purposive control." He adds that "whatever 'meaning' is, it is not merely conventional understandings based on words."[5]

The vividness and richness with which nonverbal behavior may express thought and emotion becomes clearly evident in the work of a master of pantomime like Marcel Marceau. When he is on stage the theatre is silent, but filled with most expressive silent speech.

A list of the modalities of nonverbal communication is varied and unexpected enough to surprise many readers—

1. body motion of kinesic behavior: gestures and other body movements, including facial expression, eye movement, and posture;
2. paralanguage: voice qualities, speech nonfluencies (silences and stutterings), and such nonlanguage sounds as laughing, yawning, and grunting;
3. proxemics: use of "social and personal space and man's perception of it";
4. olfaction;
5. skin sensitivity to touch and temperature;
6. use of artifacts, such as dress and cosmetics.[6]

Three Exploratory Studies of Nonverbal Behavior   Some pioneer work has been done in applying the analysis of nonverbal behavior to the supervision and education of teachers. Galloway's research in this field is outstanding. From his study of the nonverbal behavior of elementary school teachers he draws the following conclusions:

The evidence suggested that the teachers who were most encouraging tended to reveal their interest in pupils through their listening behavior, their appropriate responsiveness, and their emotional support. Teachers who displayed inhibiting communicative behaviors were disinterested in pupil talk, were inconsistent in their behavioral responses to pupils, and

[5]Ray L. Birdwhistell, *Kinesics and Context: Essays on Body Motion Communication* (Philadelphia: University of Pennsylvania Press, 1970), pp. 50, xii.
[6]Starkey Duncan, Jr., "Nonverbal Communication," *Psychological Bulletin* 72, no. 2 (1969), p. 118.

were more likely to express disapproval in their nonverbal contacts with pupils.[7]

Galloway answers a question of great moment to the clinical supervisor: Would teachers benefit from knowing about the consequences of their nonverbal behavior in the classroom?

> In conclusion, it must be stated that the meanings inherent in nonverbal expressions are used by pupils to check on the fidelity of communicative acts, and that such meanings are used by these same pupils to obtain a better picture of the self a teacher proposes to be. By interpreting and inferring from nonverbal expressions pupils may attempt to obtain the full import of a teacher's perceptions and motivations. To gain perceptual clarity and consistency each pupil feels he must be aware of the various nonverbal cues which facilitate obtaining added information. During classroom interaction, the expressive acts of a teacher's activity suggest a promissory character that is assumed by pupils to represent a more accurate reflection of the real self of the teacher. . . . Within classroom settings it is now recognized that teachers vary considerably in their ability, or in their willingness to communicate effectively when the question of competence in verbal language is raised. Teachers vary widely also in their disposition to communicate favorable feelings and attitudes toward pupils. The travesty is that too many of us are not aware of the feelings which we express toward students in our teaching. More pointedly, it might be stated that teachers are unaware of the consequences of the nonverbal messages they transmit in classroom teaching, not to mention the out-of-classroom interactions. Perhaps a failure to interpret or to be aware of the many "affective" implications of nonverbal language constantly remains a grave handicap and a profound difficulty for truly understanding the impact of one's communication with pupils.[8]

Pancrazio and Johnson have attempted to train teachers to exhibit nonverbal behaviors that would encourage classroom interaction. The categories Pancrazio and Johnson selected to work with are useful as examples of structured behaviors teachers might learn to use:

1. Initiating behaviors related to pupil participation.
   Teacher calls on pupils who obviously or subtly indicate desire to speak.
   Teacher, using direct eye contact, monitors class to see who wants to speak.

2. Initiating behaviors related to use of silence.
   Allows enough time for called-on pupil or called-on class to respond.
   Breaks silence when pupils begin to fidget, etc.

3. Responding behaviors to interested pupils.
   Listens without interruption when pupil speaks.

---

[7]Charles M. Galloway, "Nonverbal Communication in Teaching," in *Teaching: Vantage Points for Study*, ed. Ronald T. Hyman (New York: J. B. Lippincott Co., 1968), p. 70. Reprinted by permission.
[8]Ibid., p. 73.

When pupil speaks, nods in support, has eye contact.
Moves toward pupil or pupils when pupil speaks.

4. Responding behaviors to bored pupils.
STOPS whatever he was formerly doing.
Moves toward pupil or pupils to induce interest.[9]

These categories are interesting as early intimations about the non-verbal behaviors considered valuable for teachers to learn. They are further interesting as illustrations of the high level of inference that characterizes most attempts to apply what we know about nonverbal behavior. The meanings of most nonverbal behaviors have so far defied clear, explicit, and unambiguous definition. We have no dictionaries of nonverbal behavior as yet. For example, Webster defines the verb *to shrug* as "to raise or draw in the shoulders," or "to lift or contract the shoulders. . . ." This entry, however, offers two quite different additional "meanings" of the word—"to express *indifference* or *aversion*,"[10]—which are certainly quite different from the first definitions in meaning. And we can readily add other plausible definitions of our own: to express resignation or puzzlement. And if we combine a *shrug* with elbows bent and palms upturned and eyebrows raised, we can read "What does he want from me?"

As for the inferences embedded in Pancrazio and Johnson's nonverbal categories, we may note the following:

The inference in *desire*: "pupils who obviously or subtly indicate *desire* to speak."

The inference in *bored*: "responding behaviors to *bored* pupils."

These observations are not intended as disparagement. On the contrary, we applaud the categories as reasonable attempts to interpret important nonverbal behavior or to force the supervisor to make inferences about phenomena concerning which direct and unambiguous information is not otherwise available when classroom interaction is in process. Or are we to do nothing about the possibility that students may be bored until we can train them to tell us so in the course of our teaching?

A recent study by Griffard is noteworthy as a careful and painstaking attempt to adapt existing techniques for coding nonverbal and verbal communication for use in the analysis of classroom interaction. Griffard coded teacher talk, student talk, postural data on the teacher, his pacing,

---

[9]Sally F. Pancrazio and W. D. Johnson, "Comparison of Three Teacher Training Approaches in Nonverbal Behavior Which Encourage Classroom Interaction" (Paper presented at the Annual Meeting of the American Educational Research Association, 1971), p. 5.
[10]*Webster's Seventh New Collegiate Dictionary*, s.v. "shrug." (Italics added.)

other movement, and gestures.[11] He concludes that "Over time, stable patterns within individual styles [of teachers and students] can be defined for diagnostic and training use. . . ."[12]

At the present moment, what the clinical supervisor has to work with in nonverbal behavior is certainly not a highly developed theory or a body of immediately useful practices. But he does have some elements of a theory, some rudimentary practices still in the earliest stages of development, and a few fledgling categories of analysis. He has what Neal Gross has called some "sensitizing concepts." The clinical supervisor must study nonverbal behavior and master the categories that are beginning to emerge in this field. With such preparation he will be ready to make a few carefully safeguarded first tests of the applications of nonverbal behavior in clinical supervision—perhaps in simulated situations or with teachers competent and secure enough to join in such explorations. Two dangers are to be avoided: premature applications of clinical analysis to nonverbal classroom behavior and premature rejection of the whole idea.

J. H. Burnett provides an illuminating example of the teacher's and the supervisor's need to respond intelligently and emphatically to students' nonverbal behavior. In her anecdote Burnett illustrates a teacher's differential responses to the varying physical, social, and cultural behavior of students:

> . . . Suppose you [were] a teacher conducting a lesson before a group of eighth graders and had just discovered that one of the students was without a book. You ask, "Eva, where is your book?" Eva turns her head slightly, purses her lips, and casts her eyes down. What does it mean to you? The downcast eyes probably suggest that something deceptive is going on; the pursed lips that she's pouting and defiant; and the turned head a gesture of escape, or worse, haughtiness. To Eva, if she's Puerto Rican, they do not mean that at all. The Puerto Ricans often point with their lips. So Eva is pointing at the fellow student who has her book! But in those elementary-school desks she has to turn around a bit to do the pointing. Her downcast eyes are a gesture of respect, a procedure that she's being carefully taught by her parents if they really care that she be well-behaved and mannerly. It's terrible manners to stare a person straight in the eyes! Yet, I wish I had a dollar in my pocket for every time I've seen a North American teacher jerk or pull a Puerto Rican child's chin up as he, or she, talks to the child. That's the more dignified type; the more companionable, emphatic type crouch down to try to get lower than the child's eyes.[13]

[11]Charles David Griffard, "An Adaptation of the Linguistics-Kinesics Research Model to College Classroom Interaction Analysis" (Ph.D. diss., School of Education, University of Pittsburgh, 1971), p. 48.
[12]Ibid., pp. 75–76.
[13]Jacquetta H. Burnett, "Culture of the School: A Construct for Research and Explanation in Education," *Council on Anthropology and Education Newsletter* 1, no. 1 (1970), pp. 4–13.

Some Categories of Nonverbal Behavior   It may be informative to review some of the categories of nonverbal behavior now in use by researchers and clinical supervisors. (Those to be found in the work of Pancrazio and Johnson are referred to in the preceding pages of this chapter. The names of the individuals who framed each item will be placed in parentheses after the category, except when the item is framed by us.)

NONVERBAL BEHAVIOR IN INTERPERSONAL RELATIONSHIPS

Teacher helps student carry heavy equipment to laboratory.

Teacher pushes student.

Teacher listens with patience and interest. (Galloway)

Teacher ignores students and neither sustains nor encourages sharing information or expressing ideas. (Galloway)

Teacher gives student a pat on the back. (Galloway)

Quality of voice indicates pleasure or warm affection. (Galloway)

Receptivity: pose or stance suggests readiness to listen. (Galloway)

Teacher frowns, scowls, or looks threatening. (Galloway)

Teacher responds to students' signals of fatigue.

Teacher varies behavior in response to students' signals of attention-non-attention.

Teacher arranges chairs, desks, etc., to insure line-of-sight for students. Arranges seating for comfort of students who are lame, tall, short, hard of hearing.

Teacher varies classroom activities in relation to students' maturity, strength, psychomotor skills, interests, needs.

Teacher pushes, shoves, strikes students.

Teacher moves toward or away from students' territories. (Galloway)

Teacher sits with, among, students, or remains separated from them—at front of room, for example.

Teacher modifies his behavior as a result of feedback from students. Alters pace or direction of the lesson when he detects nonverbal signs of students' misunderstanding. (Galloway)

Teacher responds to or ignores signs of student discomfort.

Young female teacher smiles when meeting older adolescents in class for first time if she is in Atlanta, but not in Buffalo. Freely adapted from Birdwhistell, who notes that smiling in "particular contexts indicated 'pleasure,' in others 'humor,' in others 'ridicule,' and, in still others, 'friendliness,' or 'good manners.' Smiles have been seen to indicate 'doubt' and 'acceptance,' 'equality' and 'superordination' or 'subordination.' "[14]

(This digression about ambiguities in nonverbal behavior is inserted here to remind supervisors about the dangers of facile inference.)

NONVERBAL BEHAVIOR IN CLASSROOM CONTROL

Teacher remains silent in front of class until class becomes quiet.

Teacher rises from chair, walks toward students, and remains silent in order to establish quiet.

Teacher claps hands for order.

Teacher rings bell, strikes or taps desk with ruler to restore silence.

Teacher grants or withholds permission by nod or gesture.

Teacher reinforces by physical means. (Offers candy, prizes, etc.)

NONVERBAL BEHAVIOR AND SENSE MODALITIES OTHER THAN HEARING

Teacher teaches by having students taste, smell, touch, act, dance, walk, limp, lift, and weigh. That is, teacher uses a variety of sense modalities appropriate to different learning tasks.

MOTION IN NONVERBAL BEHAVIOR

. . . When a psychiatrist [teacher or student?] sits forward in a chair this could be interpreted by the patient [student or teacher] as a preliminary to rising and leaving and therefore of non-interest. . . . On the other hand, a more relaxed position, sitting back in the chair, suggests an openness and interest on the part of the hearer."[15] (Condon)

" 'Things like prejudice could be the result of communication problems,' Dr. Condon said, explaining that studies show black people have a fluidity and rapidity of motion and language which makes white people uncomfortable. When you are uncomfortable in a situation you avoid it, he explained."[16]

USE OF TIME AS NONVERBAL BEHAVIOR

Teacher indicates his likes and dislikes by his allocation of time to various activities. (Galloway)

STUDENTS' USE OF NONVERBAL BEHAVIOR

(As we have noted, students are not usually speaking when the teacher is. As a result, the teacher receives very little verbal feedback from students while he holds the center of the stage. It may therefore be extremely useful

[14]Birdwhistell, op. cit., p. 31.
[15]William S. Condon, in an interview with M. L. Burger: "Speak to Me Only with Thine Eyes, an Exercise in Linguistics-Kinesics." *University Times*, Pittsburgh: University of Pittsburgh, 5 March 1970, p. 5.
[16]Ibid.

for teachers and supervisors to develop competence in decoding the students' nonverbal behavior.)

Students signal that they are ready to recite or want to volunteer: by eye contact, raising hand, nodding the head.

Students signal that they are not paying attention: they fall asleep, read during a recitation, cover their ears with their hands, pass notes, play pencil-and-paper games, etc.

The Processes of Analysis of Nonverbal Behavior   As presently practiced by researchers in kinesics, the processes of analysis are far too specialized, demanding, and costly to be adopted by clinical supervisors. We need to confine ourselves to very modest objectives and develop the limited analytical procedures appropriate to our objectives and the present state of our knowledge and competence in this new field. It will be useful to begin with a study of both the basic research and the applied work of men and women like Pancrazio and Johnson, Galloway, and Griffard. From such sources the clinical supervisor may learn about the nonverbal categories and the analytical techniques likely to be most useful in these first stages of his work. The suggestions made here are given with full recognition of the very minimal help they will provide. Most supervisors are habituated to the use of audio or typed records. They therefore need help in developing the discipline of focusing on nonverbal behavior. They also need help in learning to see. Among the most useful and informative experiences they could have would be working in several two- or three-hour sessions with an experienced analyst of nonverbal behavior. Both the training in observation and the technical skills gained through such experiences could form a serviceable basis for further study.

It hardly seems necessary to mention the fact that videotape or sound-film recordings are indispensable for such study and analysis. Some of the following procedures may be useful:

1. Review film without sound. Review and check nonverbal patterns.
2. Review the film in shorter "takes." Record impressions for each take.
3. Review the entire film with sound. Record general impressions about students' learnings, students' behaviors, and the teacher's behaviors.
4. For closer analysis or micro-scanning some researchers use a time-motion analyzer, which permits the viewer to examine the sound film frame by frame. This is especially useful in identifying complex and rapid nonverbal behavior that is otherwise not apprehended by the analyst. Such sophistication should perhaps be avoided by the naive observer. Clinical supervisors might be well advised to stick to simple behavior and gross analysis at present.

Is it really feasible to analyze nonverbal behavior in clinical supervision? The men and women doing research in the analysis of nonverbal behavior are unanimous in attesting to the difficulties plaguing their work. How does one capture and code the multitudes of fleeting and often unnoticed behaviors in the act of smiling or in the complex movements of the entire body that accompany speech? In contrast to these complicated tasks, the recording, coding, and analysis of verbal behavior begins to appear deceptively simple, even "scientific." The result may be that we overestimate our power to record and make sense out of human speech. The seeming simplicity of verbal discourse derives largely from the fact that we deal with speech by ignoring most of it: most of its plural "meanings," to start with; most of its inflections, metaphors, connotations, dialects, and poetry. For proof of this statement we have only to note that in the most widely used verbal interaction analysis systems the spoken words are immediately translated into code, and the words themselves often disappear, never to surface again. The apparent simplicity of what is left lulls us into dreaming that we have abolished ambiguities, plural meanings, and high inference, and have achieved the condition of science. But of course we have not.

Can we then learn not to expect too much of our early trials at making sense out of nonverbal behavior? If we are patient, we may learn to use the few categories of analysis beginning to come into view. With such help and the limited skills we can develop, we may at least explore this new field. If we are lucky, we may gain some modest insights into the meanings of the nonverbal components of classroom behavior.

CHAPTER 14

The Conference in Clinical Supervision

A Non-definition of "Clinical Conference"

A chapter entitled "The Conference in Clinical Supervision" should, nine times out of ten, start with a definition of *conference*. Not here. The reason underlying this omission is that to look at the clinical conference as an entity in itself would be a gross error. The clinical conference defines itself in its context. It is an integral part of the processes in the cycle of supervision. All the policies, recommendations, and problems treated in this chapter are equally relevant to any other occasion on which the teacher and supervisor meet professionally. The conference is not a culmination of, nor yet the most important event in, the clinical program. It is at one and the same time a constituent and a development of everything that goes on before and after it. To approach this "contextual definition" from another angle, all working contacts between the teacher and supervisor are "conference" and should be imbued with the same purposes and governed by the same policies, care, and forethought.

The conference has outcomes affecting the teacher and supervisor directly. That is, it works out well or badly. But, in addition, each conference sets up reverberations in the social networks that are called "the school" and "the school system." What happens in a conference becomes part of a history of supervision that is transmitted into the school society. Because what happens in the conference is vitally important to teachers, it is often communicated to others. The conference, therefore, must be planned and carried out with great care.

Preconference Arrangements

Physical Setting The arrangements for the conference itself merit detailed planning. The time and place should be carefully selected. Teacher and supervisor should agree on an hour that is convenient for both. The length of the meeting will vary, but enough time should be set aside to insure that it will not have to be ended prematurely. The initial conferences should be deliberate rather than pressured in pace, and they will tend to be longer rather than shorter. If possible, a period of about two hours should be available for each meeting. Ensuing conferences will usually require about an hour.

The session should ideally be held in a room specially equipped for the review of audiotapes, videotapes, films, etc. Privacy is a requisite, and the convenience of a blackboard and the amenities of comfortable surroundings are helpful. The supervisor's office is generally not physically or psychologically suitable, at least in the early stages of the program. The teacher's classroom may serve very well, especially if it is equipped for the purposes of the conference.

The Preparation of the Supervisor for the Conference   The supervisor can and does prepare thoroughly for the conference, but he cannot go too far in *preplanning* it. Its course is unpredictable. The supervisor cannot therefore anticipate in detail how it will develop, what problems will arise, or what will force a change of direction. If he plans too far in advance, the chances are excellent that he will prestructure what is to happen and, if he persists, will force some of the anticipated events to take place. As a consequence, he may unwittingly override some of the teacher's most pressing concerns.

The character of the interaction in the conference should be participatory, responsive, and formative. It follows, then, that there are no standard formats and no best strategies. The conference is a shared exploration: a search for the meaning of instruction, for choices among alternative diagnoses, and for alternative strategies of improvement.

The process of the conference may perhaps be conceptualized as follows:

1. After the teacher has taught the lesson, he and the supervisor join forces in an effort to search out its meanings and to plan to improve upon it.
2. In the pursuit of these goals, the teacher and supervisor analyze the classroom data.
3. This examination produces a partial diagnosis of the teacher's teaching, jointly formulated.
4. Following the diagnosis, the teacher and supervisor decide on the objectives to be sought in planning for the next lesson(s).
5. They then begin to construct the plan designed to achieve their objectives.
6. They work out the criteria for the success of the plan and the procedures for gathering the data needed to evaluate its outcomes.

7. The sequence of steps set out above is not necessarily the sequence that must be followed. Nor must every step be included. For example, a decision may be made not to analyze the preceding lesson at all, or the teacher may set out at once to plan for the next lesson.

The Preparation of the Teacher for the Conference   The success of the conference is in part determined by the care with which the teacher has been prepared to take his appropriate role in it. The process of preparation is initiated in the first phase of the cycle when the teacher-supervisor relationship is developing. It continues as the teacher is inducted into clinical supervision itself. And it culminates in the process in which the teacher himself examines his own teaching performance in anticipation of the conference. At this time he (1) performs an analysis of his own instruction, (2) sets out his working hypotheses about what happened in class, (3) draws up his own questions, and (4) develops some tentative strategies for improvement. The preparation of the teacher for his role in the conference helps to transform him from an object of supervision into a colleague in it.

Objectives of the Conference

1. Certain objectives of the conference remain concealed from the supervisor until after it is under way. These are the *teacher's* objectives. For example, the teacher may want to discuss a new technique he has designed to encourage greater student participation in setting the objectives of the instruction. Or he may be concerned about an incident in the lesson that demands analysis. The teacher's objectives must therefore be identified in the course of the conference and integrated with it.

2. Another goal of the teacher and supervisor is to achieve a surer understanding of the students' behavior and their learnings. One might at first assume that teacher and supervisor would both know how the students behaved and what they learned. And occasionally they may. On the other hand, the two are sometimes so focused on their own concerns that the behavior of all students is not closely followed. In either event, however, a joint review of the patterns of students' behavior and their learnings helps both the teacher and supervisor to concentrate on important rather than trivial events that have occurred in class. Knowledge about the students is a prerequisite for the formulation of working hypotheses about the teaching.

3. Once in command of the information about what the students have

done and are likely to have learned, teacher and supervisor attempt to relate this knowledge to the teacher's stated objectives and the students' learnings. This is part of the answer to "How did the teacher do?" and the beginning of the quest for the answer to "Why?"

4. The teacher's and supervisor's next objective in the conference is to identify critical incidents and patterns in the teacher's classroom behavior. This information serves a double purpose. It elaborates and deepens the teacher's self-knowledge—his concept of his teaching self. It also identifies the factors in the teacher's behavior that will be woven into the search for plausible hypotheses about how critical incidents and the teacher's patterns of behavior relate to the students' behavior and their learnings.

5. Another outcome anticipated from the conference is an improvement in the teacher's performance of his roles in the clinical conference. He has the example, the substantive help, and the encouragement of the supervisor in these tasks. The teacher's developing competence in his roles can be a source of deep satisfaction to him. These and other learnings, combined with the pleasure of professional company in the performance of significant new tasks, may open up to the teacher a satisfying and significant new domain in his professional life.

6. The teacher's increasing competence in the processes of the conference may also help him to achieve increasing autonomy in self-supervision. In order to reinforce this trend, the supervisor should encourage the teacher to set his own short- and long-range goals in the supervisory program, with the aim of buttressing the teacher's commitment to his personal program of professional development.

It is necessary at this point to call attention to the risks involved in trying to upgrade the teacher's classroom instruction while at the same time attempting to induct him into clinical supervision. The latter process may interfere with the central objective of improving instruction. Much depends upon the teacher. Some teachers thrive on the dual program. Others may become confused about which objective takes priority. And still others may want to shift the emphasis entirely to the study of clinical supervision. Occasionally the supervisor himself oscillates between the two objectives.

In general, we have found it possible to avoid most of the dangers alluded to by completing the conference proper and then, if the moment seems opportune and the teacher not fatigued, turning the current of the discussion to the clinical process itself, in what is often both an evaluation and analysis of the session and a learning experience for the teacher. However, in spite of our optimistic view of, and easy prescription for, the problem, the supervisor should approach the job very warily, waiting until he is certain that the teacher is confident in his role as teacher-in-clinical-supervision before instructing him in the role of apprentice-in-clinical-supervision. A fairly good rule of thumb is "In case of doubt, don't." It may even be better to separate the two objectives completely, but we have rarely been able to restrain our didactic impulse to do these two things at once, especially when the teacher himself begins to reach out for them.

The Jagged Profile: A Strategy for the Improvement of Teaching

Two Common Assumptions about the Improvement of Teaching   A great many supervisors appear to base their strategy for working with teachers on two implicit assumptions. The first seems eminently reasonable: No matter what the "average" of a teacher's performance may be, he is not likely to be equally competent in every aspect of his work. The second is that the objective of their supervision is to help the teacher overcome his weaknesses and thus improve the general level of his instruction. It may be useful to examine these ideas closely and to search out their probable consequences.

If the assumption that a teacher is not likely to be equally competent in all aspects of his instruction is represented graphically, the resultant graph will be jagged rather than smooth, and will have highs, middle levels and lows. For example, let us suppose that we have a 100-point scale of competence ranging from 0 to 100, with the midpoint between competence and incompetence located at 50. Let us also suppose that a teacher "scores" as follows: 70 in *planning*, 40 in *interpersonal relationships* with students, 90 in command of *content*, 0 in use of *humor*, 80 in quality of *communication*, 30 in *diagnosis* of students' learning difficulties, 60 in *methods* of teaching, and 40 in *reinforcement* techniques. One would expect that a talented teacher would have a generally high but still jagged profile, and an incompetent teacher a generally low but also irregular profile.

The metaphor of a "graphic" representation is an obvious oversimplification when used in reference to teaching, since the quality of a teacher's performance is more appropriately viewed as the product of the interaction of various dimensions of teaching than as a graph. Nevertheless, many supervisors and teachers persist in conceptualizing the teacher's

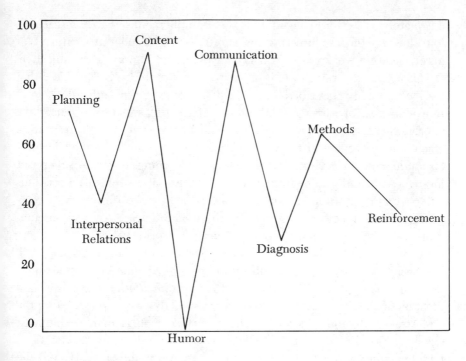

Figure 2   COMPETENCE PROFILE

performance as a bundle of separate competences having an effect that "averages out" at some general level of competence. This naive assumption strongly influences the strategies that supervisors develop to improve the teacher's performance. They diagnose a low point or a weakness in the teacher's competence profile and embark on a program to remedy it. Or, worse yet, they assume that almost all teachers suffer from the *same* weakness: they talk too much and ask too many questions requiring only recall of simple facts. The supervisors therefore promptly set about to remedy these deficiencies, hoping in this way to accomplish a comprehensive improvement in the teacher's instruction and in the students' learning. It is noteworthy that a major historical theme of school supervision has been the treatment of weaknesses. It was assumed that the normal-school graduate suffered from a deficient education and therefore needed extra supervision on the job. The liberal-arts-major-turned-teacher supposedly suffered from weaknesses in method and needed extra tutoring. As a consequence, the supervisor often still views himself as a specialist charged with filling cavities.

This "profile" approach persists even when the teacher is performing adequately or better. The supervisor still applies himself to the teacher's lowest competences, directing his efforts to the sequential treatment of purely relative weaknesses as his most logical and appropriate objective.

This attempt to remedy infirmities is justified only in the instances that we have already described as "critical." When a single critical incident threatens possibly irreparable consequences, the supervisor must take appropriate action, as noted. So, too, when a *pattern* is critical. That is, when a single aspect of the teacher's instruction is so defective as to bar his students from even minimally adequate learning, then the supervisor must focus his efforts for improvement on that pattern of weakness. This latter situation may arise when a teacher lacks even rudimentary command of his subject or when he does not communicate. In such circumstances the supervisor must give deficiencies first priority.

But when the teacher is not at such a critical juncture in his teaching, the "weakness" strategy is not likely to be very productive. The assumptions underlying it are wrong. The first is that *remediation* is the principal function of the supervisor. The second questionable assumption is that the best strategy to improve the teacher's performance is to raise his least developed competences to the level of the best developed. The third fallible assumption is that the teacher has the time, the capacity, and the motivation to attain a high flat profile of professional competences and that the supervisor has the time and talent to help him do it.

The naiveté of such assumptions about the flat profile is revealed by L. Tyler:

> For Man as a species the possibilities for development are almost unlimited. . . . In contrast, man as an individual is *limited*. This is not necessarily because he lacks any of the potentialities we attribute to the human species, but because he lacks *time*. Each individual human being thus constitutes a *selection* of a few characteristics to be developed, a selection from the vast range of possibilities initially open to him as a member of the human race.[1]

Although Tyler here refers to limitations in the development of an individual across the entire range of human potential, it seems reasonable to guess that similar constraints operate across a segment of that range, for example, across the range of potential for achieving the competences required of a teacher. It is quite clear that the appearance of men with great talent across even a narrow range of human potential is rare. We have many great artists, but few with the manifold talents of a Da Vinci.

[1] Leona E. Tyler, *The Psychology of Human Differences* (New York: Appleton-Century-Crofts, 1965), p. 505. (Italics in original.)

Common sense and psychology therefore appear to offer strong arguments against a supervisory strategy that focuses on the least of the teacher's competences. Nevertheless, in our experience it has been most difficult—occasionally impossible—to keep supervisors from concentrating on the teacher's frailties. Why is this tendency so strong? Even in the midst of an intensive six-week workshop for clinical supervisors, and after a special campaign to help supervisors-in-training, we still found them devoting most of their conference periods with obviously competent teachers to the treatment of weaknesses. The supervisor who uses this approach must ask himself why.

Is it possible that many clinical supervisors *need* to deal with the least of the teacher's competences? Are they serving their *own* needs when they do? A hypothesis suggested by Jules Henry in a discussion of what happens to students in a competitive culture may also be relevant to the behavior of supervisors. He notes that in school one student's failure makes it possible for another to succeed. This occurs in recitation when a student answers a teacher's question incorrectly. Other students are called on until the correct answer is given: "Thus Boris's failure has made it possible for Peggy to succeed; his depression is the price of her exhilaration; his misery is the occasion for her rejoicing." Henry goes on to develop his thesis by adding, "And since all but the brightest children have the constant experience that others succeed at their expense they cannot but . . . hate the success of others. . . . Along with this, naturally, goes the hope that others will fail." He sums up by saying that "a competitive culture endures by tearing people down."[2]

Do some supervisors need to affirm their special competences by demonstrating at one and the same time that the teacher has professional weaknesses and that the supervisor has professional strengths? Do some supervisors have a need to establish themselves as competent practitioners, and do they unthinkingly choose the lowest points of the teacher's competence profile as the points at which their own competence can most readily become visible? Or may they need the psychological ascendance that is almost universally evident in person-to-person interaction?

Whatever the causes underlying the remedial practices that dominate so many supervisory programs, there is a clear need for a reconstruction of the major strategies governing the conduct of supervisors. An exploratory approach to such a reformulation is proposed here.

First of all, we reiterate that critical incidents and single-factor patterns

[2]Jules Henry, "Culture Against Man," in John H. Sandberg, *Introduction to the Behavioral Sciences* (New York: Holt, Rinehart and Winston, Inc., 1969), pp. 58–59.

posing serious threats to students' learning should be dealt with as soon as they are observed and their existence has been confirmed by careful scrutiny of the relevant data. Most teachers and supervisors do not, however, face such extreme situations.

We suggest, therefore, that clinical supervisors apply more of their efforts to the improvement of existing patterns of *strength* in the teacher's performance. *Strength* as used here is relative to the teacher's own performance, not to criteria of performance external to him. This approach appears to offer many advantages:

1. To aim for the improvement of strengths is to avoid the almost inevitably painful atmosphere created by a concentration on deficiencies. To invite the teacher to apply himself to the improvement of his existing competences is to ask him to *build* rather than to *repair*. He becomes involved in sharpening and developing his best competences rather than in trying to shore up lesser skills. To work with capacity is tonic; to work with incapacity is medicinal.

2. There may be a pedagogical foundation for the strength vs. weakness approach. Harold Benjamin maintains in his appropriately titled essay "The Cultivation of Idiosyncrasy" that the learner whose "peaks of ability are built to greater heights will have his valleys of ability in other areas pulled up toward his peaks until the sum of his achievements will be far above the minimum essentials ever set by plodding plainsmen."[3] Does Benjamin's optimistic metaphor provide some support for our position? In our optimistic view it does. At the very least, we have noted many instances in which the teaching impact of some highly developed competences have been sufficient to overcome pronounced inadequacies. There may therefore be a certain pedagogical economy in leading from strength.

3. It also seems likely that the psychological reinforcement of starting from strength, together with the more frequent opportunities for rewards, may constitute a significant psychological advantage for both teacher and supervisor.

Having made a case for the primacy of strengths in the supervisory strategy, we must guard equally against excessive zeal in its application. To focus on strengths obviously does not mean that weaknesses are to be ignored or treated as though they are nonexistent. Weaknesses must be dealt with when they interact with a strength. For example, a teacher's highly developed ability to communicate complex ideas in simple form may lose some of its good effect because he fails to help his students *fix* these ideas firmly in their minds after his explanation. The supervisor can

[3]Harold Benjamin, *The Cultivation of Idiosyncrasy: The Inglis Lecture* (Cambridge, Mass.: Harvard University Press, 1949), p. 19.

help the teacher to identify this pattern and its consequences. Once this is done, it may not be too difficult for the teacher and supervisor to develop procedures to remedy the situation—encouraging students to restate the ideas in their own words, to provide examples, to invent problems, etc.

It seems likely that treating the teacher's weakness in direct connection with one of his strengths would siphon off some of the discomfort and even pain that the teacher might experience if the weakness were treated in isolation, or—worse—as one of a series of weaknesses.

In the end, however, the strength-weakness strategy proposed here will be put into operation by teachers and supervisors—that is to say, by fallible human beings. It is therefore easy to imagine what may happen. To a perfectionist supervisor every minor infirmity will be stamped *critical weakness*, and we will be back where we started from. Or a fervid devotee of the improvement-through-strength principle will be blind to the teacher's frailties. The classroom will become a stage where only perfect actors perform, and the supervisory program a joy-through-strength campaign. Which is to say that no matter how carefully the strategy of the emphasis on strength may be communicated, the best guarantee of its optimal application in clinical supervision is still the vigilance of teachers and supervisors committed to an open evaluation of their work together. No other safeguard can guarantee the preservation of the necessary strategic balance between the teacher's strengths and weaknesses in his supervisory program. No formula can do it.

Policies, Procedures, and Strategies of the Conference

"The Very First Sentence in the Conference"   The first sentence of the conference is often spoken before the conference begins at all. It is delivered when the supervisor is about to leave the classroom after an observation. The last student has gone, the teacher is standing at his door, and the supervisor is on his way out. What does the supervisor say as he passes the teacher? Most supervisors feel that they *must* make some favorable comment, whether the lesson merits it or not. If the lesson *has* been bad, they may mumble, "Very interesting." Some will say, "See you later," and then pale at the inferences the teacher might draw. Others maintain that there *has* to be something deserving praise in every lesson, so they smile and say, "Finished right on time!" and sidle out. Still others

volunteer something like "A good lesson," planning to recapture the truth later, in the conference.

Although the problem of what the supervisor is to say when he leaves seems trivial, it is not quite that. To remark to a teacher that an obviously poor lesson was "interesting" or "well done" may have serious consequences for the conference to come. What happens if the teacher believes the supervisor? Will the supervisor find it easy to reverse his field in the conference? Or what if the teacher *knows* that the lesson was bad, and concludes that the supervisor is an incompetent and really cannot tell good teaching from poor teaching? Or if he concludes that the supervisor is a hypocrite?

In truth, even if the lesson has been good, there is little to gain and much to lose by discussing it in passing. The supervisor can anticipate this problem and solve it by preparing the teacher beforehand to expect no discussion prior to the conference. Then the teacher will understand that no off-the-cuff judgments will or should be made. He should learn, too, that neither he nor the supervisor can afford to compromise their judgments about the lesson—good or bad—before it has been analyzed by both. If the teacher has learned this, then the parting words at the door will carry no meaning other than "Goodby. See you at our scheduled time." That is why we have spent so much time on "the very first sentence."

Teacher's and Supervisor's Analysis Prior to the Conference   The teacher performs an analysis of his lesson in preparation for the conference. In this process he tries to identify his own patterns and to evaluate his success in achieving the objectives set out in his lesson plan. He lists the questions he may have for the supervisor and tries to develop a strategy for the effective use of the conference time.

The supervisor carries out the full-fledged analysis, identifying critical incidents, patterns, and learning outcomes. The strategy he develops for the lesson is an attempt to anticipate the teacher's needs and his probable behavior during the conference. The supervisor organizes the data of the analysis so as to make it readily accessible. He also checks the conference room to be sure that everything is in readiness.

The Emotional Climate of the Conference   The problem of the teacher's emotional response to clinical supervision is perhaps never more pronounced than in the first few conferences. No matter how freely and confidently the teacher has participated in prior clinical processes, he may experience a certain uneasiness about the actual observation and the prospect of the session to follow. The supervisor must therefore take into account both the teacher's emotional state and the fact that in the conference the teacher will be participating in new processes and trying out new behavior.

The supervisor may find that with some teachers the early tensions of the conference are moderated if they are given the opportunity to talk first. The teacher has an opportunity to pose questions that are troubling him, or he may discuss the procedures to be followed, or he may take the opportunity to explain some incident that occurred in the classroom. Such talk sometimes helps the teacher to settle down, having had a chance to air some of the concerns uppermost in his mind. The supervisor, for his part, has an opportunity to learn something about the teacher's approach to the meeting. This information can help him to construct appropriate strategies for the occasion.

On the other hand, to offer the teacher a clear field to express himself first in the conference may turn out to be a strategic error. If the teacher is defensive, his chance to speak first may seriously compromise the course of the entire conference. For example, if he thinks his teaching was in some way deficient, he may prepare a defensive position behind which to barricade himself. He may assert that the lesson was, all in all, fine. He may affirm that the students' inattention was completely atypical and therefore not worth analyzing. Another teacher, lacking confidence in himself, may downgrade a good lesson and attempt to anticipate the supervisor's criticisms. Still a third teacher may simply desire to get right to the work at hand: the analysis of the lesson.

Whatever the reaction of the teacher, his opportunity to speak first gives him an opportunity to prestructure the conference. The advantages and disadvantages arising from this situation are substantial and sometimes crucial to the success of the session. The defensive teacher's defense may persist into the analysis, making objective analysis difficult or impossible. The teacher who is insecure about his performance may harden his own poor opinion of his work by affirming it first. The teacher who wants to turn to analysis may facilitate the entire conference process. The stakes are high in this initial decision. But they are equally high if the supervisor speaks first. What he says may also prestructure the conference. Certainly his taking the initiative and speaking first tends to put the teacher into the position of listener and into the position of the participant who does *not* have the initiative. As usual, this decision—like so many others in supervision—represents a risk that should be taken only after careful thought, but it remains a professional risk. It would very probably be even more perilous if the supervisor were unaware of the options for starting the conference and took the initiative as a matter of course.

As the conference proceeds, the teacher who has a problem he would like to discuss should be encouraged to broach it freely. If the problem is outside the domain of clinical supervision, the supervisor's least perilous response, and the one most likely to be helpful, is to listen. Beyond this, the supervisor should simply suggest consultation with competent resource people. If the problem is relevant to clinical supervision, the strategy of letting the teacher discuss it is often productive. The supervisor learns what the teacher's views are and can govern his own behavior more wisely. As for the teacher, he may sometimes recognize the answer to his problem as he states it. He may be able to devise a solution in the act of formulating his dilemma for a listener. Beyond these possibilities, the teacher's talk may have other advantages: (1) the supervisor talks less, and (2) the supervisor's interest in and readiness to listen to the teacher's ideas help to convince him that the supervisor views him as a colleague rather than as an audience.

The comfort and security of teacher and supervisor are increased if they discipline themselves to discuss behavior rather than persons. That is, to generate sentences like "The answer was wrong" rather than "You are wrong." This suggestion has been made before but is worth repeating here.

Some problems of teaching impinge very painfully upon some of the teacher's tenderest sensitivities. He may make occasional errors that the students call attention to. Or he may be unable to cope with the students' tittering or guffaws when they encounter references related to sex in their readings, ranging from lavender lines like "Girlish bust, but womanly air," to the more forthright language of modern literature. Whatever the cause, there are certain professional matters that the teacher may not really be able to discuss openly or objectively. When the supervisor becomes aware of such a situation, he may be well advised to deal with it indirectly or symbolically with the teacher—through readings, reference to similar problems occurring in other schools, or discussion of case studies.

The Teacher's Classroom Style   The kind of supervision provided for student teachers in the United States often helps to crystallize the teacher's style in a peculiar fashion. The student teacher is apprenticed to a cooperating teacher, who may be unprepared to provide constructive supervision. He may not even be a very competent teacher. The college supervisor may share these characteristics or be extremely competent, but in either case it doesn't make much difference because he rarely spends enough time with the student teacher to make a genuine difference. The student teacher, therefore, finds himself under fire from three directions at once: he must develop a teaching style that (1) really teaches his pupils something, (2) meets the cooperating teacher's criteria of good teaching, and (3) meets the college supervisor's criteria of good teaching. In his effort to operate with these three cannons trained on him, the student teacher often develops a style of teaching that we term "survival behavior," which, if successful, is hard to change or abandon: it has worked. As a result, when the novice signs his first contract to teach, it often devolves upon the clinical supervisor in the school to help him go beyond mere survival behavior. In addition, there are many other teachers who have not progressed much beyond the competences they reached in the first few years of their teaching career. How can the supervisor help these men and women to develop a style of teaching of their own?

One common way of accomplishing this aim is to have the teacher observe certain models of good teaching and help him to learn the methods and style of the model. A real or simulated model is presented to the teacher to imitate: he may visit a school where the new physics is taught, or he sees and studies films in which expert teachers demonstrate phonics or whole-word methods of teaching reading, or he simply observes "good teachers" and attempts to go and do likewise.

The use of models to change the teacher's behavior is, however, full of pitfalls. The performances supposed to serve as models have too often not been analyzed carefully. In consequence, the teacher is not quite sure which elements of a given performance make it good. That is, he may imitate the wrong behavior, not comprehending why the model's performance is good. And worst of all, the model's behavior may not be congruent with the teacher's abilities, talents, and preferences. The result of learning in this way is therefore frequently a wooden and mechanical imitation that quickly disappears after a few trials. Teachers can probably learn a few uncomplicated techniques from models, but a significant reformulation of their teaching style is rare. There is, however, a valuable variant of the process of modeling: let the teacher (or future teacher) be his own model. Help him to analyze his own teaching behavior, identify what he does well, and help him to refine and strengthen these competences. This method has the virtue of working with strength rather than weakness, and it practically guarantees that the new behavior learned will be congruent with the teacher's own style.

The techniques of using videotape records of the teacher at work in his classroom are especially well adapted to the use of the self as model. The teacher may study the videotape at leisure, or he may join the supervisor in this process. In either event, the teacher has the opportunity to help identify the best aspects of his own verbal and nonverbal behavior. After analyzing these patterns, he can isolate one or two to work on. What more congruent models can he find?

The use of self as model is especially suited to clinical supervision, in which the focus is on the teacher and in which pattern analysis brings the teacher's own strengths into clear and detailed view. Using the self as model tends to encourage autonomy rather than imitation. It also lessens the risks the teacher must run when he tries to change his classroom behavior. Where the use of others as models involves copying, the use of self-as-model encourages self-knowledge and self-discovery. The teacher's success in improving his performance through work on his own patterns may also help him build a secure foundation for experimentation with models further afield.

The Selection of Incidents and Patterns   In most of the conference strategies described in the following section, the teacher and supervisor are required to select some aspect of the teacher's behavior whose improvement will be the objective of the planning session. Some criteria for these choices are suggested here:

1. If a negative critical incident or negative critical pattern is observed and confirmed by examination of the transcript(s), the teacher and the supervisor will give this overriding problem first priority for their work together.
2. If no critical phenomena have been observed, the teacher and supervisor will elect to work on a pattern or interacting patterns of strength unless a strong argument is made for working on a pattern of weakness. For example, the teacher, having identified in his behavior a pattern of interrupting students who are in the process of making a long response, feels that he simply cannot ignore this tendency. He makes a persuasive argument for a plan to lessen or obviate such behavior before he tries anything else. If the supervisor judges that there is more to gain by acceding than refusing, the pattern of weakness may be selected to work on.
3. The pattern(s) chosen must meet the criteria of *priority, feasibility, congruence, and suitability to a short- or a long-term program.*
   a. *Priority* signifies that the pattern selected is considered to be more important than other patterns identified.
   b. *Feasibility* signifies that the teacher seems likely to possess the

capacity to achieve improvement in the pattern selected. *Example*: A teacher who successfully teaches traditional grammar proposes to extend his instruction to the teaching of modern generative grammar. This plan may be feasible if he is competent in this subject, not feasible if he is not.

c. *Congruence* signifies that the pattern selected is compatible with the teacher's style or talents. *Example*: The teacher who is successful in large-group instruction proposes that he develop similar competence in conducting an "open" classroom. The new pattern may not be congruent with his style and talents if the teacher cannot tolerate (1) noise, (2) free movement of students, and (3) absence of a fixed course of study.

d. *Suitability to a short- or a long-term program* means simply that the teacher and supervisor must decide whether a proposed pattern fits into the short-range and/or long-range objectives of the program they develop.

Some Strategies for the Conference

There is no single format for the conduct of the conference, no fixed procedure that represents "best practice." On the other hand, the supervisor (and later on the teacher) is required to prepare a plan of action designed to maximize the usefulness of the conference. Occasionally the supervisor may decide to "play it by ear." In general, however, he will improve his chances for success if he tentatively lays out a plan for the initiation and development of the sequences of the conference. Some of the strategies commonly used in the conference are described here.[4]

The Clinical Cycle Itself as a Format   The strategy of following the sequence of the cycle of supervision is a "natural." The teacher is familiar with the cycle and therefore knows the sequence to be followed: (1) truncated analysis, (2) conference, (3) resumption of planning. The truncated analysis referred to is really a joint review of the analyses the teacher and supervisor have each performed after the observation of the teacher's lesson. As the phrase indicates, the truncated analysis is short and incomplete. It terminates as soon as the teacher and supervisor agree on the aspect of the teacher's performance they will attempt to improve.

[4]Most of these strategies were tried out in the course of Supervision Institutes at Harvard University and at the University of Pittsburgh in the 1950's and '60's. Virginia S. Larrabee, a participant in one of the institutes, assessed the outcomes of some of the strategies in a paper entitled "Strategy in Supervision Interviews" (n.d.).

Many supervisors adopt the cycle strategy as standard practice and use it until the teacher has gained substantial competence in clinical supervision. At this point they begin to use other approaches if doing so seems advisable. The steps in the cycle strategy include the following:

1. The conference is initiated with the truncated analysis. The teacher usually starts by sketching in the critical incidents and patterns he has identified as most appropriate for his work with the supervisor.
2. If the supervisor agrees with the teacher's choices, he terminates the analysis and makes the transition to planning. This marks the end of one cycle and the beginning of the next.
   a. If, however, the supervisor feels that other aspects of the teacher's classroom performance also merit consideration as possible foci for the supervisory program, he goes on with the analysis and develops the data to support his views.
3. The truncated analysis continues until the two participants agree on the problems most appropriate for the work of the program at this point. They then make the transition to planning and the next cycle.
4. If no agreement is possible, they may follow the procedures set out later in this chapter under the heading "When Colleagues Differ."

The use of the strategy of the cycle has much to recommend it. Teachers readily grasp its logic and learn its sequences. Its direct approach to the teacher's problems quickly establishes the focus of the conference on central rather than peripheral questions. As a consequence, the cycle strategy tends to save time.

The weakness of the strategy lies in its very logic and directness. The momentum of the process tends to discourage digression and the consideration of alternative or radical hunches about patterns and the inferences to be drawn from them. The businesslike directness of the cycle strategy also tends to discourage "seeking behavior" and inductive approaches to the identification of patterns. Therefore, it may also foreclose the learning economies inherent in insights, intuition, and discoveries.

The Chronological Inventory of Events   In this strategy the teacher and supervisor simply recapitulate conversationally what happened in class, chronologically. The tendency is therefore to focus on the principal actor —the teacher—and to neglect the behavior of the students. As a consequence, the teacher and supervisor find themselves working with only half of their equation. Furthermore, the lack of some principle to organize the details tends to blur rather than clarify what happened in class. No topography emerges—no overall view of the terrain and its hills and valleys.

Some supervisors adopt the inventory strategy when they have failed to prepare a strategy more integrally related to the needs, style, and actual classroom performance of the teacher.

In actual use, supervisors who employ the inventory of events seem to neglect the analysis. The inventory is useful, however, when a demonstration of the *sequence* of classroom events serves to bring into high relief a weakness in the teaching. For example, the French teacher may in this process come to understand the illogicality of permitting his students to mispronounce words repeatedly in the course of the class hour, reserving the pronunciation drill for the end of the hour.

Focus on the Students' Behavior   In this strategy the teacher and supervisor focus first on a detailed analysis of the students' behavior. This behavior is then related to learning outcomes, which in turn are connected to the methods used, the pacing, etc. It is important to note in this connection that the behavior of the teacher is not treated in isolation or analyzed by itself. It is, rather, treated as method, materials of instruction, etc., in relation to students' behavior.

This plan of action is particularly successful with teachers who may react with antagonism, withdrawal, or excessive anxiety when the spotlight is on their behavior.

The Didactic Strategy   The didactic strategy is, obviously, an instructional strategy. The supervisor structures the conference, sets out the patterns he has observed in the transcript, explicates their relationship to students' behavior, identifies the pattern or patterns that are to be the focus of the planning session, and launches the session.

The weaknesses of the didactic approach are not always as great as they may appear to be from this description. The didactic is useful when the teacher genuinely wants to learn the techniques of the clinical conference and at the same time to profit from the conference in his teaching. Teachers not infrequently will request the didactic strategy in the first few sessions as a way of orienting themselves to the processes of the clinical conference before taking a participant's role. It works well with teachers who are unsure of themselves or have a strong need to perform competently or not at all. Some teachers who do not respond well to learning by doing may derive a great deal of help from the demonstration of a didactic plan for the conference. In contrast, the didactic strategy is likely to have devastating consequences if employed with a self-confident teacher who is genuinely interested in clinical supervision and is anticipating his active involvement in it with relish.

Nondirective Strategy   "Nondirective" is a misnomer here if interpreted in the Rogerian sense. It is employed simply to designate a method of encouraging the teacher to talk freely. The supervisor listens and encourages the teacher to express his thoughts and feelings about matters uppermost in his mind.

The strategy works well when the teacher feels a need to express his questions and his doubts about the clinical processes in which he is engaged. He may reveal his resistances, his dissatisfactions, and his problems. The nondirective strategy offers the teacher an opportunity to unburden himself. If he does, he may find it easier afterward to take an objective approach to the work to be done in the conference. The nondirective process is sometimes helpful when the teacher and supervisor are attempting to establish a good working rapport. The freedom to speak may lessen distrust and defensiveness.

With another teacher or with the same teacher on another occasion, the nondirective strategy may misfire entirely. The teacher may not want or need the kind of emotional release that comes from untrammeled expression. He may simply want to get on with the analysis and may resent what some teachers have wryly called the "psychoanalytic approach." Some teachers want action, not talk. As usual, supervision is risk-taking, not security.

Role-playing Strategy   If the supervisor is competent and talented enough to stage a role-playing session and carry it off successfully, he may find this strategy occasionally useful. But it takes both skill and talent. It also takes a teacher who is at least willing to try it.

Role-playing is not impossible with only two participants. It has been found useful when a teacher simply cannot comprehend the motivations behind the students' behavior. On one occasion, when a teacher assumed the role of a student to the supervisor's "teacher," he admitted afterward that he could understand some of the students' reasons for misbehaving. Role-playing should probably be used sparingly until it can be done with a group of teachers who share similar problems and who are sophisticated enough to participate fully.

Combined Strategies   Since circumstances may change in the course of a conference, the plans should also change. Certainly a procedure should be changed quickly when it is not succeeding.

The Socratic Strategy   The Socratic strategy seems to be irresistible to many clinical supervisors. Teachers, on the other hand, find it extremely easy to resist. The instructional logic behind the Socratic method is very persuasive. The supervisor makes an assertion designed to intrigue the teacher. Then, by questioning, he brings the teacher to a realization that the assertion may be doubtful. The supervisor proceeds to elicit revised "answers" from the teacher and tests them by counter-assertion until the teacher gains an insight about the true state of affairs: he gets "the right answer." The experience of insight is commonly supposed to result in more valuable learning than that gained by mere explanation.

In our experience this last assertion has been vitriolically challenged by most of the teachers who have been subjected to the Socratic strategy. Some of their reactions are worth examining:

> It is an exercise in reading the supervisor's mind.
>
> It is painful to be led like a cow by the nose.
>
> The Socratic method is an inquisition.
>
> The supervisor has a point in mind, and we have to play blindman's buff to find it.
>
> It is more damaging than outright criticism.
>
> A great deal of time is wasted.
>
> The points the supervisor is trying to make are often trivial.

A few teachers found the Socratic strategy rewarding because of the insight they gained about their own teaching.

In view of the fact that Hyman[5] and many others have painstakingly attested to the difficulties encountered in the use of the Socratic strategy, our best advice to the supervisor is not to try it unless he is certain of his competences. And we would add that the competences had better be gained through work with willing subjects rather than through practice in conferences with teachers.

The Return to Planning

The planning processes have been treated in earlier chapters, but one aspect of the return to planning at the end of the truncated analysis merits special consideration. During the conference the teacher has had an opportunity to view his own teaching analytically. He has participated in the decisions about what critical incident or pattern he and the super-

---

[5]Ronald T. Hyman, *Ways of Teaching: Vantage Points for Study* (New York: J. B. Lippincott Co., 1970), pp. 58–82.

visor will work on in the planning session. One important step, however, remains to be taken: *The teacher should commit himself to actually making the change he and the supervisor are planning for.*

The teacher's explicit commitment to carrying out the change, in contrast to simply *planning* for it, may significantly improve the probability that he will in fact change. R. C. Anderson, in a paper on learning through discussion, concludes his review of the relative influence of discussion and decision on changes in behavior by saying: "These data suggest that changes in behavior should be attributed *to making a decision rather than engaging in discussion.*"[6]

Our own experience strongly indicates that the teacher's commitment to change is confirmed in his mind during the process of planning the lesson in which it is to be tried. But his resolution obviously remains implicit. A more overt decision might, as Anderson indicates, act as an additional spur to the teacher to change his behavior. However, it would probably be counterproductive to attempt to elicit from the teacher a spoken or written "promise to change." A more adult process to be utilized at a more appropriate time can be found in a review-and-evaluation session following the completion of the lesson plan. The supervisor may begin the review by asking the teacher to recapitulate orally the behavioral changes he anticipates making in the lesson just planned. The response will often be couched in the form of sentences like "I'm going to try to let the kids know *why* I reward them when I do, instead of just saying 'Great!' or 'Good.'" Or "I'll change the plan if the students don't react right to it." Such statements are clear affirmations of decisions made in the planning session. And they arise naturally rather than on demand. In the process of recapitulating and evaluating the plan, the teacher will have ample opportunity to rephrase clearly and unequivocally the decisions he has made. The supervisor should develop fluency in creating natural opportunities for the teacher to reaffirm the behavioral decisions implicit in the latter's plan.

Review and Evaluation of the Conference

The conference, like many of the other processes in clinical supervision, has dual objectives: the supervision of the teacher and his didactic induc-

---

[6]Richard C. Anderson, "Learning in Discussions: A Resume of the Authoritarian-Democratic Studies," mimeographed (n.d.). (Italics added.)

tion into clinical supervision. Both purposes are well served by a review and evaluation of the conference. Both processes help to induct the teacher into his colleagual role. He joins the supervisor as a peer in assessing both the processes and outcomes of their work together. The supervisor also profits from the feedback he receives about his own performance in the conference. To these benefits are added the substantive knowledge he gains about the teacher in a new role.

The review and evaluation are valuable, but they should not be uniformly and inevitably incorporated into every conference session. If carried out when either teacher or supervisor is fatigued, they become a mechanical chore rather than the critical recapitulation they should be. It may also happen that certain conferences will be too unproductive or the interpersonal exchanges in them may be too deeply felt to bear the burden of immediate cognitive analysis. In sum, the review should be carried out only when it is likely to be helpful, which should be fairly regularly if the program is going well.

In the review-and-evaluation session the teacher and supervisor will examine the salient events and situations that have arisen in the course of the conference. In addition, they may on occasion find it helpful to discuss certain broad dimensions of the conference process:

1. The conference strategy:
   a. How much time and attention are devoted to working with the teacher's professional strengths? Weaknesses?
   b. Does the teacher clearly verbalize his commitment to change his teaching behavior?
   c. Are the themes of the conference related to the short- and long-term objectives of the supervisory program for the teacher?
   d. Is the strategic plan followed (1) rigidly? (2) flexibly? (3) at all?
   e. Do the teacher and supervisor develop working hypotheses characterized by low inference? high inference? moderate inference? Does either engage in psychologizing? in "therapy"?
   f. Is the supervisor person-oriented, behavior-oriented, or both at appropriate times in the conference?
   g. Is the teacher person-oriented, behavior-oriented, or both at appropriate times in the conference?
2. Leadership in the conference:
   a. Does the teacher assume leadership at appropriate times? yield leadership at appropriate times?
   b. Does the supervisor transfer leadership at appropriate times?
   c. How completely are transitions made from one phase of the conference to another?
   d. Does the supervisor help the teacher to gain competence in leadership?

    e. Is the leadership task-oriented, person-oriented, or both at appropriate times?

3. The cognitive level of the conference:
    a. Is the cognitive level of the conference best described as moderately challenging? very challenging? not challenging?
    b. Are cognitive processes generally at the level of knowledge? of analysis? of synthesis? of evaluation?
    c. Is the general trend of the conference one of negative criticism? constructive suggestion?

4. Analytic-didactic functions:
    a. Do the processes designed to further the analytic and didactic objectives—
       (1) reinforce each other?
       (2) interfere with each other?
       (3) simply not interact with each other very often?
    b. Is the data-base for the analysis consistently established in relation to patterns? to the teacher's behavior? to students' behavior? to students' learnings?
    c. Is the analysis extended beyond what is needed for the selection of the patterns to be worked on very often? fairly often? not very often? when appropriate?
    d. In what manner does the supervisor fulfill the didactic functions of clinical supervision in the conference?
    e. How may the teacher's and supervisor's performances in the formation of working hypotheses best be described?

5. Interpersonal relationships:
How may the interpersonal relationships between teacher and supervisor be characterized during the conference? Dussault provides an excellent set of categories for the evaluation of interpersonal relations in the conference. Each applies to both teacher and supervisor:
    a. security—insecurity;
    b. confidence—nonconfidence;
    c. empathy—nonempathy;
    d. understanding of anxieties;
    e. acceptance—rejection;
    f. friendliness—hostility;
    g. cooperation—aggression;
    h. honesty—playacting;
    i. support—nonsupport;
    j. autonomy—dependence;
    k. like-dislike.[7]

6. Evaluation:
    a. How well are the responsibilities for evaluation fulfilled?
    b. Who assumes leadership?

[7]Gilles Dussault, *A Theory of Supervision in Teacher Education* (New York: Teachers College Press, 1970), extrapolated from pp. 57–87.

c. Does the teacher evaluate his own work? the supervisor's?

d. Does the supervisor evaluate his own work? the teacher's?

7. Outcomes of the conference:

a. Is the plan for the next teaching session completed?

b. How could the quality of the plan best be described?

c. Does the teacher commit himself to changing his classroom behavior?

Terminating the Conference

The termination of the conference is in most instances a natural sequel to the review and evaluation. On occasion, however, special delicacy and forethought may be required on the part of the supervisor before the conference can be allowed to end, namely, when the teacher's confidence in himself is shaken. A crisis of self-confidence tends to occur when the teacher begins to doubt his own professional competence—for real or imagined reasons.

When the reasons are real, the best help the supervisor can offer is to marshal every resource at his command to help the teacher improve his work. The teacher needs all the technical and personal support the supervisor can muster—and he needs to know that this support will be fully and freely provided. The teacher facing the grim possibility that he may not really be competent does not need empty reassurances that things will get better or that they are not as bad as they seem. What he requires above all is firm knowledge of what his problems are and complete confidence that he and the supervisor have a full-fledged program under way to provide the help he needs.

On the other hand, some competent teachers may also experience a sense of genuine inadequacy from time to time—a feeling no less threatening because it is unwarranted. These teachers, too, need the full support of the supervisor. No teacher should leave a conference without full reassurance that he is professionally competent if such reassurance can be honestly given.

When Colleagues Differ

We have set the concept of the colleagueship at the heart of clinical supervision. But we know that colleagues will almost inevitably differ on professional issues. The teacher may disagree about the presence or absence of a pattern that the supervisor identifies. The supervisor may make an inference about the meaning of a pattern and find himself in a position directly opposed to the teacher's. Or the teacher may maintain that students have achieved the learnings anticipated in the plan, and the supervisor may see no evidence of these learnings at all.

Perhaps the most serious disagreements arise about the teaching strategies to be used to achieve the outcomes stated in a lesson plan. What happens, for instance, if, after a reasonable amount of discussion, teacher and supervisor are still in sharp disagreement? What happens when colleagues differ? The following suggestions for the resolution of this problem may be helpful to people engaged in clinical supervision:

1. It is the teacher who is ultimately responsible for the actual instruction, not the supervisor. The supervisor should therefore stop arguing his case as soon as a genuine reconciliation of views appears unlikely. He should then proceed to give the teacher every possible assistance in strengthening the plan for the next lesson.
2. When the plan is completed, the teacher and supervisor should clearly state their hypotheses about the outcomes they anticipate for the lesson.
3. The plan should incorporate careful provision for securing adequate feedback about the actual outcomes of the lesson. In a sense, these data will be used to test the teacher's hypotheses; that is, to determine whether the objectives of the plan are attained.
4. After the teacher has taught the lesson, an analysis of it should be made to test the teacher's working hypotheses. The purpose of the analysis is not to see "who won."
5. The professional conventions suggested here to govern the conduct of teacher and supervisor who differ on important questions may be summarized as follows:
   a. When the difference is not reconciled, the supervisor should yield to the teacher's views.
   b. The teacher for his part should not decide on a course of action without taking seriously into account the position stated by the supervisor.
   c. The teacher and supervisor together should attempt to determine the outcomes of the teacher's plan.
   d. The teacher should accept the responsibility for the outcomes of his strategy.
   e. If the strategy does not work, the teacher should be professionally obliged to change it. He cannot persist in it. (In a weak medical analogy, the responsible physician must take into account the diagnosis and treatment proposed by consultants, but the decision about treatment is his own. He is, however, required to change the treatment if the patient does not respond as he anticipates.)

Such an oversimplified and partial account of what happens when teacher and supervisor disagree is in the nature of a parable rather than a prescription. But it is a parable of *professional accountability*.

There are complexities, ambiguities, and unknowns in clinical supervision that go far beyond the teacher's and the supervisor's settling differences about what should be taught and the teacher's accepting professional responsibility for the outcomes of his plan. For instance, the outcomes of a course of action may not clearly demonstrate whether a decision was either good or bad. In addition, no matter what the outcomes, they do not prove that the procedures *not* used were better or worse. And to complicate reality still further, some differences between supervisor and teacher cannot be settled by even such poor tests as we have described above. The disagreements may not be about method but about objectives, or about the nature of the students' learning experiences. Since in most instances the determination of objectives and content is more closely related to untestable values than to demonstrable superiorities, decisions about such matters must be made and evaluated through processes of discussion, through the "weighing" of imponderables, through a logic of affect rather than through a logic of evidence, reason, and the weight of objective testing.

When decisions are to be made about questions *not* amenable to demonstration, proof, or testing in some objectively verifiable form, then we cannot help the teacher and supervisor with lists of *dos* and *don'ts*, or even with parables. In order to deal with such problems, teacher and supervisor need professional traditions and a professional way of life together. They must create a sustaining subculture of their own, strong enough to survive the ambiguities of teaching and learning. Such a culture is not mechanically constructed, nor can it be entirely communicated in a book. It is our hope, however, that something of the spirit and substance of such a professional way of life has been conveyed in this book.

References

Abercrombie, M. L. Johnson. *The Anatomy of Judgment*. London: Hutchinson and Co., Ltd., 1960.

Amidon, Edmund J., and Hough, John B., eds. *Interaction Analysis: Theory, Research, and Application*. Reading, Mass.: Addison-Wesley Publishing Co., Inc., 1967.

Anastasi, Anne. *Fields of Applied Psychology*. New York: McGraw-Hill Book Co., 1964.

Anderson, C. C., and Hunka, S. M. "Teacher Evaluation: Some Problems and a Proposal." *Harvard Educational Review* 33 (1963): 74–5.

Anderson, Richard C. "Learning in Discussions: A Resumé of the Authoritarian-Democratic Studies." Mimeographed, n.d.

Anderson, Richard C.; Faust, Gerald W.; Roderick, Marianne C.; Cunningham, Donald J.; and Andre, Thomas, eds. *Current Research on Instruction*. Englewood Cliffs, N.J., Prentice-Hall, Inc., 1969.

Association for Student Teaching. *The College Supervisor: Conflict and Challenge*. Dubuque, Iowa: W. C. Brown Co., Inc., 1964.

Association for Supervision and Curriculum Development. "Better Than Rating." Washington, D.C.: Association for Supervision and Curriculum Development, 1950.

Babin, Patrick. "Supervisors Look at Themselves." *Instructor Development* 2 (1970): 1, 3, 6.

Belanger, Maurice. "An Exploration of the Use of Feedback in Supervision." Ed.D. dissertation, School of Education, Harvard University, 1962.

Bellack, Arno A.; Kliebard, Herbert M.; Hyman, Ronald T.; and Smith, Frank L., Jr. *The Language of the Classroom*. New York: Teachers College Press, 1966.

Benjamin, Harold. *The Cultivation of Idiosyncrasy:* Cambridge, Mass.: Harvard University Press, 1949.

Birdwhistell, Ray L. *Kinesics and Context: Essays on Body Motion Communication*. Philadelphia, Pa.: University of Pennsylvania Press, 1970.

Blackie, John. *Inside the Primary School*. London: Her Majesty's Stationery Office, 1967.

Bloom, Benjamin S. "The Thought Processes of Students in Discussion." In *Accent on Teaching*, edited by Sidney J. French. New York: Harper and Bros., 1954.

Bloom, Benjamin S., ed. *Taxonomy of Educational Objectives: The Classification of Educational Goals*, Handbook I: Cognitive Domain. New York: David McKay Co., Inc., 1956.

Brandwein, Paul F. *Elements in a Strategy for Teaching Science in the Elementary School.* New York: Harcourt, Brace and World, Inc., 1962.

Broudy, Harry S. "Historic Exemplars of Teaching Method." In *Handbook of Research on Teaching,* edited by N. L. Gage. Chicago: Rand McNally and Co., 1963.

Brown, Bob Burton. "Using Systematic Observation and Analysis of Teaching." *Research Reports.* Gainesville, Fla.: University of Florida, College of Education, Institute for Development of Human Resources, n.d.

Bruner, Jerome S.; Goodnow, Jacqueline J.; and Austin, George A. *A Study of Thinking.* New York: John Wiley and Sons, Inc., 1956.

Bruner, Jerome S. *The Process of Education.* Cambridge, Mass.: Harvard University Press, 1960.

Bruner, Jerome S. *on Knowing: essays for the left hand.* Cambridge, Mass.: Harvard University Press, 1962.

Burnett, Jacquetta H. "Culture of the School: A Construct for Research and Explanation in Education." *Council on Anthropology and Education Newsletter 1* (1970): 4–13.

Carroll, John B. "Basic and Applied Research in Education: Definitions, Distinctions, and Implications." *Harvard Educational Review* 38 (1968): 263–76.

Champagne, David W. "Rationale and Design of the University Phase of an Internship for Instructional Consultants." Ed.D. dissertation, School of Education, University of Pittsburgh, 1968.

Cogan, Morris L. "Supervision at the Harvard-Newton Summer School." Mimeographed, 1961.

Cohen, John. *Behaviour in Uncertainty, and Its Social Implications.* New York: Basic Books, Inc., 1964.

Cohen, Morris R. "Reason in Social Science." In *Readings in the Philosophy of Science,* edited by Herbert Feigl and May Brodbeck. New York: Appleton-Century-Crofts, Inc., 1953.

Condon, William S. In an interview with M. L. Burger: "Speak to Me Only with Thine Eyes, an Exercise in Linguistics-Kinesics." *University Times.* Pittsburgh, Pa.: University of Pittsburgh, 5 March 1970.

Delaney, Arthur A. "Lesson Plans—Means or End?" In *Principles and Practices in Teaching in Secondary Schools,* edited by Florence Henry Lee. New York: David McKay Co., Inc., 1965.

Duncan, Starkey, Jr. "Nonverbal Communication." *Psychological Bulletin* 72 (1969): 118–37.

Dussault, Gilles. *A Theory of Supervision in Teacher Education.* New York: Teachers College Press, 1970.

Educational Policies Commission. *The Central Purpose of American Education.* Washington, D.C.: National Education Association, 1961.

Feigl, Herbert. "The Scientific Outlook: Naturalism and Humanism." In *Readings in the Philosophy of Science*, edited by Herbert Feigl and May Brodbeck. New York: Appleton-Century-Crofts, Inc., 1953.

Feigl, Herbert, and Brodbeck, May, eds. *Readings in the Philosophy of Science*. New York: Appleton-Century-Crofts, Inc., 1953.

Fisher, Helen. "Expectations for Leadership." *Educational Leadership* 16 (1959): 503–5, 525.

Flanders, Ned A. *Helping Teachers Change Their Behavior*. Final Report, N.D.E.A. Projects 1721012 and 7-32-0560-171.0, U.S. Office of Education. Ann Arbor: University of Michigan, School of Education, 1963.

Flanders, Ned A. Introduction to *Interaction Analysis: Theory, Application, and Research*, by Edmund J. Amidon and John B. Hough, eds. Reading, Mass.: Addison-Wesley Publishing Co., Inc., 1967.

Flanders, Ned A. *Analyzing Teaching Behavior*. Reading, Mass.: Addison-Wesley Publishing Co., 1970.

Freud, Anna. "The Role of the Teacher." *Harvard Educational Review* 22 (1952): 229–34.

Gage, N. L.; Runkel, Philip J.; and Chatterjee, B. B. "Equilibrium Theory and Behavior Change: An Experiment in Feedback from Pupils to Teachers." Urbana, Ill.: University of Illinois, Bureau of Educational Research, College of Education, 1960.

Gage, N. L., ed. *Handbook of Research on Teaching*. Chicago: Rand McNally and Co., 1963.

Galloway, Charles M. "An Exploratory Study of Observational Procedures for Determining Teacher Nonverbal Communication." Ph.D. dissertation, University of Florida, 1962.

Galloway, Charles M. "Teacher Nonverbal Communication." *Educational Leadership* 24 (1966): 55–63.

Galloway, Charles M. "Nonverbal Communication in Teaching." In *Teaching: Vantage Points for Study*, edited by Ronald T. Hyman. New York: J. B. Lippincott Co., 1968.

Goethals, George W. "A Psychologist Looks at Some Aspects of Helping." *Educational Leadership* 16 (1959): 472–74, 516.

Gordon, Alice Kaplan. *Games for Growth*. Palo Alto, Calif.: Science Research Associates, Inc., 1970.

Griffard, Charles David. "An Adaptation of the Linguistic-Kinesics Research Model to College Classroom Interaction Analysis." Ph.D. dissertation, School of Education, University of Pittsburgh, 1971.

Gross, Neal; Mason, Ward S.; and McEachern, Alexander W. *Explorations in Role Analysis: Studies of the School Superintendency Role*. New York: John Wiley and Sons, Inc., 1958.

Gross, Neal. "Some Contributions of Sociology to the Field of Education." *Harvard Educational Review* 29 (1959): 275–87.

Heathers, Glen. "Notes on the Strategy of Educational Reform." Unpublished paper, 1961.

Henry, Jules. "Culture Against Man." In *Introduction to the Behavioral Sciences,* edited by John N. Sandberg. New York: Holt, Rinehart and Winston, Inc., 1969.

Hone, Elizabeth B.; Joseph, Alexander; and Victor, Edward. *A Sourcebook for Elementary Science.* New York: Harcourt, Brace, and World, Inc., 1962.

Hyman, Ronald T., ed. *Teaching: Vantage Points for Study.* Philadelphia: J. B. Lippincott Co., 1968.

Hyman, Ronald T. *Ways of Teaching.* Philadelphia: J. B. Lippincott Co., 1970.

Institute of Administrative Research. *Indicators of Quality: Signs of Good Teaching.* New York: Teachers College, Columbia University, 1969.

James, William. *Talks to Teachers.* New York: Henry Holt, 1925.

Jenkins, David H., and Lippitt, Ronald. "Interpersonal Perceptions in the Classroom." In *The Adolescent,* edited by Jerome M. Seidman. New York: Dryden Press, 1953.

Johnson, D. M., and Stratton, B. M. "Evaluation of Five Methods of Teaching Concepts." In *Current Research on Instruction,* edited by Richard C. Anderson et al. Englewood Cliffs, N.J.: Prentice-Hall, Inc., 1969.

Kirscht, John P., and Dillehay, Ronald C. *Dimensions of Authoritarianism: A Review of Research and Theory.* Lexington, Ky.: University of Kentucky Press, 1967.

Kounin, Jacob S. "Observing and Delineating Technique of Managing Behavior in Classrooms." *Journal of Research and Development in Education* 4 (1970): 62–72.

Krathwohl, David R.; Bloom, Benjamin S.; and Masia, Bertram B., eds. *Taxonomy of Educational Objectives: The Classification of Educational Goals,* Handbook II: Affective Domain. New York: David McKay Co., Inc., 1956.

Kronenberger, Louis. "Speaking of Books." *The New York Times Book Review,* 7 October 1962.

Larrabee, Virginia S. "Strategy in Supervision Interviews." Paper prepared at Supervision Institute, Harvard University, n.d.

Lindsey, Margaret, ed. *New Horizons for the Teaching Profession.* Washington, D.C.: National Education Association, 1961.

Lindsey, Margaret and associates. *Inquiry into Teaching Behavior of Supervisors in Teacher Education Laboratories.* New York: Teachers College Press, 1969.

Lortie, Dan C. "Craftsmanship and Colleagueship: A Frame for the Investigation of Work Values Among Public School Teachers." Address prepared for the annual meeting of the American Sociological Association, 1961.

Lortie, Dan C. "The Teacher as Craftsman." Draft of a research memorandum, n.d.

Mager, Robert F. *Preparing Instructional Objectives*. Palo Alto, Calif.: Fearon Publishers, 1962.

Mann, Thomas. *Doctor Faustus*. New York: Alfred A. Knopf, Inc., 1948.

McAvoy, Rogers. "Measurable Outcome with Systematic Observation." *Journal of Research and Development in Education* 4 (1970): 10–13.

Mayo, Elton. *The Human Problems of an Industrial Civilization*. New York: Macmillan Co., 1933.

Medley, Donald M., and Hill, Russell A. "Dimensions of Classroom Behavior Measured by Two Systems of Interaction Analysis." *Educational Leadership* 26 (1969): 821–24.

Meier, John H. "Rationale for an Application of Microtraining To Improve Teaching." *Journal of Teacher Education* 19 (1968): 145–57.

Meux, Milton O. "Studies of Learning in the School Setting." *Review of Educational Research* 37 (1967): 539–62.

Morgan, John L. "Using the Workshop Approach as the First Stage in Creating a Helping Relationship Between Supervisors and Teachers." Paper prepared at the School of Education, University of Pittsburgh. Mimeographed, n.d.

Morse, William E. "Anxieties and Role Conflicts in an Interrelated Triangle." In Association for Student Teaching. *The College Supervisor: Conflict and Challenge*. Dubuque, Iowa: W. C. Brown Co., Inc., 1964.

Murray, C. Kenneth. "The Systematic Observation Movement." *Journal of Research and Development in Education* 4 (1970): 3–9.

Mursell, James L. *Successful Teaching: Its Psychological Principles*. New York: McGraw-Hill Book Co., Inc., 1954.

National Education Association. "Research Memorandum," No. 18, Washington, D.C.: National Education Association, 1963.

Newell, John M., and Brown, Bob Burton. "Theoretical Bases of Observational Systems." *Research Reports*. Gainesville, Fla.: University of Florida, Institute for the Development of Human Resources, College of Education, n.d.

Nylen, Donald; Mitchell, J. Robert; and Stout, Antony. *Handbook of Staff Development and Human Relations Training: Materials Developed for Use in Africa*. Washington, D.C.: National Training Laboratories Institute for Applied Behavioral Science, n.d.

Pancrazio, Sally F., and Johnson, W. D. "Comparison of Three Teacher Training Approaches in Nonverbal Behavior Which Encourages Classroom Interaction." Paper presented at the annual meeting of the American Educational Research Association, 1971.

Popham, W. James. "Performance Tests of Teaching Proficiency: Rationale, Development, and Validation." *American Educational Research Journal* 8 (1971): 105–17.

Remmers, H. H. "Rating Methods in Research on Teaching." In *Handbook of Research on Teaching*, edited by N. L. Gage. Chicago: Rand McNally and Co., 1963.

Robinson, James A. "Simulation and Games." In *The New Media and Education*, edited by Peter H. Rossi and Bruce J. Biddle. New York: Doubleday and Co., Inc., Anchor Books, 1967.

Rogers, Carl R. "A Theory of Therapy, Personality, and Interpersonal Relationships." In *Psychology: A Study of Science*, vol. 3: *Formulations of the Person and the Social Context*, edited by Sigmund Koch. New York: McGraw-Hill Book Co., 1959. Cited in Gilles Dussault, *A Theory of Supervision in Teacher Education*. New York: Teachers College Press, 1970.

Rogers, Carl R. "Significant Learning: In Theory and Education." In *Teaching: Vantage Points for Study*, edited by Ronald T. Hyman. Philadelphia: J. B. Lippincott Co., 1968.

Rogers, Carl R. *Carl Rogers on Encounter Groups*. New York: Harper and Row, 1970.

Rosenshine, Barak. "Interaction Analysis: A Tardy Comment." *Phi Delta Kappan* 51 (1970): 445–47.

Rosenshine, Barak. "Evaluation of Classroom Instruction." *Review of Educational Research* 40 (1970): 279–300.

Seager, G. Bradley. "Development of a Diagnostic Instrument of Supervision." Ed.D. dissertation, Harvard University, 1965.

Silberman, Charles E. *Crisis in the Classroom: The Remaking of American Education*. New York: Random House, 1970.

Simon, Anita, and Boyer, E. Gil. *Mirrors for Behavior: Anthology of Classroom Observation Instruments*. vol. 1. Philadelphia, Pa.: Research for Better Schools, Inc. and Center for the Study of Teaching, Temple University, 1967.

Simpson, Elizabeth Jane. "The Classification of Educational Objectives, Psychomotor Domain." *Illinois Teacher of Home Economics* 10 (1966–67): 111–44.

Skinner, B. F. "The Science of Learning and the Art of Teaching." *Harvard Educational Review* 24 (1954): 86–97.

Thelen, Herbert A. *Education and the Human Quest*. New York: Harper and Bros., 1960.

Torrance, T. Paul. "Teacher Attitude and Pupil Perception." *Journal of Teacher Education* 11 (1960): 97–102.

Tyler, Leona E. *The Psychology of Human Differences*. New York: Appleton-Century-Crofts, 1965.

Wilson, L. Craig; Byar, T. Madison; Shapiro, Arthur S.; and Schell, Shirley H.

Sociology of Supervision: An Approach to Comprehensive Planning in Education. Boston: Allyn and Bacon, Inc., 1969.

Zilsel, Edgar. "Physics and the Problem of Historico-sociological Laws." In *Readings in the Philosophy of Science,* edited by Herbert Feigl and May Brodbeck. New York: Appleton-Century-Crofts, Inc., 1953.

Index